A Student's Guide to A2 Music

for the **Edexcel** Specification
2008–2009

by

Paul Terry and David Bowman

Rhinegold Publishing Ltd
241 Shaftesbury Avenue
London WC2H 8TF
Telephone: 020 7333 1720
Fax: 020 7333 1765
www.rhinegold.co.uk

Rhinegold Study Guides
(music series editor: Paul Terry)

A Student's Guide to GCSE Music for the Edexcel Specification
Listening Tests for Students (Books 1, 2 and 3): Edexcel GCSE Music Specification
A Student's Guide to AS Music for the Edexcel Specification
Listening Tests for Students (Books 1 and 2): Edexcel AS Music Specification
A Student's Guide to A2 Music for the Edexcel Specification
Listening Tests for Students (Books 1 and 2): Edexcel A2 Music Specification

Similar books have been produced for the AQA and OCR Music Specifications. Also available are:

A Student's Guide to GCSE Music for the WJEC Specification (separate English- and Welsh-language versions)
A Student's Guide to AS/A2 Music Technology for the Edexcel AS and A2 Specifications
AS/A2 Listening Tests for Music Technology

The following book is designed to support all GCE music courses:

A Student's Guide to Harmony and Counterpoint (for AS and A2 Music)

Other Rhinegold Study Guides

Students' Guides to AS and A2 Drama and Theatre Studies for the AQA and Edexcel Specifications
Students' Guides to AS and A2 Performance Studies for the OCR Specification
Students' Guides to AS and A2 Religious Studies for the AQA, Edexcel and OCR Specifications

Rhinegold Publishing also publishes Classical Music, Classroom Music, Early Music Today, Music Teacher, Opera Now, Piano, Teaching Drama, The Singer, British and International Music Yearbook, British Performing Arts Yearbook, Music Education Yearbook, Rhinegold Dictionary of Music in Sound.

First published 2001 in Great Britain by
Rhinegold Publishing Limited
241 Shaftesbury Avenue
London WC2H 8TF
Telephone: 020 7333 1720
Fax: 020 7333 1765
www.rhinegold.co.uk
Reprinted 2002, 2003, 2005, New Edition 2005, Reprinted 2006, New Edition 2007

You should always check the current requirements of the examination, since these may change.
Copies of the Edexcel Specification may be obtained from Edexcel Examinations at
Edexcel Publications, Adamsway, Mansfield, Notts. NG18 4FN
Telephone 01623 467467, Facsimile 01623 450481, Email publications@linneydirect.com
See also the Edexcel website at http://www.edexcel.org.uk/

A Student's Guide to A2 Music for the Edexcel Specification (2008–2009)
British Library Cataloguing in Publication Data.
A catalogue record for this book is available from the British Library.
ISBN 978-1-906178-19-2
Printed in Great Britain by Thanet Press

La musique exprime ce qui ne peut être dit
et sur quoi il est impossible de rester silencieux.

Music expresses that which can not be said
and on which it is impossible to be silent.

Victor Hugo (1864)

Contents

The authors

Paul Terry was director of music at the City of London Freemen's School for 15 years. He currently works as a music editor, engraver and publisher. He was a music examiner for more than 25 years and has worked as a consultant to various examination boards. Paul has served as a member of the Secondary Examinations Council and its successor the Schools Examinations and Assessment Council. He was chief examiner for the Oxford and Cambridge Schools Examinations Board (now part of OCR) and he was a chief examiner for London Examinations (now part of Edexcel).

Paul Terry's publications include three books on aural (all with CDs) for A-level music, and six *Student Guides* to AS and A2 Music, all written in collaboration with David Bowman (see below), and he has contributed to *Music Teacher* and *Classroom Music* magazines. He is also co-author with William Lloyd of *Music in Sequence, a complete guide to MIDI sequencing* (1991), *Classics in Sequence* (1992) and *Rock in Sequence* (1996), and also *Rehearse, Direct and Play: A Student's Guide to Group Music-Making* (1993), all published by Musonix/Music Sales.

David Bowman was for 20 years director of music at Ampleforth College and was a chief examiner for the University of London Schools Examination Board (now Edexcel) from 1982 to 1998. He now spends more time with his family, horses and dogs.

David Bowman's publications include the *London Anthology of Music* (University of London Schools Examinations Board, 1986), *Sound Matters* (co-authored with Bruce Cole, Schott, 1989), *Aural Matters, Aural Matters in Practice* and *Listening Matters* (all co-authored with Paul Terry, Schott, 1993, 1994 and 2003 respectively), *Analysis Matters* (Rhinegold, Volume 1 1997, Volume 2 1998), and six *Student Guides to AS and A2 Music* (co-authored with Paul Terry, Rhinegold, 2000 onwards). He has also written sections in a number of Rhinegold's *Student Guides to GCSE Music* and he has written numerous analytical articles for *Music Teacher*. David Bowman is a contributor to the *Collins Classical Music Encyclopedia* (2000) edited by Stanley Sadie and is author of the *Rhinegold Dictionary of Music in Sound.*

Acknowledgements

The authors would like to thank Dr Hugh Benham, Edexcel's Chair of Examiners in Music, for his expert advice so freely offered throughout the preparation of both the original edition and this new edition of the Student Guide. Nevertheless, if any errors have been made it is only right to state that these are the responsibility of the authors. We would also like to thank Dr Lucien Jenkins of Rhinegold Publishing for so much help and encouragement in the preparation of the entire series of Rhinegold Study Guides.

Introduction

This book is intended to assist students preparing for the Edexcel A2 Music examination. Like other *Rhinegold Study Guides* it is intended to supplement, but not supplant, the work of teachers.

The full Advanced GCE in Music is made up of six units, three AS and three A2. This book deals only with the three A2 units.

We have included many suggestions and tips which we hope will help you do well in performing and composing, but the main emphasis is on preparation for the paper in *Analysing music*. As part of this unit you will be extending your knowledge of **one** of the areas of study that you covered for AS *and* you will also be working on **one new** area of study.

The basic information for each of the areas of study is given in **A Student's Guide to AS Music for the Edexcel Specification** and we have not repeated those details here, so you will need to refer to the AS guide during your A2 studies.

A Student's Guide to AS Music for the Edexcel Specification from 2005 by Paul Terry and David Bowman. *Rhinegold Publishing Ltd.* ISBN: 0-946890-90-0.

In this book each of the chapters dealing with an area of study concentrates on the topics of 'continuity and change' and 'special focus' works that are prescribed for study in the A2 exam. The questions during the course of these chapters will help you check your understanding of the context, style and technical features of the music – they are not intended to be representative of actual exam questions. If you have difficulty with these, you will generally find the right answers by rereading the preceding pages. The sample questions in these chapters are more demanding and these should be worked under examination conditions. For examples of the questions that are likely to be encountered in the exam, you should be guided by the specimen and past papers published by Edexcel, and by the Listening Tests published by Rhinegold.

Listening Tests for Students for the Edexcel A2 Music Specification by Hugh Benham and Alistair Wightman, *Rhinegold Publishing Ltd.* Book 1 (ISBN: 1-904226-46-9) and Book 2 (ISBN 1-904226-67-1). CDs with answer booklets are available for both volumes.

A glossary of technical terms is given at the end of the AS guide. If you need further help with terminology you encounter during the course, we recommend you consult **The Rhinegold Dictionary of Music in Sound**. This comprehensive resource not only gives detailed explanations of a wide range of musical concepts, but also illustrates them using a large number of examples on a set of accompanying CDs and scores.

The Rhinegold Dictionary of Music in Sound by David Bowman. *Rhinegold Publishing Ltd.* ISBN: 0-946890-87-0.

Planning is the secret of success. Initial ideas for composing are best formulated early in the course and plans for performing need to get under way as soon as possible. Preparation for the *Analysing music* unit needs to be completed in time to allow for revision and the working of complete papers in the weeks before the actual exam.

Remember that it will help enormously if you can perceive the many varied connections between the music you hear, the music you play and the music you compose. Understanding the context and structure of music will not only enhance your enjoyment when listening, but will also inform your performing and illuminate your composing. Composing, performing, listening and understanding are all related aspects of the study of music, and this integration of activities is fundamental to the Advanced GCE in Music.

A2 Music

There are three units: *Performing and composing, Specialist options* and *Analysing music*. Each of the first two of these accounts for 30% of the total A2 mark, while the third is weighted at 40%.

Performing and composing

There are two parts to the *Performing and composing* unit, both of which build on work you undertook for AS music:

- An assessment of your performing during the course. For this you will need to keep a log of the pieces you have performed and then choose the best four for assessment (you must include at least one solo piece and at least one ensemble item). The work will be assessed by your teacher and the mark moderated by Edexcel (for moderation purposes a recording of one **solo** piece of performing during the course is required).
- A timed test in compositional techniques, marked by an Edexcel examiner. For this part you will work in greater depth on **one** of the compositional techniques you studied for AS.

Specialist options

You must choose one of two different pathways through this unit, both of which are marked by an Edexcel examiner:

- **Either** you will have to write two compositions (together lasting at least six minutes) each based on a different topic from a given list; one of these must be on the same topic you chose for AS
- **Or** you will have to perform a 20-minute recital of music, which will be recorded for assessment purposes.

Analysing music

There are two separate papers for this unit, which are taken one after the other in the same three-hour exam session. Both are marked by Edexcel examiners:

- A listening paper, consisting of three questions on music on a CD that you can play as many times as you wish within the 60 minutes allowed for the test; the music will be selected from a wide variety of styles
- A two-hour written paper based on questions about **two** areas of study you have prepared from the *New Anthology of Music*, an unmarked copy of which you may use for reference in the exam.

The *New Anthology of Music* is published by Peters Edition Ltd, ISBN: 1-901507-03-3 (CDs, ISBN: 1-901507-04-1), and is available from Edexcel publications (see page 2) or all good music retailers.

The details of the specification are correct at the time of going to press, but you and your teachers should always check current requirements for the exam with Edexcel as these may change.

Key Skills

Key Skills are becoming increasingly important for success at work, entry into higher education and making the most of everyday life. A2 Music offers a number of opportunities for you to develop your knowledge and understanding in five of the six Key Skills: Communication, Information Technology, Working with Others, Improving own Learning and Performance, and Problem Solving. You are therefore recommended to discuss with your teachers the ways in which the work you undertake for A2 Music might also be used as evidence for your acquisition and development of skills for these Key Skills units at Level 3.

Performing and composing

1. Performing during the course

This section accounts for 50% of the marks for the *Performing and composing* unit. Like the similar component in AS Music it offers an excellent opportunity for you to receive credit for the performing you do during the course. This needs careful planning and record-keeping, and you need to meet all of the following requirements:

- You must submit four *different* pieces for assessment; these must not include any items that you offered for AS Music nor, if you are opting for performing as your *Specialist option*, any piece that you present in your recital
- At least one of the four pieces must be a solo
- At least one of the four pieces must be an ensemble item
- Performances must be completed in time for your submission to reach the examiner by 15 May in the exam year
- One solo item must be recorded for moderation purposes
- Your teacher must have been present for at least three of the four performances.

To be sure of meeting all these requirements it is going to be essential to make your plans at the start of the A2 course and to discuss with your teacher the practicalities of the last two points above. Remember that there may be little time to arrange performances at the start of the summer term in the exam year.

You can include a performance in which you were the director or conductor of an ensemble, but you may submit only one such piece. In this part of the exam you are allowed to include performances that encompass improvisation if you wish.

The combined length of the four pieces you submit must be at least 7–8 minutes, but there is no maximum time limit. The difficulty of the music is taken into account in assessment and is expected to equate with grade 6 standard (your teacher will help explain what this implies if you do not take graded exams). The mark scheme allows credit if the music is of a higher standard. Although the highest marks are not available if the pieces are below grade 6 in level of difficulty, you will probably get a much better mark if you choose music that is well within your capabilities rather than pieces that are so hard that they will cause you to struggle and perhaps even break down in performance. When choosing pieces remember that, while accuracy is expected, the majority of the marks at this level are awarded for your **interpretation** of the music.

The performances can be given in class to your fellow students, or they may include events such as lunchtime concerts, rock gigs, music festivals or concert tours – but remember that your teacher must be present for at least three of the performances you submit. You may include playing on any instrument or singing, but marks are awarded for quality and not variety, so there is no advantage in including music on instruments that you don't play well.

There must be an audience at the performances, even if it is only a couple of people, and for that reason you are not allowed to include performances given at music exams or auditions in which there is no audience in the normal sense of the word. However you can include exam and audition pieces if you perform them on some more open occasion.

Ensemble performances can be of many different kinds – piano duets, wind trios, string quartets, jazz bands, rock groups, choirs or orchestras. However a piece in which you are the one dominant performer throughout does not count as an ensemble. Thus in a piece for flute with piano accompaniment the flautist cannot submit the work as an ensemble item, although the accompanying pianist can. When choosing ensemble performances to include on your list, remember that the work will need to be assessed – this may be difficult if it is a piece in which you have played a very minor role in a large ensemble.

Some advice on solo performing is given later in this guide, as part of the section on the recital. A useful handbook which will give you many ideas for getting the best out of ensemble performing of all kinds is:

Rehearse, Direct and Play by William Lloyd and Paul Terry.
Musonix Publishing, 1993. ISBN: 0-9517214-3-7, £4.95.
Order from http://www.musonix.co.uk

Keeping a performance diary

You will need to keep your own diary of performances, which should include the following information:

✦ The precise title of the work you performed and the movement(s) performed if it was not complete

✦ The name of the composer

✦ A note of whether it was a solo or ensemble item

✦ The nature of the occasion (such as a lunchtime recital, a rock concert, an arts festival, etc)

✦ The role in which you participated (such as flute in wind trio, second trumpet in county youth orchestra of 80 players, bass guitar in rock group, one of 12 altos in choir of 60, etc)

✦ The date and whether it was an internal event at your centre or an external event that occurred elsewhere.

Remember that you will need a recording of one of the solo items which you submit, and a photocopy of your part in the piece.

By early May in your exam year you will have to select the four best pieces from your diary, in accordance with the requirements listed on the previous page, and transfer the details to a log form provided by Edexcel. When you do this be careful not to include any piece more than once, and do not include any pieces that you offered for assessment in your AS Music examination or that you performed in your recital (if you have chosen this as your *Specialist option* for A2 Music).

2. Compositional techniques

This section accounts for the remaining 50% of the marks for the *Performing and composing* unit.

You have to continue and extend your study of the same techniques topic that you chose for AS Music. You will be required to sit a timed exam paper in which you will have to complete an exercise in your chosen technique. During the exam you will be allowed access to a musical instrument and/or music-technology equipment (but not to any written notes or other reference materials).

The exercise to be undertaken will be related to the coursework you did for AS Music, but it will be more demanding, not only because it must be completed as a timed test but also because you will be required to supply more music in your answer.

The table below shows the choice of topics. Remember that you must choose just **one** technique, and it must be one of those that you chose for AS. The table also summarises how the requirements at A2 differ from those you undertook for AS Music.

Compositional technique	AS coursework	A2 exam
A1 Baroque counterpoint Complete an upper part to a given figured bass	12–16 bars	18–24 bars
A2 Minimalism Complete a given opening to make a piece lasting about one minute	For keyboard	For three melody instruments
B1 Bach chorale Add three lower parts to a chorale melody	Harmonise the cadences only	Harmonise the whole passage
B2 32-bar popular song Realise the middle-eight and turnaround	Add a bass part from given chord symbols	Add chord symbols and a bass part
C1 Renaissance counterpoint Add a third part to two given parts	8–10 bars	12–16 bars
C2 Serialism Extend a given opening	For solo instrument, about 12 bars in length	For two instruments, about 20 bars in length
D1 Extended instrumental techniques Develop one of two given openings to make a one-minute piece which exploits: vocal contrast, prepared piano, woodwind chords, glissandi or vocalising through the instrument	Exploit one of the listed techniques in your piece	Exploit two of the listed techniques in your piece
D2 Electro-acoustic music Record a given ostinato, then add material to make a piece lasting about one minute which exploits: envelope shaping, filtering, pitch shifting, sampled sounds, reversing or looping.	Add one track and employ one of the listed processes in your piece	Add one or two tracks and employ two of the listed processes in your piece

In the case of electro-acoustic music you are required to submit a recording as well as some form of notation (not necessarily a score). You will be allowed time to set up the equipment and to record the given ostinato outside the timed part of the examination.

Detailed help on compositional techniques A1, B1, B2 and C2, along with many tips and practice exercises, is given in **A Student's Guide to Harmony and Counterpoint** by Hugh Benham. *Rhinegold Publishing.* ISBN: 1-904226-31-0.

We have given some general guidance on the various options below. Your teacher will explain to you the specific techniques required, since these are very detailed and vary greatly between options, but in all cases it is important to listen to, study and hopefully perform examples of the music concerned. Make sure that you work through plenty of exercises and, most important of all, try to learn from any mistakes you might make in those workings.

Baroque counterpoint

Useful books on this topic include **Bach: Chorale Harmonization and Instrumental Counterpoint** by Malcolm Boyd, published by *Kahn and Averill*, ISBN: 1-871082-72-2, and **A Practical Approach to Eighteenth-century Counterpoint** by Robert Gauldin, published by *Waveland Press* (USA), ISBN: 0-88133-853-2.

You will be required to complete an upper part to fit with a given figured bass in the style of Corelli, Handel or their contemporaries. The passage will be 18–24 bars in length. It is likely that the music will include modulations and you may be expected to find opportunities to use imitation and develop the given melodic material. In addition to the harmony you encountered when studying for AS music (first and second inversions, 7ths, 9–8 and 4–3 suspensions and accidentals) the passage may contain the following figuring: $^{6}_{5}$, $^{4}_{3}$, $^{4}_{2}$ and 7–6. Remember that stylistically appropriate melodic decoration is important, that leading notes and 7ths must be correctly treated, and that you must check for consecutives. It will be useful to study (and perhaps play) some of Bach's two-part inventions, Corelli's violin sonatas and Handel's flute sonatas.

Minimalism

You will be required to complete a given opening to make a piece for three melody instruments lasting one minute. Be prepared to use both treble and bass clefs. If you use a MIDI workstation for the task remember that you must nevertheless write for acoustic instruments, taking into account their ranges, characteristics and practicalities in performance. As the required length is only one minute it will not be practical for ideas to unfold slowly, as often happens in this style. Try to study some of the early works of the 'New York minimalists' listed on page 19. Note how, when motifs are shifted out of phase with one another (as occurs in *NAM 12*) new patterns arise from the resulting combination, and notice the free use of unprepared dissonance in this style of music.

Bach chorales

Useful books for this topic include **Bach: Chorale Harmonization and Instrumental Counterpoint** by Malcolm Boyd, published by *Kahn and Averill*, ISBN: 1-871082-72-2 and the examples of Bach's own harmonisations in **Bach: 371 Harmonized Chorales**, edited by Riemenschneider, published by *Schirmer / Music Sales.*

You will be required to add three lower parts to a given chorale melody, in the style of Bach. Revise your AS work for this topic, since the correct harmonisation of cadences is essential to the style. Much of the rest of the harmony can often be established by working progressively backwards from the cadences. Examiners will be looking for strong bass lines, good spacing of parts, the use of quaver passing notes and suspensions. Check your work thoroughly for inappropriate use of second inversions and forbidden consecutives.

32-bar popular song

A useful general resource for this topic is **Songwriting: a complete guide to the craft** by Stephen Citron, *Hodder and Stoughton*, ISBN: 0-340-48872-7. Best of all is to make a study of the harmony in some of the many AABA forms in albums of songs by Cole Porter, Irving Berlin, Jerome Kern, George Gershwin and Richard Rodgers, and of the songs in the various collections of jazz and pop standards.

You will be required to complete an AABA popular-song structure by writing a chord sequence **and** bass part for the 'middle eight' (the B section). Your chords should contrast with the given harmony of the A section and should introduce one or more passing modulations to keys such as IV, ii, iii or vi (more remote keys may be appropriate in some styles). You should end with a turnaround that prepares for the return of the A section in the tonic key. The bass part should include passing notes, and appropriate licks and fills. The examiners are likely to be more impressed with a strong and stylish use of a wide harmonic vocabulary (including secondary dominants and other chromatic chords) rather than memorised stock chord progressions that are poorly suited to the context.

Renaissance counterpoint

A useful reference book for this topic is **Modal Counterpoint, Renaissance Style** by Peter Schubert. *Oxford University Press.* ISBN: 0-19-510912-0.

You will be required to add a third part to two given parts, in a late 16th-century style. The passage will be 12–16 bars in length and may be either sacred or secular vocal polyphony. You need to remember that control of dissonance is a key feature (including 4ths with the bass), and that the sharpened leading-note will be required in most cadences. Remember to spend time trying to find natural points for imitative entries. Aim for correct underlay of the text, with stressed syllables usually falling on accented beats.

Serialism

Useful books for this topic include **Serial Composition and Atonality** by George Perle. *University of California Press*, ISBN: 0-520-22921-5, and **Serial Composition** by Reginald Smith Brindle, *Oxford University Press*, ISBN: 0-19-311906-4.

You will be provided with a note row, from which you must construct a piece for two instruments of about 20 bars in length. In addition to using the four basic versions of the row (which you should identify with the letters O, I, R and RI above the staves) you should look out for the opportunity to use transpositions of the row, to exploit patterns such as hexachords and trichords in the given material, and to use more advanced techniques such as rotation. Examiners will look for a musical result with imaginative use of the row, development of ideas and a clear sense of structure.

Extended instrumental techniques

Useful works to study for this topic include *NAM 10, 11* and *40*. See also *Stripsody* by Cathy Berberian, an excerpt of which can be found in *Sound Matters* (Bowman and Cole), and *Eight Songs for A Mad King* by Peter Maxwell Davies. The latter includes a wide range of extended techniques for all its performers.

As at AS you will be required to develop one of two given openings to make a one-minute piece, but at A2 your composition will have to use **two** of the techniques listed on page 9. You can employ both techniques in a work for a solo performer, or you could write for two or more performers and use the techniques in different parts. Whichever you choose, you must identify in the score which techniques you have employed. Your piece must be performable and you should also give a full explanation in the score of how the techniques are to be realised. The examiners will be looking to see how well your use of the techniques integrates with the musical intentions of the piece, so you should avoid writing music which is merely a study or experiment in the use of technical effects.

Electro-acoustic music

As at AS you will be required to record a given ostinato which you must loop or repeat to produce the basis of a one-minute piece. To this you must add one or two tracks which feature **two** of the processes listed on page 9. Your added material could be derived from the given ostinato, or it may be entirely new. It can be either electronic or acoustic, but if you use any pre-existing samples you must identify these and credit their source. The examiners will be looking for a good sense of balance, a clear stereo image and full use of the audible frequency range, as well as appropriate organisation of your musical ideas. For this topic your work should be submitted as a recording, but you should also include written documentation (a computer-printed score, graphic notation, track diagram, table or flow chart) that includes a description of the processes you have used.

What the examiners look for

Whichever topic you choose, examiners will award marks for:

- A clear and accurate presentation of your score (or recording)
- An outcome that is creative and musical, and which responds to the demands of the question
- An awareness of style and a fluent use of technical procedures
- A coherent and controlled use of structure in your work.

Specialist option A: Composition portfolio

You must choose one of two different pathways through the unit entitled *Specialist option*, depending on whether you want to focus on composing or performing. Turn to page 23 for the latter.

For Pathway A you have to write **two compositions**, based on two different topics from the following list. One of your topics must be **the same one that you chose for unit 2 in AS Music**.

- Variations
- Romantic miniatures
- Neo-classicism
- Post-modernism
- The popular song
- Club dance and hip hop
- Fusions
- Film and television
- Music theatre.

The score should be appropriate to the style of the music. It may be fully notated, a lead-sheet, track sheet or annotated diagram.

The two compositions together must last at least six minutes. You have to present both works as scores *and* in recorded format. You will also have to submit a short written description of each piece. Your work must reach the examiner by **15 May** in the exam year.

Planning

Start planning your compositions early in the course, as you will need plenty of time to develop initial ideas, make preliminary sketches and try these out in performance before you even start on the final scores and recordings.

You will first need to decide on the resources you are going to use. Be realistic in what you have time to achieve. While it may be tempting to write for an orchestra, band or large choir, this will require a lot of work and it may prove impossible to get the necessary resources together when needed. It is usually better to write for people who will be available to work with you during the whole composing process, such as the other students in your group or people with whom you regularly rehearse and perform.

You could write for just a solo instrument, especially if it is a harmony instrument such as the piano or guitar, but at this level it is good to be a little more ambitious, and two or three players will give you much more flexibilty and textural variety. Consider combinations such as piano duet (either two pianos, or two players on one piano), piano with solo instrument or voice, acoustic guitar and flute, as well as trios or quartets of various kinds.

As we recommended in the AS Guide, start by discussing with your performers how the characteristics of their instruments and/or voices can best be exploited. Try to identify the skills (and weaknesses) of each performer so that you can use their individual strengths in your composing. Discuss what sort of things are easy and what are difficult for each instrument or voice, and try some improvising both separately and together.

Research

Begin by investigating some of the existing music in your chosen topic area. You may find examples in the music you play as well as in the *New Anthology*, but you will also need to investigate what can be found in libraries, and in scores and recordings that you may be allowed to borrow from your teacher or music department. Aim to make a **detailed** study of several examples that differ in style, mood and resources, and make notes on:

- **Melody**: is there a melody line? If so, what makes it distinctive or memorable? What role does rhythm, particularly rests and repeated notes, play in its construction? Does it have a point of climax? Is the melody regularly phrased? Is it developed? Is it formed from smaller motifs and are these developed separately? How is the melodic material distributed around the various performing resources? Is there any contrapuntal interest?
- **Accompaniment**: is there a distinct accompaniment or do all the parts have equal melodic interest? Does the accompaniment possess musical interest of its own? Is there rhythmic variety in the accompaniment? Does it have a strong bass line? What role does the accompaniment have when there is less interest in the main melody? What role is played by repeated notes and rests in the accompaniment?
- **Structure**: how is the music given shape? How much repetition is there? Is it varied repetition? How much contrast? Do areas of contrast sound as if they are part of the same piece? Why? Are changes of key used to provide areas of contrast? How are these established? Are there distinct sections in the piece? If so, how are they linked? How does the piece begin? How does it end?
- **Texture**: how are different textures used to provide variety? How are the voices and/or instruments exploited? How do changes in texture contribute to climaxes in the music? What use is made of different tone colours within various textures?

In addition, make a note of any useful **techniques** that relate to your chosen topic and try to identify any potential problem areas that you could encounter in your own composition. You will soon begin to accumulate a store of information that will be enormously helpful in planning your own work.

While it is possible to start a composition at bar 1 and gradually work through to the end, you will find your task easier if you first plan out the structure and main events, leaving the detail to be sketched in later. This also makes it easy, if you get stuck, to leave the current section and try out some ideas for later in the piece.

Musical style

Compositions may be in any style that is appropriate to the topic you choose, but you will want to show the best you can do, so it is probably best to opt for a format that will allow you to use a variety of textures and techniques. If you adopt a style that is exceptionally repetitive or very slow-moving it may be advisable to write a relatively long work so that you can achieve some variety and a sense of development in your composing.

Whichever topic you choose, note that you are **not** expected to write in the style of a specific composer. For instance, if you decide to compose a romantic miniature you are not required to write in the style of Chopin or Schumann – you might decide on a modern interpretation of this genre. Similarly, variations are not expected to be realised in the style of Bach or Mozart – you may want to write jazz variations or an electro-acoustic piece in a modern cross-over style that uses a ground bass formed from a tape loop.

The topics simply provide you with broad guidelines, which you should interpret imaginatively, and we have suggested some ideas to help you with this later in the chapter. However your two compositions should be in different styles – you should not, for example, write two similar songs for a musical and submit one as a popular song and the other as music theatre.

Information technology

You may find it useful to use a MIDI workstation to develop your compositions, but unless your work is intended only for electronic realisation (as may be the case with club dance and some types of film music) reread the advice on pages 13–14 of the AS Guide, paying particular attention to the notes about computer-generated scores. Don't become so engrossed with the technology that you neglect the composition, and remember that music technology will not give you feedback on the practicality (or enjoyability) of your music that you can expect from live performers.

Developing the brief

Painters often begin with a number of preliminary pencil or charcoal sketches, sometimes followed by some drafts in watercolour, before starting work on the final canvas. A similar procedure can work well for composing. Improvising, either alone or in a group, can be a good start. Each student could contribute a variation to a given theme, or all could arrange a given passage for the ensemble each intends to use in their own compositions.

More specific exercises may involve you trying several alternative sketches for key features of your piece – such as different layouts for the opening, a central climax, or a complex contrapuntal section. You may want to experiment with different voicings in the scoring, or provide alternative treatments for a passage that is technically difficult. Once drafted in rough, ideas for short sections can be tested at the piano or MIDI workstation, and then trialled in performance workshop sessions. Record these for later playback and analysis, noting if some sections seem to flag, fail to cohere, are unplayable, or do not achieve the effect you desire.

Reread pages 16–17 of the AS Guide, noting the following points:

✦ Aim to **balance unity and diversity** in your work. Too much repetition will lead to a lack of variety, but too much new material will prevent the piece hanging together. Use your research to suggest ways in which ideas can be transformed, adapted and developed, so there is a sense of moving forward during the work and a sense of completion when it ends. Pay particular attention to ends of phrases and sections, where the music can easily lose its impetus. Explore your musical ideas in depth, exploiting the potential of individual motifs, not just manipulating complete tunes, and experiment with unusual changes of key and more complex types of structure. Watch out carefully for unwanted predictability, such as too many four-bar phrases in succession or rondo/chorus structures in which it is all too obvious where the theme will come round yet again.

- Remember that **variety of texture is essential** for success. All parts should be musically interesting and ideally all should play a leading role at some point in the piece. Use instruments or voices in different parts of their ranges, and remember that rests are more valuable than notes in providing changes in texture. Check that you have contrasts in dynamics and articulation, and ensure that accompanying parts are rhythmically interesting. Remember that long melodies can often be split into shorter motifs that can be assigned to different parts within the texture, and that a counter-melody or some short contrapuntal motifs can add interest to the repetition of a section. Plan points of tension and areas of relaxation carefully, using changes in texture, dynamics and articulation to heighten their contrast.
- Plan your schedule to allow time for testing in performance and subsequent refinement of ideas, before embarking on the final recording and neat copy of the score. Unsatisfactory sections may need to be replaced, and the work as a whole polished. Sometimes a work can get totally stuck, and if this happens you may need time to start afresh on something new.

Presentation

Reread pages 14–15 of the AS Guide and use the composition checklist on page 15 to ensure that you haven't missed anything. If you submit a lead-sheet or chord chart instead of a score, note that it must contain **all** significant cues and performing directions. Similarly, track sheets must include **full** details of the processing you used. For each of the two compositions you will have to submit a score (which may be a lead-sheet or track list if appropriate to the musical style), a recording and a structured commentary which will require answers to the following questions:

- How does your composition relate to the chosen topic?
- What musical resources have you used?
- What is the form or structure of the piece?
- What improvements were made in the process of composition?

Use the commentary to make your intentions clear to the examiner. It is not necessary to explain how you discovered the dominant 7th, or how you mislaid your computer disk and had to start again. Nor should you write a programme note about the piece. However you should draw the examiner's attention to any points about the piece that you feel are important and identify any material you have used that is not original (such as lyrics, samples, or someone else's theme on which you have written variations).

Composition topics

Variations

Listed below are just a few of the more accessible works that use variation form. Aim to make a *thorough* study of about five works, selected from different periods.

Variations for solo instruments

Excerpts from Bach's Chaconne in D minor, Brahms' *Variations on a Theme of Handel* and other works in variation form can be found in *The Rhinegold Dictionary of Music in Sound*. The third movement of Webern's Variations appears in *Sound Matters* (Bowman and Cole).

Bach's Passacaglia in C minor for organ, *Goldberg* variations, and the Chaconne from Partita in D minor for unaccompanied violin. Mozart's Piano sonata in A, K331 (first movement) – his complete piano variations are also available. Haydn's Variations in F minor, Beethoven's *33 Variations on a Waltz by Diabelli* and Schubert's Impromptu in B♭ (Op. 142 No. 3). Chopin's *Variations brillantes* (Op. 12), Mendelssohn's *Variations sérieuses* (Op. 54) and Brahms' *Variations and Fugue on a theme by Handel* (Op. 24). Ives' *Variations on 'America'* and Webern's Variations (Op. 27). Also look out for CDs of 19th-century virtuoso piano music, such as **The Earl Wild Collection** (*Vanguard* OVC 4033) which includes a number of works based on variation technique.

Variations for small ensembles

Ground-bass arias by Purcell can be found in *NAM 36*, *Aural Matters* (Bowman and Terry), *Sound Matters* (Bowman and Cole) and *The Rhinegold Dictionary of Music in Sound* (A75).

The slow movement (theme and variations) of Haydn's String Quartet in B♭, Op.9 No.5, can be found in *Sound Matters* (Bowman and Cole). Excerpts from the variations in Haydn's *Emperor* quartet can be found in *The Rhinegold Dictionary of Music in Sound.*

Pachelbel's Kanon (a canon over a ground bass), Purcell's Chacony in G minor (for strings) and various ground-bass arias (see *left*). Mozart's Duo for Violin and Viola in B♭, K.424 (last movement), his piano trios in G, K.496 (last movement) and K.564 (second movement) and Clarinet Quintet, K.581 (last movement). Haydn's *Emperor* quartet (second movement). Beethoven's *Harp* quartet (last movement) and his trio in B♭, Op. 11 (third movement). Schubert's *Death and the Maiden* quartet (second movement) and *Trout* quintet (fourth movement). Mendelssohn's Variations concertantes for cello and piano. Stravinsky's Octet (second movement).

Orchestral variations

The second movements of Haydn's symphonies Nos. 94 (*Surprise*) and 103 (*Drumroll*). Mozart's piano concertos in B♭ (second movement) K.450, and in G (third movement) K.453. Brahms' *Variations on a theme by J Haydn* (also for piano duet) and the last movement of his Symphony No. 4 in E minor (a passacaglia). Tchaikovsky's *Variations on a Rococco Theme* (for cello and orchestra). Reger's *Variations and Fugue on a Theme of Mozart* (based on K.331 above). Richard Strauss's *Don Quixote*. Elgar's *Enigma* variations. Schoenberg's *Variations for Orchestra*. Dohnányi's *Variations on a Nursery Tune* (for piano and orchestra). Vaughan Williams' *Five Variants of Dives and Lazarus.* Britten's *A Young Person's Guide to the Orchestra* (subtitled *Variations and Fugue on a Theme of Purcell*). Walton's *Variations on a Theme of Hindemith*. Lloyd Webber's *Variations* (compare with Rachmaninov's *Rhapsody on a Theme of Paganini*).

When you study (and hopefully perform) some of these pieces, note how the theme is constructed and harmonised, as well as how the entire work is structured. Many sets of variations build up tension by using increasingly complex figuration as they proceed. Some provide contrast with a slow and/or minor-key variation before an exciting finale (which may be less clearly associated with the theme). Some end with a short coda which refreshingly refers back to the theme in its original form.

Notice how most themes are simple and based on strong chord patterns – these usually offer the greatest potential for exploitation in the ensuing variations. Make detailed notes on the types of variation used and the differing moods that these can create. The methods employed may include any of the following (often two or more of these techniques will be used simultaneously):

- Elaborating the melody with many types of decoration
- Redistributing the notes of the melody between different hands (in piano music) or between different instruments
- Changing the harmony and/or tonality
- Altering the rhythm, metre or tempo (or a combination of these)
- Fragmenting the theme
- Developing a new theme from the fragments
- Reusing the harmony but creating a new melody above it
- Treating the theme contrapuntally by using imitation or adding a counter-melody.

If you decide to adopt a theme-and-variations structure, consider whether you want to write your own theme, or use an existing one. Composition will be more straightforward if the theme has a clear melodic outline and strong harmonic structure. You could instead use a freer variation structure (such as a fantasia on a theme) or a tighter one (such as a ground bass or chaconne), although the latter can be a much harder format within which to work.

Double themes and variations were frequently used by Haydn. For example, in the slow movement of his *Drumroll* symphony a theme in C minor is followed by one in C major, and this pair of themes is then varied in each of the following sections. Explore ways in which you can vary the often predictable variation plan. The slow movement of Stravinsky's Octet repeats the first variation as a sort of rondo after some of the later variations, and ends with a repeat of the theme, giving the form $A–A^1–A^2–A^1–A^3–A^4–A^1–A$.

Aim to include a range of variation techniques, not just different embellishments of the melody line, and if you are working in a tonal idiom, plan how you will achieve variety of key – it is all too easy for sets of variations to get stuck in one key with little or no modulation. Beethoven avoided this as early as 1802 in his Six Variations (Op. 34). The theme is in F major and the variations fall in thirds through D, B♭, G, E♭, C minor and back to F major.

Decide whether your variations are going to proceed in discrete sections or if you are going to link them into a through-composed format, like the free variations on a double theme which form the foundation of Richard Strauss's tone poem, *Don Quixote*. This work is of a type known as 'character variations' – each variation portrays one of the fantastical adventures of the hapless old knight. Similarly, each of Elgar's *Enigma* variations portrays the character of one of the composer's friends. Perhaps there might be an idea here for a set of variations characterising your own friends or emotions, or perhaps reflecting various favourite places you have visited.

Finally, remember that variation technique pervades many types of music – it is fundamental in serial music, jazz improvisation, the Indian *rag* and in the simultaneous variation of gamelan music.

Romantic miniatures

A 'romantic miniature' could be a song, a dance form such as a waltz or short ballet movement, an entirely abstract piece (e.g. a prelude, intermezzo or impromptu) or a 'character piece' that aims to suggest a specific idea, such as a mood, person or place. You could write a piece in the form of a study for your instrument, but studies often concentrate on just one technique, which may make it difficult for you to show a range of skills in composing.

NAM 23 consists of three miniatures from *Kinderscenen* by Schumann. See also *NAM 24* (Debussy) and *NAM 39* (Fauré). Romantic miniatures in the *Rhinegold Dictionary of Music in Sound* include works by Chopin, Mendelssohn's *Venetian Gondola Song*, an excerpt from Liszt's *La Lugubre Gondola I*, a waltz from Grieg's *New Lyric Pieces*, the Trepak from Tchaikovsky's *The Nutcracker* and extracts from *Préludes* by Debussy and from Saint-Saëns' *Carnival of the Animals*.

Romantic miniatures can be found in many instrumental teaching books and in collections of graded exam pieces. Some of the well-known collections for piano include Schubert's *Moments musicaux*, Mendelssohn's *Songs without Words*, Chopin's preludes, nocturnes, waltzes and mazurkas, Grieg's *Lyric Pieces* and *Poetic Tone Pictures*, and the various cycles of short piano pieces by Schumann, such as *Papillons*, *Carnaval*, the *Davidsbündler* dances, the *Album for the Young* and *Kinderscenen*. In addition, there are many attractive works in this genre by minor composers such as Burgmüller, Fibich, Gurlitt, Karganoff, John Field and others.

The character piece proved enduringly popular, so there are many examples from later 19th-century composers such as Tchaikovsky, Borodin, Cui, Dvořák and Smetana. Remember that you are not necessarily expected to compose in a romantic style. Debussy's *Préludes*, Kabalevsky's *24 Pieces for Children*, or Bartók's shorter piano pieces (such as those in *For Children* and *Mikrokosmos*) will reveal how 20th-century composers reinterpreted this genre.

If you are writing for solo instrument with piano or small ensemble, look out for some of the popular arrangements and encore pieces such as Elgar's *Salut d'amour*, *Chanson de matin* and *Chanson de nuit*, Raff's *Cavatina*, Massanet's *Méditation* from *Thaïs*, Monti's *Czardas* and Dvořák's *Humoresque*. If you want to work on a more ambitious scale, look at movements from Grieg's *Holberg* and *Peer Gynt* suites, Dag Wiren's *Serenade for Strings*, movements from Saint-Saëns' *Carnival of the Animals* and the individual dances in Tchaikovsky's ballet scores, such as the 'characteristic dances' from *The Nutcracker*. Singers should remember that many German *Lieder* and 19th-century French *chansons* are essentially types of romantic miniature, as are such popular art songs as Tchaikovsky's 'None but the lonely heart' and Dvořák's 'Songs my mother taught me'.

From this wealth of material you should be able to deduce that the romantic miniature is short, focused on a single musical idea and usually memorably melodic, all ingredients that make for easy listening. Note the forms used, which are often quite basic (binary, rounded binary or ternary) perhaps with a short introduction and coda. It may be difficult to sustain your own piece for three minutes or more with such simple forms, so look carefully at what happens in longer works. You could, if necessary, write a matching pair of movements, perhaps both based on the same theme.

Notice that while some works in this genre have abstract titles, such as prelude or 'album leaf', others specify the style of the piece (march, waltz, song without words) and still others (such as those in *NAM 23*) suggest very specific images. You can use whatever is appropriate to your own work, but try to make the title relevant to the musical content.

Although melody is important, you should notice that harmony is often quite luxuriant. Try to analyse why. You should spot that chromatic chords such as secondary dominants and diminished 7ths are often used, and tertiary modulations (shifts to a key a 3rd away, such as G to E♭) are employed to give an exotic effect. Notice how dissonances are created by lingering on non-harmonic notes and by using long appoggiaturas, often with resolutions that are so brief that they seem almost to be an after-thought.

Neo-classicism

Three movements from Stravinsky's *Pulcinella* suite are printed in *NAM 7* – try to listen to the rest of the suite or the original ballet score. Stravinsky arranged some of these movements for violin and piano in his *Suite Italienne* (also available for cello and piano) – this version would be particularly useful for study. Other well-known neo-classical works by Stravinsky include the concerto for piano and winds, the Symphony in C, *Oedipus Rex* (modelled on baroque oratorio) and *The Rake's Progress*.

The *Bransle Simple* from Stravinksy's neo-classic ballet *Agon*, is included in *Sound Matters* (Bowman and Cole) No.42.

The Rhinegold Dictionary of Music in Sound includes an extract from Ravel's *Le Tombeau de Couperin* (C33) – compare it with the extract of a Forlane by Couperin (C32) in the same publication.

Works by other composers include Prokofiev's *Classical* symphony (try to hear at least the third movement, which is a modern version of a gavotte), Hindemith's *Ludus Tonalis* for piano, and Satie's *Sonatine bureaucratique* (a satiric paraphrase of a classical piece by Clementi). The clear textures of neo-classicism can be found in the work of a number of other early 20th-century composers, including Bartók (Dance suite for orchestra), Poulenc (see *NAM 19*) and Shostakovich (*NAM 25*).

Your own piece could take the form of a sonatina or trio sonata, a contrapuntal form such as a fugue, or perhaps some linked dance movements, using pre-1800 dance forms interpreted in a bitonal idiom. While it is possible to base your work on existing music, this technique was quite rare among the neo-classicists – the only other work by Stravinsky which does so is *The Fairy's Kiss*, in which he reworked compositions by Tchaikovsky.

Post-modernism

A good starting point for research is the early work of the 'New York minimalists': *In C* (Terry Riley), *Music in Similar Motion*, *Music in Fifths* and *Another Look at Harmony* (Philip Glass), *Phase Patterns* and *Drumming* (Steve Reich). An excerpt from Reich's *Clapping Music* is included in the *Rhinegold Dictionary of Music in Sound* (C89) and his *New York Counterpoint* is in *NAM* (No. 12).

Other post-modernist music in the *Rhinegold Dictionary of Music in Sound* includes extracts from the music of Giles Swayne (C91), Sylvie Bodorová (C96) and James MacMillan (C97).

Look out for larger-scale works such as Stockhausen's *Stimmung*, and John Adams' *Harmonium* (1981) and *Harmonielehre* (1985). Certain post-modernist pieces became immensely popular in the closing years of the 20th century, particularly Jonathan Dove's comic opera, *Flight* (1998), Henryk Górecki's third symphony, John Adams' *Short Ride in a Fast Machine*, and the works of Arvo Pärt and John Tavener (both influenced by the mystical style of Eastern Orthodox church music). Tavener's *The Lamb* is in *NAM* (No. 32) and an excerpt from his much earlier *Ultimos Ritos* can be found in the old London Anthology, No. 119. Look out also for his cello concerto (called *The Protecting Veil*) and *Song for Athene*.

Because musical change tends to occur over a long time span in minimalist music, you will need to consider how you can show a range of skills if you choose this style – it may be necessary to write

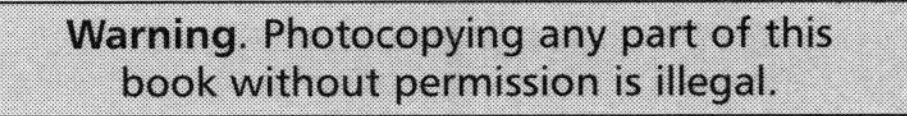

a piece rather longer than the minimum requirement. In addition to art music (choral works, instrumental pieces, etc.) you could choose other formats in which a contemporary musical style is appropriate – educational pieces that might incorporate parts for children, music intended for a sound installation (e.g. music for a science exhibition or a virtual-reality experience) or a suite of music for a computer-games program (splash-screen music, mood music to underline fear, safety, excitement and aggression, location music for different levels of the game, and so forth). If you are tempted by this last category, remember the need for consistency (a 'brand image') across separate items, be sure to include some more extended pieces as well as shorter looped tracks, try to avoid items that are purely sound effects, and concentrate **on the music** as CD-ROMs, artwork or videos are not required. However you can submit your work on tape, CD or minidisk, accompanying it with explanatory diagrams or a flow chart.

The popular song

You could write a song with accompaniment for piano or guitar, or a more elaborate setting that includes backing vocals, rock group, jazz band or even orchestral parts. Any style is acceptable (including folk, jazz, soul, reggae, as well as contemporary styles) but remember that you will need to show a good range of skills within a single composition, so try to avoid types of music in which there is much repetition and little variety. Your song will be expected to feature a vocal line (the lyrics of which will not be assessed). You are permitted to submit your work as a lead-sheet, but the accompaniment must be fully worked out on the recording. Aim for a strong bass line, and remember that you will be expected to show imagination in your choice of chords and modulations, and in the musical detail you assign to backing instruments. Aim for an interesting structure, perhaps with varied treatment of verses and choruses, a middle section in a more remote key, and additional sections such as an intro, an instrumental bridge and a coda. Consider how these might be unified through the use of a hook line or common chord pattern. Pay attention to stylish licks and fills, and aim for some variety when writing drum patterns.

There are many songs for you to study in the popular music and jazz section of the *New Anthology*, and in the jazz and pop section of *Sound Matters* (Bowman and Cole). Most pop music is published in easy arrangements for voice and piano/guitar; however, this format does not form a good model for study as too much important detail is missing. Instead look out for the detailed transcriptions that are published in the *Rock Scores* series by Music Sales and in the *Off the Record* series from IMP, as well as collections such as *Beatles: The Complete Scores* (Music Sales).

There are also detailed scores of 17 classic hits from the 1950s to the 1990s, with hints on sequencing, in *Rock in Sequence* (Lloyd and Terry), published by Music Sales.

Club dance and hip hop

At first sight this topic may appear rather confusing: hip hop developed in 1970s New York as a cultural movement of the urban ghetto, in which music (and specifically rap) is only one element. Club dance music, on the other hand, can encompass a broad range of music that may include anything from 'golden oldy' tracks by Abba and Queen, through house, techno, trance, garage, jungle and Nu-NRG to eclectic mixes by that night's DJ. In Britain, hip hop became popular in the early 1980s, quickly being adopted by the strong club scene. This commercial, dance-orientated style (which has been disparagingly called trip-hop) tends to avoid the violent subject matter and frank language sometimes found in rap itself.

However the intention here is to give you the opportunity to submit modern dance music and not to limit you to one particular style. It is likely that your work will include tightly sequenced rhythms, carefully set at the appropriate speed (bpm) for the intended dance style, and it may well include samples of pre-recorded material. You may choose to include a vocal part, either sung or rapped, or you may prefer to write a purely instrumental dance track.

Research will need to be mainly by ear from existing recordings, since this type of music is not normally notated, although magazines and web sites on hip hop may be useful. You may wish to produce a score of your own piece but this is not necessarily expected – a good-quality recording plus a fully annotated track diagram showing the processes used will be fine. Note that it is essential to identify all samples used in your recording.

Your composition should show variety in its use of textures and drum patterns, so you should adopt a style in which this is possible. Work at this level should be ambitious in structure, with a variety of well-balanced tracks and an imaginative use of sampled sounds, perhaps modified by various effects processes, in order to achieve a rich mix of stylish material.

Fusions

Here again there is the opportunity to work in any one of a huge range of styles, the essential requirement being that the music draws on different cultural traditions, combining elements from both to produce a distinctive style of its own. Originally the term fusion was applied to the rock-influenced jazz style adopted by Miles Davis in the late 1960s, and taken up by groups such as Weather Report. Other types of fusion popular at this time included folk-rock, the Latin-American based rock of Carlos Santana, the art-rock interpretations of classical music by Emerson, Lake and Palmer, and the vocal jazz arrangements of Bach performed by the Swingle Singers.

Recent decades have witnessed a still greater range of fusion styles, including bhangra, salsa and celtic rock. Indeed, many multicultural pop styles can be seen as a type of fusion, arising from the influence of western pop music on local cultural traditions. In addition there has been further exploration of the ground between pop- and art-music styles in the work of cross-over artists such as Steve Martland and John Casken. It might also be useful to explore some earlier examples of the use of popular styles in art music, such as Debussy's *Golliwogg's Cakewalk*, Satie's *Parade*, Walton's *Façade*, Stravinsky's *Ragtime* for 11 instruments and Peter Maxwell Davies' *St Thomas Wake* (a 'Foxtrot for Orchestra').

Casken's *Piper's Linn* and Martland's *The World is in Heaven* appear in *Sound Matters* (Bowman and Cole). Martland's *Principia* and folk-rock from Steeleye Span can be found in *Aural Matters* (Bowman and Terry). Both these books also include examples of world music that may be useful for this topic. *The Rhinegold Dictionary of Music in Sound* includes excerpts from Debussy's *Golliwogg's Cakewalk* and the *Popular Song* from Walton's *Façade*.

Your work may be in any appropriate form, but it should exploit the idea of fusion and draw on appropriate elements from the different styles and idioms involved.

Film and television

The *New Anthology* provides one of the most useful sources of research material for this topic. There are also a number of books and websites about film music composition. Themes from many famous films are available as sheet music, but such publications are usually simplified arrangements for piano, and thus omit many important details, and they seldom include more than the main title theme so they are unlikely to be very helpful. However it would be useful to look out for scores and CDs of the following works, which are all based on film music: Prokofiev's *Suite from Lieutenant Kijé*, Walton's *Henry V Suite*, Copland's *Our Town Suite* and Vaughan Williams' Symphony No. 7 (based on his music for the film *Scott of the Antartic*).

Your own music could be for an existing film or video, an imaginary one, or perhaps one that is being made by other students at your school or college. You may submit your work as a recording dubbed on video if you wish, but this is not required – a clear account of the image that the music is intended to underscore is sufficient.

The subject could be historical (possibly giving the opportunity for some pastiche of an old musical style), a travelogue such as a video of a school foreign trip (perhaps including local musical styles to give a sense of location to the various scenes), a cartoon, a sports sequence or an extended commercial. Try to choose a topic with some dramatic content as this is likely to give you the opportunity for some interesting and vivid contrasts in your music.

It is acceptable to submit several short extracts for this topic – perhaps a title theme, a piece of illustrative music, various link passages (eg bridges that are designed to change mood) and a sequence for the final credits. Try to maintain a consistent style in such a submission and, if appropriate, link the sections thematically. Aim to convey a clear sense of mood, paying attention to the way music is used in the visual media to heighten and release emotional tension, as well as to create atmosphere. This will need careful attention to scoring.

Music theatre

For exam purposes this topic covers any type of music that involves a staged element in its presentation and so includes opera, operetta, ballet, musicals and rock opera, as well as the type of small-scale, semi-staged work in which the instrumentalists frequently take a dramatic role and which is often specifically described as music theatre. This last category includes works such as Stravinsky's *The Soldier's Tale*, Schoenberg's *Pierrot Lunaire* (which is often staged), Britten's church parables, such as *Curlew River*, and Peter Maxwell Davies' *Eight Songs for a Mad King* and *Vesalii icones*.

One of the songs from *Pierrot Lunaire* is in *NAM* (No. 40) and an extract from another is in *The Rhinegold Dictionary of Sound*. An excerpt from *Vesalii Icones* can be found in *Sound Matters* (Bowman and Cole).

Your own composition could be a short section of a musical or other music-theatre work, perhaps including a vocal introduction, a solo or duet, and ending with a dance number or a finale in which you could combine several voices and a chorus. It is not essential to score the accompaniment for full orchestra – you could confine yourself to a piano reduction (as used in rehearsals) or you could write for just a small ensemble of accompanying instruments. You could instead choose to write purely instrumental music designed for a dramatic work, such as an overture, music for a contemporary dance production, or incidental music for a play.

Choose a subject that will give you the opportunity to show a dramatic quality in your music, and a sense of theatre. A slow, dreamy ballad might be part of the submission, but it would be best to include some points of tension and conflict as well.

Specialist option B: Recital

If you choose pathway B for the specialist option, you will have to perform a solo recital instead of submitting the composition folio described on pages 12–15.

Requirements

You will need to plan a program that lasts at least 20 minutes. The minimum size of audience is two (your teacher and one other person) but you may feel that performing to such a small group seems more like an exam than a recital. Some people find that a class concert presented to a group of friends and fellow students is more natural, and provides a good focus for the preparatory work involved, but the occasion can be on any scale, including a lunch-time or evening concert at your school or college, or a gig at a public venue. Note, though, the requirements that your teacher must be present and that the recital must be recorded, so you need to discuss the proposed occasion with your teacher.

Any music that you play which is intended to be accompanied must be performed with accompaniment. This can be provided by a keyboard instrument, a group of other performers, or by a tape or electronic backing. It is important that you should feature clearly in a solo capacity in any ensemble pieces you choose to include, such as jazz improvisations or rock numbers. Remember that the examiners need to hear and assess only your part, and not the playing of other musicians.

If you are at all unsure if a particular piece would be regarded as a solo, check with your A level teacher, since Edexcel provides guidance on this matter.

You can include just selected movements from longer works if you wish, and if there are long sections in which only the accompaniment plays (as may occur in a concerto) these can be curtailed. But in other respects the music must be complete – you should not omit sections that you find too difficult.

You may use more than one instrument in your recital. For example trumpeters may wish to include a piece for cornet or flugelhorn, or perhaps a baroque piece for trumpet in D. Similarly a recorder player may wish to include works for both descant and treble instruments, and percussionists should certainly plan to show their skills on a range of both pitched and unpitched instruments.

Note that there are no marks for diversity. For example, if you are primarily a singer who can also manage a bit of piano playing, there is nothing to be gained by including an easy piano piece – it would be better to concentrate on achieving a high standard in your vocal repertoire. If you do play a second instrument to the same standard as your main study, the music for that instrument should be chosen with regard to achieving a coherant overall program.

Difficulty level

The technical difficulty of the music you choose also needs careful consideration. Easy pieces played musically are much more likely to be successful than difficult pieces marred by hesitations and breakdowns. In order to be able to achieve the highest marks the pieces need to be of grade 6 standard or higher (if you do not take graded exams your teacher will help explain what this implies). If the majority of works are at grade 7 standard (or higher) your mark will be scaled up accordingly. There is no need to struggle to reach a high difficulty level (and risk a potential disaster if it proves too hard) since you will be given credit for what you can do with the music you offer, but you should be capable of presenting a recital in which all of the pieces are *at least* of grade 5 standard if you choose this option. If the pieces are below grade 6 in standard, or if the recital is less than 20 minutes in length, your mark will be scaled down.

Whatever your technical standard it is better to choose music that you can perform with confidence than to attempt a difficult work which stretches your technique to its limit. Works that are too demanding will leave no leeway for the inevitable nervousness that *will* arise under the conditions of a live assessment. The anxiety and tension they generate will be communicated to the listener, and will inevitably impede your musical interpretation.

Choice of music

The minimum 20 minutes length for the recital can include time for applause and any brief spoken introductions you choose to make. Audiences greatly appreciate the latter – it provides a moment of human contact rather than just seeing you sneak on and off without apparent awareness of others in the room. However keep to a short announcement of the work and perhaps a word or two about your reaction to the piece – such as why you enjoy performing it. Avoid a lecture about its date and form, and try to be positive – if you sound miserable and scared, your audience will be, too.

Choose pieces that you enjoy playing and that allow you to show a range of skills. Note that you must not include any items you offered for AS Music, or that you performed during the course as part of the *Performing and composing* unit. A surprising number of pieces, whether single-movement classical works or pop songs, are only about three minutes in length, so make sure that you have enough repertoire to last at least 20 minutes.

A programme with some variety is likely to serve you best. Your audience (and that includes your examiner) are likely to be more impressed by items which vary in style, mood and speed than a succession of all-too-similar slow movements. Try to start with something that grabs the attention, but that is not necessarily too difficult, such as a baroque allegro, or a lively electric-guitar solo. Alternate slow pieces with more lively items, and try to end with something destined to leave the audience still wanting more – a humorous modern work or a hard-rock number.

Also remember to pace yourself carefully. Don't start with the most challenging work – if it goes wrong, your nerves may be shattered for the following items. Plan some items for the middle where you can relax a bit, such as an expressive slow movement or a lazy blues. This is especially important if you are a wind player or singer as you will need the opportunity to recover your breath and/or lip. Note that the recital can consist of a single long work, such as a concerto or song cycle, since this will by its very nature include the necessary variety for both performer and audience.

Preparation, performance and assessment

Reread the advice on pages 10–11 of the AS Guide, noting the importance of performing the complete programme in advance to someone who can give you some dispassionate feedback. Adequate rehearsal with the accompanist (if applicable) is vital, and a run-through in the final venue is essential.

You are required to provide programme notes on a form supplied by Edexcel. Mention the characteristics of each piece and how you intend to convey them, and also give reasons for your choice and order of items. After the event you can, if you wish, add a comment about the extent to which your intentions were realised in the recital. Note that the examiner will require photocopies of your solo part(s) as well as a recording of the event and programme notes.

Analysing music

There are two parts to this unit:

- a one-hour listening test that accounts for just under 40% of the marks for this unit, followed immediately in the exam by …
- a two-hour written paper that accounts for just over 60% of the marks for this unit.

1. Listening test

The test is presented on CD and you will be given your own copy of this CD which you are allowed to play as many times as you wish in the 60 minutes allowed. Each extract is recorded only once, so you will need to be familiar with the controls of your CD player in order to locate and repeat individual tracks efficiently; you will also need to pace yourself carefully so that you have time to answer all three questions in the test.

Context

1. You will hear **three** different passages of music for which no notation is given. For each passage you will have to give a context for the music by answering questions on matters such as its style (e.g. baroque, minimalist, jazz, etc), its genre (e.g. anthem, opera, 12-bar blues, etc) and any prominent elements (e.g. atonality, irregular metre, etc). You will be asked to suggest a date of composition and to name a person (composer or performer) likely to be associated with the music.

Comparison

2. You will hear **two** excerpts of music for which no notation is given. You will have to answer questions on the similarities and differences between the two excerpts in matters such as instrumentation, shared material, technique, style and so forth. The two extracts may be from different parts of the same piece or they may be from two different pieces by the same composer or band, that are related in style. Note that there may well be more differences than similarities, and that you may also be asked to identify the type(s) of music, and how they are related.

General test of aural perception

3. You will hear **one** excerpt of music for which a two-stave skeleton score will be provided. There will be three questions on pitch and rhythm, of which you must answer two:

    (a) Three short rhythms or melodies will be printed, and you must locate where in the score each of these is heard
    (b) You will be asked to notate the rhythm of a specific short passage heard on the CD
    (c) You will be asked to notate the pitches of a specific short melody heard on the CD (the rhythm will be given).

    In addition you will have to answer two further questions:

    (d) You will have to identify four specific keys, key relationships, chords or chord progressions in the music
    (e) You will have to write a short commentary on important features of the music that you can hear in the recording (and that are not obvious from the score or covered in the preceding questions) and place the extract in context.

I, II, IV, V (root position or first inversion)
III and VI (root position only)
VII in first inversion
V^7 in root position or any inversion
Ic, II^7b, diminished 7th
augmented 6th, Neapolitan 6th.

In 3(d) questions on tonality will require you to identify specific keys, and they may involve recognising the following simple key relationships: dominant, subdominant, relative minor/major, and tonic major/minor (eg a change from C major to C minor, or vice versa). Questions on chords may involve identifying any of the chords listed left. Questions on chord progressions might include recognising the standard types of cadence, the circle of 5ths, and patterns such as V–I, I–V, IV–I, I–IV and V–VI.

Bass part played by bassoon.
Opening phrase repeated octave higher.
Second section develops the opening motif.
Ascending chromatic scale in third section, followed by oboe and flute in dialogue.
Dominant pedal prepares for the recap.
Flute imitates clarinet near the end.
Homophonic texture in the coda.

In question 3(e) you will be asked to mention significant features of the music that are not immediately obvious from the skeleton score and that have not been identified in the other questions on this extract. You can answer in note form or continuous prose. You are likely to get one mark for each accurate point, so if eight marks are available you should aim to make eight points about the music. If you refer to specific events in the music you should give their location. For instance you should write 'imitation between flute and clarinet near the end' – not just the single word 'imitation'. An example of a successful type of answer is shown *left*.

If you include a general point about the impact of the music, make sure it is justified with evidence. For instance, you might state that 'a jolly mood is created by the major tonality, frequent cadences and lively articulation'. Just saying that it sounds happy, without giving reasons, will not be rewarded with a mark.

None of the music extracts in the listening test are linked to any particular area of study, so you are likely to encounter music which will be unfamiliar. In order to gain confidence in answering questions on identification it will be essential to listen to a wide range of music and to practise recognising its main features.

Beware of jumping to conclusions too quickly. For example the presence of a harpsichord in orchestral music might seem an obvious clue that the music is baroque – but if the orchestra also includes horns then the extract might actually be early classical, perhaps from the period 1750–1780, when the harpsichord was still in common use. You need to listen for further evidence – if the phrase lengths run mainly in clear four-bar periods and the textures often consist of a melody with subordinate accompaniment, early classical would seem likely. But if the texture is more contrapuntal, and the parts are formed from short motifs that are spun out into long melodic lines, then late baroque might seem more probable. Similarly, remember that although church music might be sung by an unaccompanied choir, not all unaccompanied choral music is church music – it could be a madrigal or an excerpt from an opera, for instance. Get into the habit of tuning into a radio station such as Classic FM and trying to identify what you hear.

Listening Tests for Students (Edexcel A2 Music Specification) by Hugh Benham and Alistair Wightman, *Rhinegold Publishing Ltd.* Book 1, ISBN: 1-904226-46-9. Book 2, ISBN: 1-904226-67-1.

Listening Matters by David Bowman and Paul Terry. *Schott and Co Ltd.* ISBN: 1-902 455-08-8.

Aural Matters by David Bowman and Paul Terry. *Schott and Co Ltd.* ISBN: 0-946535-22-1.

Aural Matters in Practice by David Bowman and Paul Terry. *Schott and Co Ltd.* ISBN: 0-946535-23-X.

Sound Matters by David Bowman and Bruce Cole. *Schott and Co. Ltd.* ISBN: 0-946535-14-0.

The Rhinegold Dictionary of Music in Sound by David Bowman. *Rhinegold Publishing.* ISBN: 0-946890-87-0. This includes a chapter on 'Style, genre and historical context'.

Your teacher will help you with practice materials (some are listed *left*), and you could also make your own listening tests by devising questions on a short extract from a piece that you play and could perform for the rest of the group to use as an aural test. You can also develop your skills in dictation by writing down the rhythm and pitch of short melodic fragments you know by heart, and then checking the results by playing them on an instrument.

2. Written paper

For this part of the unit you must prepare **two** of the following areas of study:

- Music for large ensemble
- 20th-century art music
- Music for small ensemble
- Keyboard music
- Sacred vocal music
- Secular vocal music
- Music for film and television
- Popular music and jazz
- World music

One of your choices **must be an area of study that you offered for AS Music**. For A2 you will extend your earlier work by:

a) Studying a prescribed 'special focus' work (or works) from the area of study, **and**

b) Investigating a topic of continuity and change that relates to the area of study as a whole.

Your other area of study must be one that you did **not** offer for AS Music. For this area of study you are required only to prepare a prescribed 'special focus' work (or works). You do not have to learn about the other works in the area of study.

The music for each of these areas of study is provided in the *New Anthology of Music* (referred to as *NAM* in the rest of this book) with recordings on a companion set of four CDs. You are expected to use an **unmarked** copy of the anthology in the exam.

In the examination you will have to answer five questions, four from Section A and one from Section B, as follows:

Section A

There will be three questions on each of the 'special focus' works. You must answer **two** questions on the prescribed work(s) from the Area of Study that you also offered for AS Music **and two** questions on the prescribed work(s) from the new Area of Study that you have chosen for A2 Music.

The rest of this book is based on the Special Focus Works and Topics set for examination in 2008 and 2009. Different works and different topics will be set in later years.

Section B

There will be two questions on each Area of Study. You must answer **one**, which must be on the Area of Study that you started for AS Music and have extended for A2.

There is no division of works into list A and list B, as there is for AS Music. For A2 you need to study all of the works that relate to the prescribed topic of continuity and change. However remember that you only study **one** such topic – the one set for the Area of Study that you began at AS and that will appear in Section B of the paper. For the other Area of Study, the one that you start specially for A2, the only requirement is to study the prescribed 'special focus' work(s).

Preparation

Reread pages 21–23 of the AS Guide, noting the importance of focusing your studies on the music itself, not on peripheral matters such as learning biographies of composers or quotations of what other people have said about the pieces.

It is important that you have a clear understanding of technical terms relating to the music you study. Terminology is not an end in itself – it is merely a convenient way of explaining to other musicians precisely what you mean in as few words as possible. But remember that if you use technical terms incorrectly it will confuse rather than elucidate. We haven't included a glossary of terms in this guide, but you should refer to the glossary in the AS Guide if you encounter any term about which you are unsure. The most important thing is to be certain you know how the term relates to the sounds you hear – if you need further help, look up the word in the *Rhinegold Dictionary of Music in Sound*, play the example(s) on its associated CDs and check the notation in its set of scores.

For A2 it becomes increasingly necessary to listen to an extensive range of music, not only to prepare for the listening test but also to help you amplify your answers in the written paper. Try to make use of the holidays for this enjoyable task, remembering to listen for pleasure as well as for understanding.

The rest of this Guide consists of chapters on each Area of Study. These cover the information you are likely to need to know for the exam and sometimes include suggestions for additional listening and reading. During the course of each chapter there are a number of questions headed 'Private study' that are designed to help you check your understanding – these are not necessarily the type of question that you will encounter in the exam and in most cases the answers should be clear by carefully rereading the preceding paragraphs or the related section in the AS Guide. At the end of each main section you will find a set of 'Sample questions' which will give you some exam practice, particularly in your final weeks of revision. Some notes on how to revise effectively are given on pages 24–25 of the AS Guide.

Remember that your revision plan needs to include rereading the introductory information on your Areas of Study given in the AS Guide, as well as a thorough reappraisal of your AS notes for the Area of Study that you are carrying through from AS to A2.

Exam technique

In Section A you will have to answer four questions – two on each of your 'special focus' works. Each of these four questions attracts 10 marks (out of a total of 60) and your answer can be written in continuous prose, or note form, or as a set of bullet points. A good rule of thumb is to reckon that there will be one mark for each valid point that you make. A 'valid point' is one that helps answer the question directly. Just stating a fact about the music will not gain a mark if it is irrelevant.

Support your points by making frequent references to the music, usually by means of bar numbers (e.g. 'a modulation to the dominant is confirmed by a perfect cadence in bars 13–14'). Be precise, adding the name of the part and/or the beat number(s) if necessary to avoid ambiguity. A widely understood method is to use small superscript numerals for beat numbers: for example, bar 4^3 means bar 4, beat 3. Be aware that giving detailed and relevant references to substantial points in this way can often gain you extra marks.

In this book we often use expressions such as 'motif x', 'the second subject' or 'the third episode' when explaining music. If you do this in an exam answer, remember that it is *essential* to show the examiner exactly what you mean – for instance, 'the second subject (in the violin part of bars 15^4–26^3).

Make sure you answer the correct number of questions (four in Section A and one in Section B). Pace yourself carefully so that you are not rushed towards the end of the paper and that you have a few minutes to check your answers at the end of the exam. Choose your questions with care. Don't just dive in as soon as you happen to recognise the general gist of a question – first consider if you have enough knowledge to provide a really full answer.

For each of the four questions in Section A you are going to need to make 10 valid points in under 20 minutes. Although you have to answer only one question in Section B, it attracts 20 marks and must be written in continuous prose, as a short essay. It would therefore be wise to allow yourself 40 minutes to complete this question.

Essay writing

Developing a good clear style in writing prose will not only help your exam technique but will also prove useful in later life if you are required to write reports, evaluations or proposals. This takes practice, so it is important that you write essay answers (including some timed examples) during the course, as you work your way through your chosen specified topic.

The assessment will include your skill in written communication (which can gain you extra credit if it is good, and not just lose you marks if it is weak). If this is an area you find difficult, remember that one of the most useful tips listed below is to keep to short sentences. Make a point and then follow it up with an example (see the first essay on the next page). It will also help to make a brief plan of the essay, so you get an overview of all the points you wish to make, and can then arrange them in a logical order. Having to change tack in mid-essay in order to go back to some point you had previously forgotten can make your reasoning difficult to follow.

Nine tips for a good essay

- Make sure that you understand the requirements of the question.
- Plan the structure by making a note of the main areas to cover. It can be useful to devote one paragraph to each of these areas.
- Begin by immediately addressing the question – don't waste time trying to 'set the scene' with background information.
- Keep to the point. If you run out of ideas, it is better to examine the score carefully to see what you may have missed rather than to start introducing irrelevant facts.
- Try to support each one of your arguments with evidence from the music itself, given in the form of references to specific bar numbers.
- Avoid repetition. You don't get extra marks for repeating a point, even if you clothe it in different language.
- You should normally stick to factual information – if a personal opinion is required remember that it (like all your arguments) should be supported by reference to specific examples in *NAM*.
- Avoid long sentences whenever possible.
- Aim for handwriting that is legible and unambiguous.

Many of the Section B questions require you to make a specific evaluation of the works you have studied – such questions often begin 'Compare and contrast …' or 'To what extent does … '. The examiners will be looking for a balanced argument in your answer: 'In these respects there are similarities … but in these respects there are differences …'. Check that all your points relate to the question posed, since there is no credit for irrelevant information.

The ticks in these two examples show the type of points that are likely to be given credit, but they do not represent an official markscheme. In practice, the examiners will have agreed on a detailed markscheme for each question after an initial evaluation of a large number of answers.

As you can see from the example below, it is possible to cover a large number of points in a short essay if you are concise and stay focused on the question. When you look at this, and the essay on the next page, **remember that there is no one way of tackling a question – these are merely examples of different styles and neither represents a mythical 'right answer'.**

13a. Compare the structures of the Sarabandes by Bach and Debussy

Bach's Sarabande is in binary form,✔ typical of most baroque dances. The two sections are defined by their tonality.✔ The first ends in the dominant at bar 12.✔ The second is longer✔ and modulates more widely✔ before returning to the tonic at bar 29.✔ At this point there is a modified restatement of the opening material.✔ This is known as rounded✔ binary form.

The movement is based on a continuous development of the opening material.✔ For example, the sequence beginning in bar 5✔ is derived from the motif in bar 1✔ and the second section begins with a transposition of bars 1-2.✔

Debussy's Sarabande is also in two sections of unequal length,✔ separated by a double barline in bar 22, although the sections are not repeated.✔ It also returns to the opening material in the second section (at bar 42).✔ But whereas Bach's Sarabande is monothematic, Debussy uses a variety of independent themes.✔ There are two in the first section (bars 1 and 9),✔ the first of which is repeated at bar 15.✔ He uses a new theme for the second section (bar 23)✔ and another new theme at bar 50.✔ Unlike Bach, he ends the movement with a coda, starting at bar 63.✔

While Bach uses tonality to define the sections of his form, Debussy's melodies are modal and his harmonies are complex, using key more as a means of colour than as a way to define structure.✔

This is a first-rate answer which directly addresses the question by means of a valid point in every sentence. The structure is clear: the first half is devoted to Bach's Sarabande, the second to Debussy's, and comparisons are clarified in constructions such as 'Debussy's Sarabande also …', 'But whereas Bach …', and 'Unlike Bach …'.

The short sentences are unambiguous and almost every point is backed-up with references to specific bar numbers in the music. The use of technical language is secure, and the concluding paragraph is perceptive, showing an understanding that it is tonality which defines structure in Bach's Sarabande, but not in Debussy's.

Now, can you see why the following answer is less successful than the first? It is the same length, but relevant points appear far less frequently and there are no references to specific bars in the music.

13a. *Compare the structures of the Sarabandes by Bach and Debussy*

The sarabande is one of the dances of the Baroque suite. Bach's partita, which is really a suite, was published in 1728 and is in D major. Debussy's sarabande was written in 1894 and is a more modern version of the old dance.

Both works are lovely pieces, but Bach's music sounds more lively because it is often played on the harpsichord while Debussy's music is more dreamy because it is played on the piano.

Debussy uses thicker chords than Bach, to make his piece more interesting, and he uses more themes ✔ with several laid back tunes that pop up as the piece goes on.

● *Not everyone appreciated Debussy's music. Someone said 'he doesn't like the piano much'. That seems an unfair criticism.*

Bach uses binary form ✔ but Debussy doesn't. He uses some other form. Another difference is that Debussy uses several different themes in his Sarabande. It is hard to work out the form because he doesn't write in clear keys for different sections like Bach ✔ does, but it looks like he has two sections and the second is longer, like Bach's. ✔

Debussy wrote a lot of other pieces, with titles like 'La Mer' and 'The Girl with the Flaxen Hair'. These were all composed after Bach had died so they are romantic pieces. ●

Neither sarabande would be very good music for dancing to, because they are both too slow.

There is nothing inaccurate in the first two paragraphs, but neither tells us anything about structure. The first is 'scene setting' narrative while the second consists mainly of subjective opinion.

Not until the third paragraph is there an attempt to tackle the question. The slang terms in the colloquial expression 'laid back tunes that pop up as the piece goes on' are not appropriate to this style of writing – it would be better to support the good first point by giving some examples (by bar number) from the score. The fourth paragraph throws in a memorised but unattributed quotation (it is actually from Debussy's piano teacher) which doesn't contribute to answering this question about structure.

The fifth paragraph is much more successful, with several valid observations (although the point about Debussy using more themes has already been made). The sixth introduces some irrelevant information, while the conclusion is unrelated to the question and misses the point that neither Sarabande was written for dancing.

Of course in reality most answers tend to fall between these two extremes, but hopefully these made-up examples will help you to develop your own written style in a clear and focused way.

Note that it is not necessary to copy out the question at the start. Some people find it helps to keep the wording in focus, but just writing the question number is sufficient.

Special Focus Work for 2008 and 2009	
NAM 1 (page 7)	CD1 Track 1
Northern Sinfonia of England	
Directed by George Malcolm	

Bach, Brandeburg Concerto No. 4 in G: movement 1

Before starting on this section you should work through (or revise) the information about the context and structure of this music given on pages 27–28 of the AS Guide. Make sure that you understand all of the terminology used on those pages.

Instrumentation and scoring

This is a movement from a **concerto grosso** in which the **concertino** consists of a solo violin and two solo recorders and the **ripieno** consists of parts for two violins, viola, cello and double bass. The size of this string ensemble can vary since most (if not all) of the ripieno parts can be played by several performers.

There is no **figured bass** shown in *NAM 1*, but an example from another work by Bach can be seen on page 288 of *NAM*.

Both groups are accompanied by a **continuo** ensemble consisting of at least one bass instrument (such as a cello) plus at least one harmony instrument (such as a harpsichord or lute). The latter improvises harmonies in accordance with the conventions of the time and guided by any figuring given in the bass part.

There is a clear distinction between the virtuoso solo violin part and the less taxing recorder parts. The violin is allowed long, sparsely accompanied solos (bars 83–102, for instance), but the recorders nearly always work together, often in **parallel 3rds or 6ths**. This distinction is most noticeable in the extrovert violin solo in bars 187–209, where the recorders supply unobtrusive accompaniment figures in 6ths and 3rds (bars 187–192) that are little different from the duet for ripieno violins in the next six bars.

Context

Bach's six *Brandenburg* concertos were written between 1717 and 1722 for the small but very competent court orchestra of Cöthen, one of the many states into which Germany was then divided, and where Bach was director of music. He subsequently presented a score of the six works to the ruler of the much larger state of Brandenburg, hence their title. It is not known if the concertos were ever played at Brandenburg, but most were forgotten after Bach's death in 1750. Even after the rediscovery of Bach's manuscripts in the 19th century performances were rare. It was not until the 20th century, when recording made the *Brandenburg* concertos available to a wide audience, that these works became established as some of the best-loved instrumental music of the baroque period.

Brandenburg Concerto No. 4 is modelled on the type of concerto that was perfected by the Italian composer Vivaldi, who was ten years older than Bach. Bach studied Vivaldi's concertos by making his own (more complex) arrangements of them. The most famous is Vivaldi's Concerto Op. 3, No. 8, RV 522 – a concerto grosso for two violins and strings, that Bach transcribed as a solo piece for organ (BWV 593). The first movement is only half the length of NAM 1 and in both versions the rondo-like form is simpler and has clear thematic differences between the loud ritornellos and the quieter episodes that separate them. Both are available in budget price recordings so, if at all possible, try to listen to them several times as an aural preparation for NAM 1.

Rhythm and metre

As in most of Bach's instrumental music – and much of his sacred music too – dance rhythms are clearly in evidence. The unvarying one-in-a-bar triple metre is enlivened by the **syncopated rhythms** of the recorders in bars 4, 6, 15, 17, 43–47 and so on, and by **hemiolas** (the *basso continuo* in bars 79–80 effectively goes into one bar of $\frac{3}{4}$ time, as shown *right*). These bars contain the most joyful and complex rhythms of the whole movement. The upper strings accentuate the second, first then the third quavers of each bar (and are therefore out of phase with the bass hemiola), while the recorders accentuate the intervening quavers (and are therefore in phase with it). But all of the parts agree on the characteristic syncopated rhythm at the cadence, where the second quaver of bar 82 gets particular emphasis because the chords change at this point (IV^7–V^7). Bach uses this startling collection of syncopations elsewhere in the movement, always to signal the end of an important section, thus underlining the structure of the music.

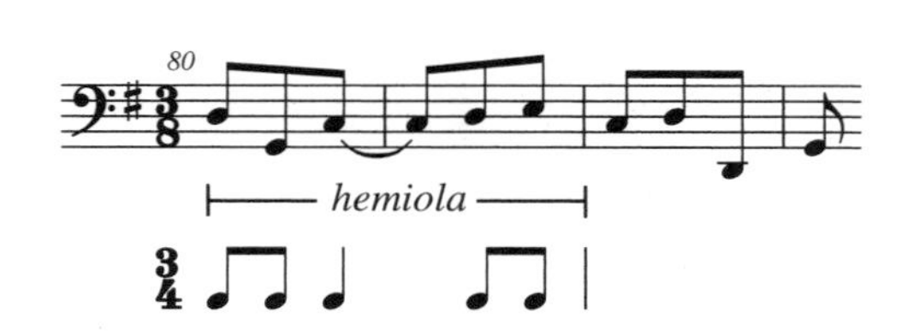

Melody and motif

Bach's melodic lines often include arpeggio figures that outline the underlying chords. For example, the second recorder's arpeggios in bars 1–2 clearly trace the triads played by *ripieno* strings (chords I and V). Variants are two-a-penny: for instance, a triad of E minor is as clear in the upper string parts in bar 14 as it is in the second recorder's arpeggio in the same bar. Such harmonically charged melodic lines are particularly obvious in the extended violin solos. For instance, the unaccompanied violin in bar 84 clearly changes the G-major triad of bar 83 into the dominant seventh of C major. Even when Bach writes scale-based figures, as in bars 187–208, the harmonic implications are almost as clear. For instance, in bar 202 the violin part changes the underlying G major triad into the dominant 7th of C major and so initiates the lead into C major for the third ritornello (bars 209–235).

Some of these melodic figures are more important than others since they are seeds from which long melodic passages later flower, often by sequential development but sometimes merely by repetition. Motif *(a)*, shown *right*, is immediately repeated a 4th lower to form a sequence in bars 1–2, followed in bar 3 by the last three quavers of motif *(b)*. Bars 4–6 consist of the whole of motif *(b)* plus a sequence of its first four notes overlapping the start of a repeat of the first six bars in bars 7–12.

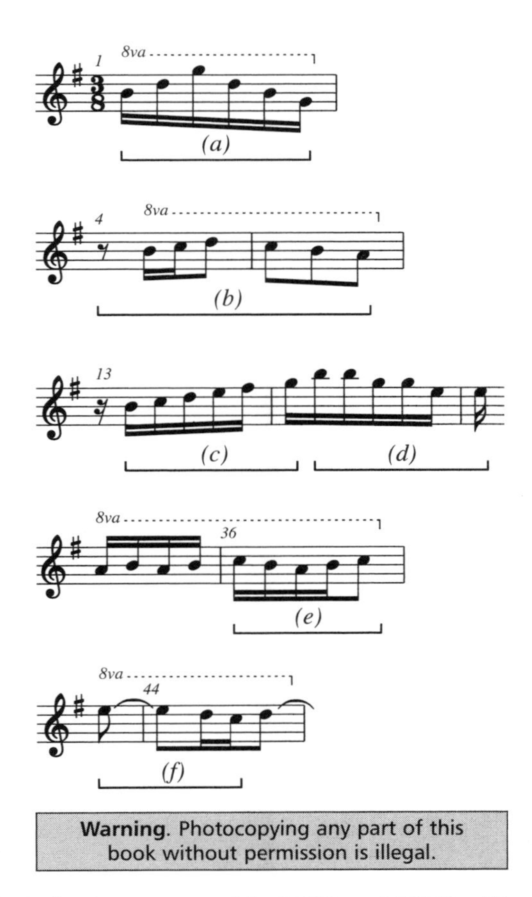

Motifs *(c)* and *(d)* come from the violin solo that starts in bar 13. Bach develops these into an extended melody that begins with a rising sequence built out of both motifs. Then, in bars 18–22, a descending sequence is built out of motif *(d)* alone. This organic growth of a melody from the seeds of mere motifs is called *Fortspinnung* in German. It means 'spinning-out' and the process is typical of late-baroque melodies.

There are just two other motifs, labelled *(e)* and *(f) right*. Sometimes *(e)* is preceded by four semiquavers, but more often it appears on its own. Look at the first recorder part that begins in bar 35. Motif *(e)* is first heard in bar 36 and is attached by a tie to a varied repetition of itself in bar 37. Bar 38 is an inversion of motif *(c)* and this leads to a sequential repetition of the whole phrase in bars 40–43, at which point motif *(f)* first appears. This syncopated motif is twice repeated in a descending sequence (bars 43–47). Simultaneously the continuo, solo violin and ripieno violin parts provide **counter-melodies** fashioned out of motif *(d)*.

In almost every bar of this movement one or more of the melodic strands derive from these six motifs: together they provide the thematic glue that holds the structure together.

Harmony and tonality

Functional harmony refers to the use of chord progressions, particularly cadences, that establish the main key(s) of the work, and which thus help to give it structure.

Throughout the movement the harmony is **functional** and mostly **diatonic**, with chord changes or an octave leap in the bass at each barline. In bars 1–13, for instance, chords I and V (or V^7) in root position establish the tonic key of G major. A modulation to the dominant is engineered by way of a pivot chord in bar 14 (E minor being chord VI in G and chord II in D). Root positions continue until bar 19, enlivened by suspensions with decorated resolutions (bar 15, first recorder; bar 17, second recorder).

The harmony is not always this simple. Look at bar 22, where the recorders outline a chord of A^7 followed by a chord of D in bar 23. However, under the A^7 in bar 22, the bass instruments outline a triad of D major. This strange combination of tonic and dominant harmony is the result of Bach's relentless pursuit of the sequence of one-bar units begun by the solo violin in bar 18, then imitated in the bass starting in bar 20. A similar effect occurs in G major in bar 56 and there are further examples later in the movement.

Harmonic sequences abound. In bars 33–35 there is a perfect cadence in D major. The addition of C(♮) from bar 36 onwards changes the function of the triad from the tonic of D major to the dominant 7th of G major and the perfect cadence in this key (bars 38–39) reflects the previous cadence. The same process leads to a perfect cadence in C major (bars 42–43). Such modulating harmonic sequences moving through keys a 5th apart (in this case a descent from D through G to C) are typical of late baroque harmony: there are many more examples in this movement.

Another typical harmonic sequence occurs in bars 43–47. It is in G major and entirely diatonic. Beginning on the second quaver of bar 43, three root-position chords (IV–II–VII^7) fall in 3rds. A similar progression is then stated three times, each time a tone lower and always starting on the second quaver: III–I–VI^7 / II–VII–V^7 / I–VI–IV^7. Above this progression the recorders trace a prominent melodic sequence, the first recorder adding a suspension on the first beat of each bar and a resolution on the second beat (hence chord VII^7, VI^7, V^7, and IV^7 at the beginning of bars 44–47). This whole progression, including the decorated suspensions, is typical of this movement in particular and of much late-baroque music in general. A new harmonic sequence in G major begins in bar 48. See if you can identify the chords and suspensions in it.

Hemiola rhythms occur before the cadences that mark the end of all but one of the ritornellos. In every case the hemiola proper is harmonised with part of a common type of harmonic sequence known as a **circle of 5ths**, as in bars 79–80 where the bass notes are B–E–A–D–G–C. As in most circles of 5ths, alternate intervals rise a 4th instead of descending a 5th (the harmonic effect is the same) because a literal succession of descending 5ths would take the part below the range of most bass instruments. The whole progression in bars 79–83 is typical of this movement in its diatonic simplicity, in its reliance on mainly root-position chords and in the faster rate of chord change at the approach to a cadence (compare the following with bars 75–78, in which there is only one chord per bar):

Now see if you can describe the similar progression in bars 153–157.

Structure

The whole movement is a fusion of **ternary** and **ritornello form.** Viewed as a ternary (ABA) structure the movement consists of the following three sections:

Section A (bars 1–83) ends with the complex hemiola rhythms discussed earlier (bars 79–83). Since this section also contains most of the thematic material for the central section, and because it is repeated at the end, it functions as an extended ritornello in relation to the movement as a whole.

Section B (bars 83–344) consists of an alternation of solo and tutti passages in which the motifs identified earlier are deployed in the construction of lengthy melodic lines. A sense of purpose is generated by modulations in the solo passages to related keys. Once these have been firmly established transposed passages from the first ritornello are restated by the combined forces of the concertino and ripiano. As in section A, so in section B the end is signalled by hemiola rhythms and a perfect cadence (this time in B minor) in bars 342–344.

Section A (bars 345–427) is an exact repeat of bars 1–83.

The ritornello structure

Within the overall ternary form there is a **ritornello structure** of alternating ritornelli and episodes, as shown *right*. Bach elaborates this plan further by including solo passages within the ritornello sections and adding interjections from ripieno strings within the soloists' episodes:

Bars	*Structure*	*Key*	*Timing*
1–83	Ritornello 1	G	0:00
83–137	Episode 1		1:23
137–157	Ritornello 2	E mi	2:14
157–209	Episode 2		2:36
209–235	Ritornello 3	C	3:28
235–323	Episode 3		3:55
323–344	Ritornello 4	B mi	5:21
345–427	Ritornello 1	G	5:44

Ritornello 1

Bars 1–23 contain an exposition of motifs *(a) – (d)* in G major followed by a modulation to the dominant (D major, bars 15–23). The concerto principal of alternating solo and tutti passages (bars 1–13 and 13–23 respectively) is already apparent.

Bars 23–35 are a repeat of the solo section (bars 1–13) transposed to D major with some changes of scoring. The three perfect cadences that so firmly established the tonic key in bars 1–13 now firmly establish the dominant key (bars 24–25, 28–29 and 30–31).

TIP
If you need to write about motifs in an exam answer, you must show exactly which notes you are referring to, perhaps by using a short music example, otherwise the examiner will not know what you mean by expressions such as 'motif a' or 'motif e'.

Bars 35–57 consist of a long tutti passage in which motif *(e)* is introduced by the recorders (bars 36–37) while prominent C♮s initiate a return to G major (V^7–I in bars 36–39). A harmonic sequence (bars 36–39 / 40–43) effects a brief visit to C major, but G major returns with the F♯s in bar 44. They coincide with the first statement of the syncopated motif *(f)* in the recorder parts and the tutti ends with a perfect cadence in the tonic (bars 54–57).

Bars 57–69 are another repetition of bars 1–13, this time in the tonic key.

Bars 69–83 start with an ascending sequence in which motifs *(d)* and *(f)* are combined, leading to the syncopated cadence-phrase that marks the end of the ritornello. There are no changes of key – the chromatic notes belong to secondary dominant chords (V^7 of IV, V^7 of V and V^7 of VI in bars 70–71) that add excitement to the ascending sequence without altering its tonality.

Bach has now laid firm foundations for the central section, which is explained below in note form, leaving you to identify Bach's use and manipulation of the six motifs, *(a)–(f)*.

Episode 1 (bars 83–137)
G major then D major in bars 102–128, modulating to E minor in bars 129–137): violin solo with recorder and ripieno interjections.

Ritornello 2 (bars 137–157)
E minor. A transposed repeat of bars 63–83.

Episode 2 (bars 157–209)
Beginning in E minor it modulates to B minor (bars 166–170) then A minor (bars 175–185). From bar 165 the texture is that of the baroque trio sonata (two recorders and a bass part). In bars 185–209 the music begins in A minor then modulates through G major (bar 201) to C major (bars 202–208). The whole episode is dominated by a non-thematic violin solo of great virtuosity.

Ritornello 3 (bars 209–235)
C major. A transposed and varied repeat of bars 57–83. The ascending sequence based on motif *(f)* in the recorder parts of bars 69–75 is simplified in the solo violin's double-stopping in bars 221–227.

Episode 3 (bars 235–323)
C major, G (bars 244–257) and D (bars 258–263). The violin solo is closely imitated by ripieno strings (bars 235–238 and 251–254) and is punctuated with recorder interjections based on the first two bars of the movement (bars 241–243 and 249–251).

Musical analysis involves interpretation as well as fact. You could argue that bars 263–285 form Ritornello 4 and bars 285–323 constitute Episode 4. This would mean that the movement ends with Ritornello 6 followed by the repeat of Ritornello 1.

In bars 263–285 Bach introduces a varied repeat of bars 35–57. This could be viewed as another ritornello (see *left*). However, the first 34 bars of the original ritornello are omitted and, unlike the main ritornelli which each end in the key in which they begin, this interjection modulates from D major through C major in bars 268–271 to G major (bars 272–285).

After this interruption, Episode 3 resumes in bars 285–323 with a series of more rapid modulations, starting in G major and passing through E minor, A minor, G major and D major before reaching a perfect cadence in B minor in bars 319–323.

Ritornello 4 (bars 323–344) and Ritornello 1 (bars 345–427)
B minor. A repeat of bars 63–83 transposed from G major to B minor with some changes of scoring. Two bars based on motif *(d)* link this ritornello to an exact repeat of the first ritornello (bars 345–427 being a restatement of bars 1–83).

Private study

1. Name one chordal instrument and one bass instrument that might be used to play a continuo part in baroque music.
2. Explain the difference between the ripieno and the concertino.
3. In ritornello form, what is the name for the passages of music heard between the main ritornello sections?
4. In bar 1, which note of a G-major triad is played by the violas – is it the root, third or fifth of the chord?
5. (a) In bar 388, the recorders play the notes C and E above a chord of D major. What is this harmonic device called?

   (b) Explain how the music of bar 388 is treated in bars 389 and 390.
6. All of the keys in this movement are related to the tonic key. Explain how each of the following keys relates to G major (the final answer has been given):

   D major C major E minor
   B minor: the relative minor of the dominant.

Sample questions

In the exam there will be three questions on this work, from which you must answer **two**.

(a) Give examples of the ways in which Bach uses melodic ideas heard in the first 48 bars during the rest of the movement.

(b) Comment on the structure of this movement, identifying its main sections and keys.

(c) Describe the characteristic features of Bach's style evident in this special focus work.

Continuity and change in structures and tonality

For examination in summer 2008 and 2009

You do not need to study this topic unless *Music for large ensemble* is the Area of Study that you undertook for AS Music and which you are now extending for A2.

Before starting work on this topic you need a thorough understanding of the material on *Music for large ensemble* in the AS Guide (pages 26–39). Remember that for A2 the topic draws on works from across the **entire** Area of Study, not just those in one of the two lists, A or B.

Introduction

It is important to be aware that tonality refers to the relationship between keys in music – it is nothing to do with the tone colour of musical sounds. *NAM 1* and *NAM 2* were written in the 18th century, at a time when harmony was primarily functional. This means that certain chords (particularly the dominant and tonic) had the specific function of defining keys and forming cadences.

NAM 3, *NAM 4* and *NAM 5* were composed in the 19th century, at a time when the clear-cut relationships of functional tonality were becoming increasingly obscured by the ambiguities and exotic colours of chromatic harmony. In the 20th century there were many different approaches to harmony and tonality, from the use of highly dissonant chords and atonality (music that avoids the use of keys) to works that draw on harmonic ideas from the modal systems of folk and pre-baroque music, or on ideas from the blues or other types of world music. *NAM 6* is typical of this trend – it is strongly influenced by the modal styles of early music, and contains little in the way of functional harmony.

Bach

NAM 1 (page 7) CD1 Track 1
Northern Sinfonia of England
Directed by George Malcolm

We looked in detail at Bach's use of stucture and tonality in the first movement of *Brandenburg* Concerto No. 4 in the previous section. The essential point to remember is that its various sections are defined through the use of related keys. For example, when regarded as simple ternary form, the A sections begin and end in the tonic, while the central B section explores a variety of related keys.

Viewed as ritornello form, section A is an enormous ritornello that frames the central section. It begins with an alternation of tonic and dominant chords that form four perfect cadences, leaving no doubt about the home key of G major. The pivot chord of E minor facilitates a modulation to the dominant (D major). In this key there is a repetition of the first 13 bars (starting at bar 23) followed by a harmonic sequence that passes through G and C major. The tonic key is re-established by diatonic harmonic sequences and a perfect cadence in bars 54–57). The first 13 bars are then repeated in G major, a key that remains undisturbed by the chromatic chords in bars 69–71 and that is confirmed by the perfect cadence in bars 82–83.

Now reread page 36 and note how, in the central section, all of the solo episodes modulate from one key to another, while the three main ritornelli in this section end in the key in which they began (E minor, C major and B minor).

The final ritornello then re-establishes the home key of G major by repeating the first 83 bars.

Haydn

NAM 2 (page 31) CD1 Track 2
Academy of Ancient Music
Directed by Christopher Hogwood

This opening movement of Haydn's Symphony No. 26 is in sonata form, one of the principal musical structures of the classical period. Unlike *NAM 1*, distinct melodic themes are assigned to specific keys, each established by functional and largely diatonic harmony. The movement's structure consists of three sections: an **exposition** in which the two main themes (called 'subjects') are established, a **development** in which these themes are manipulated in various ways, and a **recapitulation** in which they are restated.

Exposition (bars 1–44): D minor and F major

First subject (bars 1–16). Statements of a syncopated theme (bars 1–8 and 13–16) ending with a perfect cadence. Between them a 'sighing' motif is heard four times (bars 9–12). All 16 bars are in the tonic key of D minor with entirely diatonic harmony

Second subject (bars 17–44). A harmonisation of a fragment of plainsong that remains in F major (the relative major of D minor) throughout. There is only one chromatic chord (bar 33) and, of the 28 bars, 20 contain just tonic and dominant chords. At the end the new tonality is emphasised by two perfect cadences (bars 40–41 and 42–43).

Development (bars 45–79): Modulations through related keys

The first phrase is a repetition of bars 1–8 transposed to F major. A move away from this key is initiated by a sequential treatment of the 'sighing' motif (F major in bars 53–54 and G minor in bars 55–56). In the next nine bars a modulating **circle of 5ths** is defined by the first bass note of each bar: B♭–E–A–D–G–C♯–F–B–E). These notes form the foundation for a sequence that passes through D minor in bars 62–63 and ends on the dominant of A minor sustained as a **pedal** on E in bars 65–68. The expected tonic chord of this key is delayed by the dramatic intervention of a pair of diminished 7th chords (VII^7c of A minor) in bars 69 and 71, both resolving to chord Ib. After a perfect cadence in A minor (bars 73–74) the music returns to D minor via F major (V^7c–V^7b–I in bars 76–78), only regaining the tonic at the last moment (V^7b–I in D minor in bars 79–80).

Recapitulation (bars 80–126): D minor and D major

First subject (bars 80–99). A repeat of bars 1–14 in the tonic key, followed by an extension (bars 94–99) ending on V of D minor.

Second subject (bars 100–125). A repeat of bars 17–42 transposed down a minor third to D major, the **tonic major** key (sometimes called the **parallel major** key).

Coda (bars 126–133), The last two bars of the exposition are enlarged into a coda (closing section) in which the tonic major is hammered home by dominant-tonic harmony and a final cadence phrase (I–VI–IIb^7–V–I in bars 130–133).

Berlioz

NAM 3 (page 42) CD1 Track 3
London Symphony Orchestra
Conducted by Colin Davis

Although Berlioz called *Harold in Italy* a symphony, this third movement from the work has little to do with traditional structures such as the sonata form of *NAM 2*. So we should not necessarily expect tonality to be used to define form. Nor, despite the fact that it features a solo viola accompanied by an orchestra, does it have anything much to do with the concerto structure of *NAM 1*.

In fact, *Harold in Italy* doesn't even fit into the 19th-century tradition of pitting an impressive display of solo technique against the power of a full orchestra. Its modest solo part is as suitable a vehicle for virtuoso display as a Zimmer frame would be for an athlete (which is why the highly accomplished Paganini refused to play it, despite having the highest regard for Berlioz's music).

There are, however, two tenuous structural connections with the earlier works we have studied. Firstly, the saltarello (bars 1–31) is repeated (bars 136–165) at the end of the serenade proper (bars 32–135) just as the first ritornello is repeated at the end of Bach's concerto movement. So, like the latter, this tone poem could be viewed as a ternary structure were it not for the facts that:

- Berlioz follows the repeat of the introduction by a closing section (bars 166–208) in which he combines the saltarello rhythms (tutti violas) and serenade tune (solo viola) with the *idée fixe* that occurs in all four movements (flute and harp harmonics)
- Whereas Bach's ritornello is the source of motifs used throughout *NAM 1*, in *NAM 3* there is no other connection between the introduction and the serenade proper except the common key of C major.

C major almost totally dominates the movement. Modulations to other keys are not there to help define the structure but to add a touch of colour to Berlioz's picture of life in the Italian mountains. The introduction is underpinned by a **double pedal** on C and G (tonic and dominant of C major), representing the drone of folk-like bagpipes. To accommodate the flat 7th common in bagpipe music (B♭ in bars 15 and 17) Berlioz doesn't modulate – he uses a secondary dominant (V^7b of IV resolving to IV), briefly dropping the pedal on G, although the tonic pedal continues.

At first sight it might seem that the Allegretto resembles a sonata-form structure similar to that of *NAM 2*:

- ✦ Four phrases (bars 34–41, 41–48, 48–52 and 53–58) are stated in the manner of an **exposition**
- ✦ A little like a **development**, this material is repeated with some significant changes starting at bar 59. Phrases 2, 3 and 4 are combined with the *idée fixe* (viola) in bars 65–95, phrase 3 is subjected to melodic variation in bars 75–91 and the new key of G major is established in bars 89–96.
- ✦ All four phrases are repeated in bars 99–121 as they might be in a **recapitulation**.
- ✦ The Allegretto ends with a serene **coda** in C major, starting at bar 122, based on phrases 1 and 2.

It is only when we compare the keys of these sections with Haydn's tonal structure that we realise that this analysis is flawed because:

- ✦ Berlioz's first section begins and ends in C major and passes through F major, A minor, D minor and G minor in bars 49–54 (instead of the two clearly defined keys in Haydn's exposition).
- ✦ Instead of exploring a range of related keys, more than half of Berlioz's central section is in the tonic (bars 59–80). It then modulates to the dominant (bars 81–89), remains in G major for eight bars and ends on chord V of D minor in bar 99.
- ✦ Instead of being in the tonic, Berlioz's repeat at bar 99 starts with 17 bars in D minor. The fourth phrase returns in its original keys (G minor and C major in bars 116–122). So only the last three bars of the third section are in the tonic key of C major.

In other words Berlioz is using tonality as an expressive rather than a functional device.

Wagner

NAM 4 (page 65) CD1 Track 4
Vienna Philharmonic Orchestra
Conducted by Georg Solti

In order to read this orchestral score accurately, you need to learn the following points about the transposing instruments:

- ✦ The cor anglais sounds a perfect 5th lower than printed
- ✦ Clarinets in A, and the bass clarinet, sound a minor 3rd lower than printed
- ✦ Horns F sound a perfect 5th lower than printed
- ✦ Horns in E sound a minor 6th lower than printed
- ✦ Trumpets in F sound a perfect 4th higher than printed.

In addition, some parts are written in the C clef (𝄡), which wraps itself around the stave line that represents middle C.

One of the most famous aspects of this work is a deliberate tonal ambiguity that arises from lingering on sustained and sometimes unresolved dissonances. The first chord heard in the prelude is so closely associated with the entire opera that it has become known as the **Tristan chord** (see *right*). In bar 3 this dissonance resolves to V^7 of A minor (A and A♯ are passing notes), but instead of being followed by chord I there is a long silence.

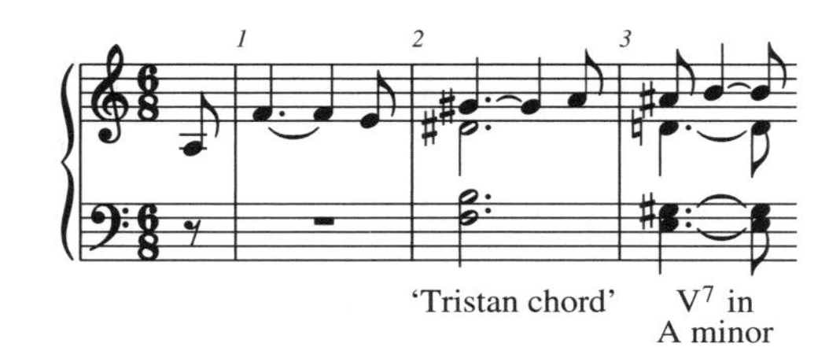

These bars are then transposed to end on V^7 of C major in bar 7 and again there is no resolution – only a silence. Another transposition leaves the music poised on an unresolved V^7 of E major in bar 11. This progression is repeated an octave higher in bars 12–13, and then just its last two notes are repeated in bars 14 and 15. In bars 16–17 the melody chromatically surges to a climax – but instead of the long-awaited perfect cadence in A minor, there is an **interrupted cadence** (V^7–VI) with a long and highly dissonant **appoggiatura** on B above a chord of F major (see *right*).

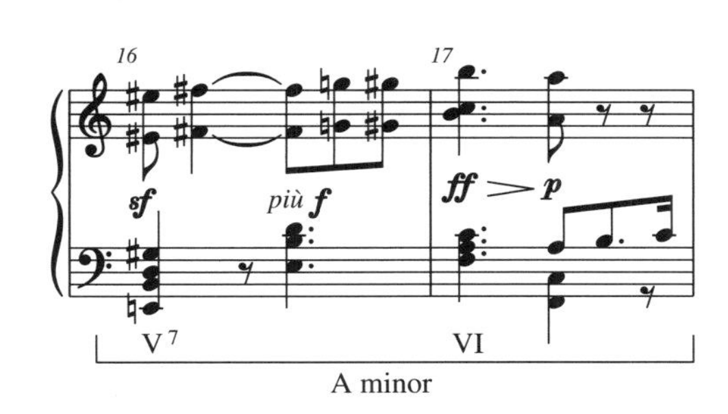

This process of hinting at a tonic, rather than defining it through functional cadences, is one of the ways in which this work differs from the movements we have studied by Bach and Haydn. The two earlier composers used tonality to define form, whereas Wagner used it as an expressive agent to foreshadow the longing of the doomed lovers in the opera that begins with this prelude.

Similarly, Wagner's melodies are not presented as clearly contrasting themes in different keys, each helping to clarify the structure of the movement, as we saw in Haydn's symphony. Instead, Wagner builds his melodies from **leitmotifs** (some of which are identified in the AS Guide) that continually mutate and overlap in order to create a sense of 'unending melody'.

There are several ways to analyse the resulting structure, of which the following (summarised *right*) is just one.

Bars	*Structure*
0–24	Exposition
24–65	Middle section
66–83	First recapitulation
84–111	Second recapitulation

Exposition (bars 0–24): A minor/major

Theme 1 (bars 0–17) begins and ends in A minor, concluding with a massive interrupted cadence. It is fragmented into five phrases by lengthy silences (which are omitted in later recapitulations).

Theme 2 (bars 17^4–24, cellos then violins) starts in A minor but then modulates rapidly through D minor and B major to reach the first perfect cadence in the tonic (A major) in bar 24.

Middle section (bars 24^6–65): shifting tonality centred on A

This part forms an ABA^1 ternary structure.

Section A begins with **theme 3** – the eight-bar cello melody in bars 24^6–32^4. This theme starts in E major and ends on the tonic note (A) without a cadence. It is made out of motifs from theme 2, played in reverse order. Section A ends with a repeat of bars 17^4–21 (the beginning of theme 2, now on wind).

Section B (bars 36^4–44) starts with antiphonal development of a motif from theme 2 and ends on a root-position chord of A major.

Section A^1 (bars 45–65) is a reworking of section A. The dominant pedal on E in bars 63–70 links this section to the next.

First recapitulation (bars 66–83): A minor/major modulating to V of E♭ minor

The start of this section is signalled by two statements (by oboes and cor anglais) of the motif first heard in bars 2–3. The second initiates a compressed recapitulation of the exposition in which the rests are omitted and some of the motifs are telescoped (woodwind, bars 68–74). Meanwhile the strings continue to develop the motif first heard in bars 17^4–18^3 until, at bar 74, they repeat the first four bars of theme 2.

The last part of this section modulates to E♭ minor (the most distant key possible from A minor) for the principle climax of the entire prelude. In bars 81–83 Wagner contrapuntally combines all three themes over harmony which swings between II^7 (an enharmonic respelling of the 'Tristan chord') and V^7 of E♭ minor in each bar. In the example *left*, the themes are identified by the names of the motifs given in the AS Guide. In addition to the parts shown, added excitement is provided by rapidly ascending from the violins while a timpani roll provides a continuous pedal on F.

When the climax arrives in bar 83 the 'Tristan chord' reveals its tonal ambiguity by resolving not to V^7 of E♭ minor in bar 84, but to V^7 of A minor (as shown *below left*) ready for a recapitulation of the opening few bars in their original key.

Second recapitulation (bars 82–111): A minor modulating to C minor

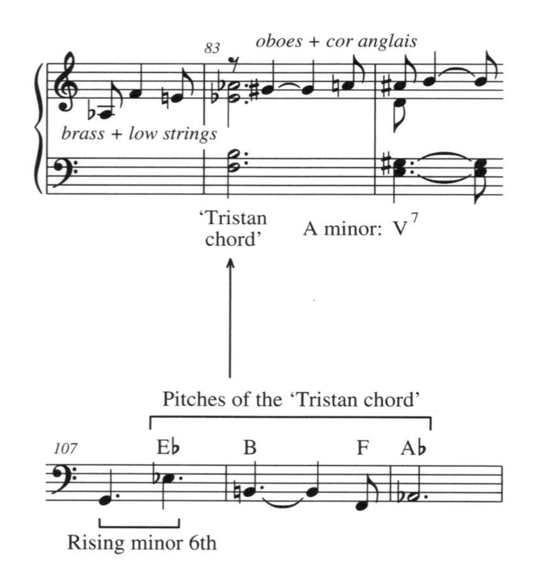

This second restatement of the principal motifs overlaps the first recapitulation when the opening motif of the prelude is begun by brass and low strings, and continued by oboes and cor anglais (see *left*). However, instead of the long silences heard in the exposition, the phrases are now linked by motifs in the strings.

The interrupted cadence recurs in bars 93^4–94 and, as in the exposition, theme 2 (beginning in the cellos at bar 94^4) overlaps the resolution of the appoggiatura. However, the end of the phrase is modified to lead to an imperfect cadence in C minor in bars 99–100.

Woodwind instruments attempt to start another recapitulation (bars 100^6–106^3 are a rescored repetition of bars 0–7) but an intermittent dominant pedal on G, played by the timpanist, anchors the tonality to C minor. The final unaccompanied melody for cellos and double basses links the rising minor 6th with which the work began (G–E♭ in bar 107) with the notes of the 'Tristan chord' played melodically. (As shown *left*, D♯ and G♯ are notated as E♭ and A♭).

There is a particular reason why Wagner ends on the dominant of C minor, despite having started the work in A minor. The prelude leads straight into the opera, which begins with a young sailor singing a melancholy unaccompanied ditty in a modal version of C minor. However, when the prelude was first performed in a concert in 1859 (six years before the complete opera was staged) Wagner adopted a more conventional approach, and wrote a special ending in A major to balance the A-minor opening – in other words, he ended the movement in the parallel tonic major key, something we saw that Haydn did in *NAM 2*.

Stravinsky described Debussy's *Prélude à l'après midi d'un faune*, written in 1894, as 'the first masterpiece of the modern era'. In the way chords are treated as sound events, valuable in themselves rather than as tools to define tonality, this is certainly true. Yet there are many tonal and structural connections with Wagner's *Tristan* Prelude. The **chromatic** flute melody of the first two bars swings across the tritone between C♯ and G♮, giving no clear idea of a key. The second half of the flute solo sounds modal, and the first chord (oboes and clarinets) is an inconclusive added 6th on C♯ minor.

Debussy

NAM 5 (page 86) CD1 Track 5
Concertgebouw Orchestra
Conducted by Bernard Haitink

But when the harp enters, its glissando forms an arpeggiated chord of A♯–C♯–E–G♯, which is a transposed 'Tristan chord' (the version in bar 81 of *NAM 5* is shown in the example *below right* for ease of comparison). As in bars 2–7 of Wagner's prelude, Debussy follows this chord with a dominant 7th (harp and strings, bar 5) followed by a rest and a repeat of the same two chords (strings and harp in bars 8–9). But the differences are as great as the similarities:

The other notes in this glissando are enharmonic equivalents of the chord notes – a technique that allows the harpist to produce an arpeggio rather than a scale when running the fingers across the strings.

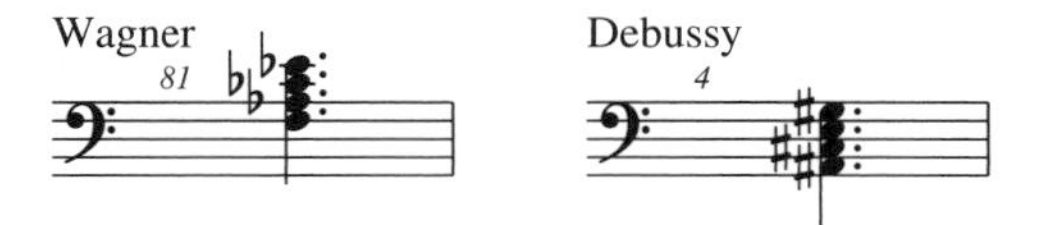

- Wagner resolves the 'Tristan chord' to an adjacent dominant 7th. Debussy shifts to a chord that *looks* like a dominant 7th but *sounds* like a static event to the ear, the only connection between the chords being two common pitches (A♯=B♭, G♯=A♭).
- Wagner's repeat of the two-chord progression is part of a harmonic sequence that leads to a clear interrupted cadence in the tonic key of A minor. Debussy's repeat is at the same pitch with the 'dominant 7th' leading back to a harmonised repeat of the chromatic flute melody and a perfect cadence in the tonic key – which turns out to be E major (bar 13).

Wagner's aim was to frustrate the listener's expectation of resolution in order to portray a sense of unfilled longing, Debussy's aim was to represent a world of sensual delight that *is* fulfilled in cadences that mark points of articulation in what is otherwise a free fantasia. The most significant examples are:

(a) Bar 13: The perfect cadence (V^{13}–I in E major) is masked by the horn adding a 6th (sounding C♯) to the E-major chord.

(b) Bars 19–20: V^7b of F♯ minor resolves to $E^{add\ 6}$ in bar 21.

(c) Bars 29^3–30: V^{13}–I in B major is a point of repose that is negated by a harmonised variant of the opening flute melody in bar 31 followed by **whole-tone scales** (clarinet and flute, bars 32–33) that suspend any sense of tonality.

(d) Bars 51–55: A dominant pedal on A♭ leads to a perfect cadence in D♭ major (bars 54–55), the principal key of the central section.

(e) Bar 78: The chord of D♭^{7} irregularly resolves to a first inversion of E major in bar 79 – a 'side-slip' rather than a modulation.

(f) Bars 105–106: The cadence (V^{13} and V^9 resolving to I in E major) is decisive, but the coda (bars 106–110) contains chromatic triads above a tonic pedal (bar 107) and final references to the same 'Tristan'-like chord as those in bars 4 and 7.

As in Wagner's prelude the structure is deliberately vague, but Debussy's key signatures and use of strongly contrasting themes suggest a ternary structure in which:

Section A (bars 1–54) consists of variants of the opening flute melody centred on E major, followed by a transition (bars 31–36) to a new theme (bars 37–54) that begins in E major before modulating to a perfect cadence in D♭ major (see (d) *above*).

Section B (bars 55–78) has a completely new theme in D♭ major, which, at its second appearance (bars 63–74) is entirely diatonic. A third repetition of the theme (first violins, bars 75–77) is cut short by the cadence described in (e) *above*.

Section A¹ (bars 79–106) begins with a rhythmically augmented version of the flute theme in E major alternating with a scherzando version of it (oboe) in C major. From bar 94 there can be no doubt about the tonality as the flute theme plus the triplets from the central section are harmonised above a tonic pedal on E, followed by the perfect cadence and coda described in (f) *above*.

Tippett

NAM 6 (page 120) CD1 Track 6
Academy of St Martin-in-the-Fields
Conducted by Neville Marriner

The principal sources of Tippett's harmonic and tonal style in the *Concerto for Double String Orchestra* are the modal styles of pre-baroque music, and the lively, pungent discords employed by a number of early 20th-century composers, including Stravinsky. Let's consider each of these in turn.

Sing the first orchestra's melody in bars 1–4 in free rhythm with each note roughly equal in length and you will discover it sounds like a fragment of medieval music. You might also discover that it uses all five pitches of a pentatonic scale (A, B, D, E, G). So, although it sounds modal, we do not have enough information to identify a particular mode (like major and minor scales, ancient modes all have seven pitches). But look at both of the melodies in bar 5 and you will discover the missing notes (C and F) of the **aeolian mode.**

The **aeolian mode** uses the same pattern of pitches as the natural minor scale: A, B, C, D, E, F and G.

Now look at the second orchestra's four-bar melody starting in the first bar. Notice that, like most medieval melodies its range does not exceed an octave and that it includes all of the notes of the aeolian mode transposed up a tone (B, C♯, D, E, F♯, G, A and B). In early music, a single chromatic alteration of the mode is common, particularly to avoid outlining a tritone (e.g. between F and B). In terms of the aeolian mode on B, the two C♮s are chromatic notes needed to avoid outlining a tritone from the low G to C♯ (bars 2–3) and a tritone from C♯ to the high G (bar 4).

When combined, these two versions of the aeolian mode fight with each other to produce a seemingly random assortment of harmonic intervals. But there are only two discords (the 9th on the first quaver of bar 2 and the 7th on the second quaver of bar 3) and they both resolve correctly by falling a step to a consonant interval. In this and other aspects of his two-part counterpoint, Tippett was following the practice of the Tudor composers he so admired – but the **bimodality** of the first four bars (and other more complex passages) owes nothing to the past.

Pandiatonic refers to music based on the free use of unresolved dissonances from the diatonic scale. These often appear in the form of added notes (e.g. the note D added to a C major triad, making C$^{add 2}$).

In such neoclassical works as *Pulcinella* (*NAM 7*), Stravinsky cultivated a 'deliberate wrong note' style, sometimes known as **pandiatonicism**, that was another important influence on Tippett. In bars 85–89 of the first movement from the *Concerto for Double String Orchestra*, there is a terrifically exciting passage in C♯ major. If you find it difficult to think in this key (in which every degree is sharpened) just forget the accidentals and imagine it to be C major. Sing or play the melodic strands and you will find they all make perfectly good tonal sense, whether they descend conjunctly from the dominant to the tonic (e.g. second orchestra, violin 1, bars 85–88^1) or leap about the notes of the tonic chord (e.g. cellos, bar 86). Add them together and it becomes apparent that the counterpoint in bars 85–86 strongly suggests chord Ib (even though there's an added 2nd in bar 85 and an added 4th in bar 86).

A perfect cadence is formed between a spicy version of chord V in bar 87 and an astringent version of chord I in the next two bars. But when we look at the intervals between the parts, on every quaver we find the same random collection of concords and discords as that in the first four bars – and this time they don't resolve 'correctly'. So, every note in these four bars is diatonic, and standard chord progressions can be detected. But the chords are infested with 'wrong notes' that ginger-up these conventional progressions. This is what is meant by pandiatonicism.

Now let's examine the second subject (bars 39–67) of this sonata-form movement where we will find more important features of Tippett's harmonic and tonal style. The passage revolves around G major, a tone below the tonic of the whole movement.

The most tonal passage in the whole movement occurs in bars 39–50. Essentially it is **an extended perfect cadence in G major**. In bars 39–42 chord I is implied by a melody that starts and ends on G and includes all but one of the degrees of a scale of G major (and no other pitches). In bars 43–45, alternating parallel root-position triads of D and C major (violins) over root-position arpeggios of D (violas, cellos and basses) make chord V^7 of G major (with an added 9th and 11th). The perfect cadence is completed when this chord resolves to the tonic in bar 46. Finally, bars 39–42 are repeated an octave lower to form bars 47–50, with the melody again implying chord I. The only modal touch is F♮ (bar 46) which, in this context, suggests a descending mixolydian scale (G–G on the 'white notes').

In bars 51–57, bass arpeggios outline a progression of root-position chords, shown *right*. All three primary triads of G are present (I, IV and V) but this functional harmony is coloured by modal-sounding chords on the flat 3rd and 7th degrees. This underlying harmonic progression is decorated with alternating root-position triads that are similar to those in bar 43. Here they sound very modal because of the flat 7ths they add to the arpeggios. None of these decorative chords turns the basic triads into dominant 7ths because none of them resolves. Listen out for Tippett's Tudor-like **false relations** (such as F♯/F♮ in bar 51) and notice the **lydian 4th** (F♯) in bar 56. The main tonal centre of the second subject (G major/minor) returns in bars 57–59, then alternating roots similar to those already discussed lead back to G again (bar 65) but the descending scale is cunningly bent towards E minor at the start of the development.

Bar 51^1	D	=	V of G major
Bars 51^2–52^1	F	=	♭VII of G major
Bars 52^2–53^1	B♭	=	♭III of G major
Bars 53^2–56	C	=	IV of G major
Bar 57	G	=	I of G major

The development (bars 68–128) contains many passages where tonality disappears. The best example starts in bars 113–117 with cellos and basses outlining major triads of A♭, C and E. Tippett wilfully sustains the A♭ of the first chord so that it grinds against the G♮ of

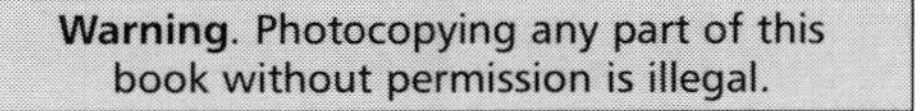

the second chord (likewise the C of the second chord clashes with the B of the third chord). Now listen to the violin parts – can you spot the patterns based on a decorated **whole-tone scale**, starting at bar 113? In bars 113–117 five-note segments of this atonal scale (which we encountered in *NAM 5*) clash violently with the three major chords we have already discussed. In these bars this scale (which lacks clearly-defined tonality) clashes violently with the three major chords we have already discussed. But in bars 118–122 Tippett introduces an **augmented triad** (C–E–G♯) which surges upwards in the bass against a repetition of the decorated whole-tone scale. The augmented triad is the only type of triad that can be constructed from the pitches of a whole-tone scale and is just as tonally ambiguous – its dissonant effect clamouring for resolution. This comes when the ascending whole-tone patterns 'morph' into the ascending melodic minor scale of the tonic key (bars 126–128) leading to the recapitulation of the first subject, which starts at bar 129. Despite the best efforts of the lower strings of the second orchestra there can be no doubt about the aeolian tonality now that the violins of the second orchestra supply all degrees of this mode. As in classical sonata-form movements, the second subject (bars 165–193) is now in the tonic major (as in bars 100–133 of *NAM 2*).

Exposition (bars 1–67)
- First subject (bars 1–20)
  - tonal centre A
- Transition (bars 21–38)
  - aeolian on A and lydian on C leading to ...
- Second subject (bars 39–67)
  - tonal centre G

Development (bars 68–128)
- Unrelated tonal centres such as A (bars 68–75), C♯ major (bars 80–89) and A♭ major (bars 107–112)

Recapitulation (bars 129–193)
- First subject (bars 129–146)
  - tonal centre A
- Transition (bars 147–163)
  - modified to maintain A as the chief tonal centre
- Second subject (bars 165–193)
  - tonal centre A

Coda (bars 194–232)
- more unrelated tonal centres but ending with a cadence that features the two chief tonal centres: G (now lydian in bars 228–231) and A (with a bare-5th chord in the last bar)

The structure of the whole movement is defined by modes as well as by major keys – but both often contrast with passages in which a sense of tonality seems to disappear. Continuity is evident in a sonata-form structure that even Haydn might have recognised – but he would have been surprised to find that tonic–dominant polarity (or minor–relative major polarity in *NAM 2*) had been replaced with tonal centres a tone apart (A and G). Be that as it may, we are now in a position where we can discern this overarching tonal structure, summarised in the box *left*.

Private study

1. Describe the difference between the relative major key and the tonic major key, giving examples of both from *NAM 2*.
2. Name the three main sections of a sonata-form structure.
3. Explain how functional harmony helps to determine tonality.
4. Which of the following are likely to strengthen a sense of tonality and which are likely to weaken it?

   whole-tone scales   perfect cadences   related keys   atonality
   dominant pedals   the aeolian mode   the 'Tristan chord'

Sample questions

In the exam there will be two questions on this topic, from which you must answer **one**.

(a) Show how sonata form differs from ritornello form, using examples from two of the works you have studied.

(b) Discuss the differences and similarities between Debussy's use of tonality in *NAM 5* and Wagner's use of tonality in *NAM 4*.

(c) Contrast the different approaches of Haydn and Tippett to structure *and* tonality evident in *NAM 2* and *NAM 6*.

Stravinsky, *Pulcinella* Suite: Sinfonia, Gavotta, Viva

Special Focus Work for 2008 and 2009

NAM 7 (page 139) CD1 Tracks 7–9
Academy of St. Martin-in-the-Fields
Conducted by Neville Marriner

Before starting on this section you should work through (or revise) the information about the context and structure of this music given on pages 41–43 of the AS Guide. Make sure that you understand all of the terminology used on those pages.

Genesis

When Serge Diaghilev re-formed his *Ballets Russes* in 1917, it was at a time when Europe was still torn apart by the first world war and his patron, Tsar Nicholas II, had been deposed in the Russian revolution of that year. Lacking the resources to continue commissioning ballets on the scale of Stravinsky's *The Rite of Spring* that had caused such a sensation in 1913, Diaghilev asked the Italian composer Tommasini to produce some simple orchestrations of baroque keyboard sonatas by Domenico Scarlatti. Although now largely forgotten, *Les Femmes de bonne Humeur*, with its characters dancing in Venetian masks, was a great succes. Diaghilev therefore decided to repeat the formula, handing his old collaborator Stravinsky a selection of 18th-century music that they both believed to have been written by Pergolesi.

In fact, of the 21 movements that Stravinsky selected for the ballet, only ten were actually by Pergolesi (who died in 1736), the rest being by a variety of other 18th-century composers.

Stravinsky adapted the music for a 32-piece chamber orchestra of 18th-century proportions: pairs of flutes, oboes (no clarinets), bassoons and horns, a trumpet, and strings divided into concertino (soloist) and ripieno (full) sections in the manner of a baroque concerto grosso. Since most of the genuinely Pergolesi excerpts are vocal, there are also three singers (soprano, tenor and bass) who rather unusually perform from the orchestra pit. Even more novel was the inclusion of a trombone part that would be more at home in a circus band than in any 18th-century orchestra.

Pulcinella was premiered by the *Ballet Russes* at the Paris Opéra on 15th May 1920. As usual, Diaghilev gathered together the finest talents of the age. In addition to music by Stravinsky, the sets were by Picasso, the choreography by Léonide Massine (who danced the title role) and the orchestra was conducted by Ernest Ansermet.

Despite some revivals in recent years, *Pulcinella* has never entered the mainstream ballet repertoire – its convoluted plot (see *right*) full of disguised characters and unlikely dramatic resolutions, together with a large cast and a disjointed succession of 21 tiny movements (most under two minutes in length), was not a formula for success.

Context
The story of *Pulcinella*

Pulcinella is a masked character from traditional Italian *Commedia dell' arte* (see the picture on the front cover of this book). He is a rascal (the origin of Punch in Punch and Judy) who ignores his fiancé Pimpinella in order to flirt with the girls of Naples. Their own jealous fiancés plot to kill Pulcinella, but he outwits them by getting his friend Fourbo to dress as his double. The double pretends to die at the hands of a stranger (who is actually the real Pulcinella in disguise).

With the much-envied Pulcinella now out of the way, the young men each disguise themselves as Pulcinella in the hope of becoming more attractive to their respective girlfriends. The real Pulcinella then returns, disguised as a magician and mysteriously revives the 'corpse' – who turns out to be neither dead nor actually Pulcinella. Finally, the magician throws off his disguise to reveal *himself* as the real Pulcinella. Magnanimously bearing nobody any malice, he arranges for all the couples to get married and for his own betrothal to the long-suffering Pimpinella.

Thus it is that the work is much better known in the concert hall than in the theatre, through the suite of eight movements that Stravinsky compiled in 1922. The three movements in *NAM 7* relate to this suite (and the full ballet) as follows:

Sinfonia	Movement 1 of the suite Overture of the ballet
Gavotta	Movement 6 of the suite No.16 in the ballet (Scene VI)
Vivo	Movement 7 (*duetto*) of the suite No.17 in the ballet (Scene VII)

Neo-classicism

In art music, **neo-classicism** was a 20th-century style popular between the two world wars. It was a reaction to the sometimes overblown and emotionally-charged romanticism of the previous century. Composers sought to create a more detached and purer type of music by reinterpreting, in a modern idiom, some of the basic principles of 18th-century music.

However, the term 'neo-classical' is confusing since composers usually found their inspiration in the baroque music of the first half of the 18th century, rather than in the classical style of the late 18th century – hence the neo-classical slogan of 'back to Bach' and the preference of some writers to call the style 'neo-baroque'.

Pulcinella was a first step on the road to neo-classicism for Stravinsky – a style that was to dominate his music for the next 30 years. It is unusual among neo-classical works in consisting of novel arrangements of 18th-century music. More commonly, composers wrote entirely original music, as in Prokofiev's *Classical* symphony of 1917, one of the earliest neo-classical works. It uses a small, 18th-century-sized orchestra along with the forms, clear textures and balanced phrasing of classical music – it even includes an antique gavotte as its third movement. But its widely leaping melodies and pungent harmonies are clearly of the 20th-century. Prokofiev described his first symphony as a work that 'Haydn might have written … had he lived in our day'.

Stravinsky's approach in *Pulcinella* was rather different. And yet it is neither pastiche (an attempt to copy something as faithfully as possible) nor merely an arrangement. Stravinsky himself described his technique as one of 're-composition'. Let's see what he meant.

Most of the sources for *Pulcinella* were pieces with two- or three-part textures. Stravinsky retained much of this original material, confining his changes to:

- Creating unusual timbres through innovative instrumention
- Adding precise details of articulation and vivid contrasts in dynamics
- Highlighting individual notes with accents and doublings, often in order to add (or emphasise) syncopation
- Realising ornaments and adding new melodic decoration
- Thickening musical textures by devising extra parts, additional doublings, pedal points and ostinati
- Eliding sections or inserting bars in order to produce unexpected phrase lengths
- Deliberately weakening bass-lines, destabilizing cadences and adding dissonances to create harmonic ambiguity.

Stravinsky becomes increasingly adventurous in his use of such techniques as the music unfolds. The inattentive listener might believe that the opening Sinfonia is genuinely 18th-century, but gradually the mask is lifted and by the time the Vivo is reached (some two-thirds of the way into the complete ballet score) there is no doubt that it is Stravinsky who is pulling the strings.

Sinfonia

The Sinfonia is in **rounded binary form**, one of the most common structures used in short instrumental movements of the baroque period. Its has two sections, both based on similar material:

- The shorter first section (bars 0^4–15^3) establishes the tonic key of G major and then modulates to the dominant (D major)
- The longer second section (bars 15^4– 44) begins in the dominant, wends it way back to the tonic via a range of related keys, and includes a varied restatement of the opening, starting at bar 33.

This ABA^1 structure may seem like ternary form, but there is an important difference. In ternary form the first A section ends in the tonic and so can be repeated exactly to conclude the piece. In rounded binary form, the first A section ends in a related key (often, as here, the dominant) and so has to be modified when it returns in order that the movement can end in the tonic. Also, in ternary form the B section is frequently much more contrasted with the A section than it is in any type of binary form.

It is this 'rounding off' of the second section, by returning to the opening material in the tonic key, that gives rounded binary its name.

Stravinsky's source for the Sinfonia was the first movement of a Trio Sonata by Domenico Gallo (born in Venice, *c.*1730) – a work for two violins and cello. Confusingly, baroque trio sonatas require a fourth performer to fill out the harmonies on an instrument such as the harpsichord. This is done by improvising chords based on figures given in the cello part (known as a 'figured bass').

Stravinsky adds detailed performing directions (including bowing at some points) but retains Gallo's first violin and cello parts largely intact – usually, but not exclusively, in his own first violin and cello parts. Gallo's second violin part (often altered) is treated more freely with phrases from it appearing in various orchestral parts.

Stravinsky also adds numerous doublings and additional notes. For instance, he blurs the harmonies in bar 3 by adding A to the G-major chord of beat 1 and G to the D-major chord of beat 2, seizing the opportunity to use bare 5ths on open strings (G–D–A) on both beats in the second violin parts. The second oboe repeats a low B throughout the bar, adding to the harmonic richness – so F♯, G, A and B all cluster on beat 2, while the B adds a major 7th to the C-major chord on beat 3.

In bars 7–9 Stravinsky adds new countermelodies to the texture (in the bassoon, second violin and solo cello parts) and then trips-up the metre by inserting an extra beat ($\frac{2}{4}$ + $\frac{3}{4}$ = five beats), allowing a crafty extra repetition of Gallo's little cadence figure:

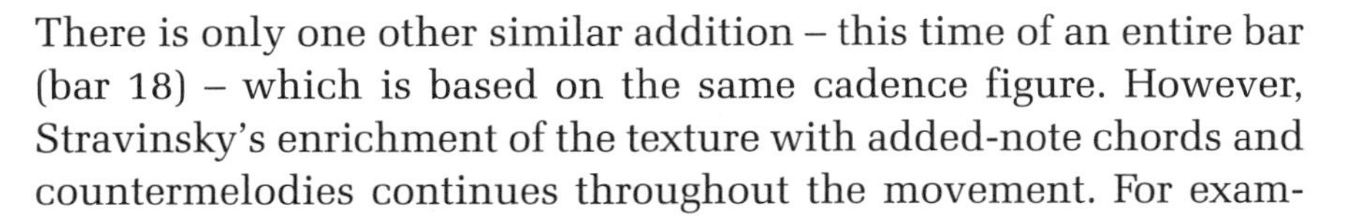

There is only one other similar addition – this time of an entire bar (bar 18) – which is based on the same cadence figure. However, Stravinsky's enrichment of the texture with added-note chords and countermelodies continues throughout the movement. For example, in bars 24–26 the two original melodic parts are assigned to second violins and violas, so that the first violins can be given a newly-invented and gently dissonant descending scale that intertwines with Gallo's own suspensions and descending sequences. See if you can spot how Stravinsky gives this passage another new treatment when it returns in bar 37 (Gallo's material appears in the parts for solo violins and orchestral bass – all else is added).

The circle of 5ths progression in bars 24–27[1] is disguised by Stravinsky's added violin scale, mentioned in the paragraph above. The basic progression consists of the chords Em – A – D – G – C♯ dim – F♯ – Bm.

As in most binary-form movements, the second section modulates more widely than the first, passing sequentially through G major (bar 21), A major (bar 22) and B minor (bar 23). A **circle of 5ths** progression in bars 24–27 ends with repeated perfect cadences in B minor (bars 26[4]–28) and then another modulating sequence quickly visits E minor (bar 29), D major (bar 30), A minor (bar 31) and finally the tonic, G major (bar 32).

The return of the opening material in bar 33 is done with typical Stravinskian whimsy. Shorn of its anacrusic start, it creeps back in on horns and bassoons, and it is only with the ***f*** tutti entry in bar 35 that we realise that a recapitulation is already under way. Despite a chromatic passing note (C♯ in bar 36), the music remains in G major for the rest of the movement.

The Sinfonia has a largely **homophonic** texture with one dominant melody supported by subordinate parts. It varies in density from the three-part writing of bars 29–30, which comes straight from the original trio sonata (except that the bass has been transposed up two octaves) to passages such as bars 37–39. Here, Stravinsky's reinterpretation of the figured bass involves a dense accompaniment, with solo strings sustaining, and tutti strings repeating, harmonies that are smudged by the violas' insistence on sounding a double pedal (on E and B) through every one of the six different chords.

Gavotta

This movement was originally part of a keyboard suite by Carlo Ignazio Monza, published around 1735. The gavotte is a fairly fast duple-metre dance and Monza followed it with six *doubles* (that is, variations in shorter notes) of which Stravinsky used the first and fourth.

Another example of simple binary form from the baroque period occurs in *NAM 15* – see the diagram on page 64.

The gavotte is in simple **binary form**. The A section (which ends at the repeat sign in bar 10) first establishes the tonic key of D major and then modulates to the dominant (A major). The B section, as usual, modulates more widely. It starts with a four-bar phrase in G major (bars 11–14) that is repeated sequentially a tone higher in A major (bars 15–18). The first two bars of this phrase are then heard in bars 19–20, adapted to cadence in F♯ minor, and these are sequentially repeated in E minor (bars 21–22) and D major (bars 23–24). The final eight bars remain in the tonic and consist of a four-bar phrase (bars 25–28) that is repeated in decorated form in bars 29–32.

The variations follow the same pattern, each being in binary form, except that the shorter note values in the second variation allow it to be compressed into half of the number of bars.

Monza's original keyboard gavotte has a mainly two-part texture (one note in each hand) except for bars 19–26, where the left hand has chords. Stravinsky's principle contributions are the distinctive scoring for wind and the addition of numerous countermelodies and accompaniment figures. In the first ten bars, Monza's melody appears in the first oboe part and his walking bass (albeit with a few changes) in the second bassoon. Everything else has been added by Stravinsky.

Later additions include the sighing horn part (starting in bar 11) and the filling-in of Monza's bass with bassoon glissandi (starting in bar 15) – although the latter are unfortunately unconvincing on the *NAM* recording. Bar 19 sees a thickening of texture by the conventional device of doubling the tune in 3rds and 6ths. In bars 25–28 Stravinsky veils the melody in sustained notes above and below and adds an inverted tonic pedal, designed to deliberately weaken the effect of the perfect cadence:

In total contrast, the final four-bar phrase is just as Monza wrote it, the original trill in bar 31 being notated in full.

Variation I is in the style of a gigue – a lively baroque dance in compound time. At the start, the first oboe plays Monza's melody, the second horn plays his bass part (with some simplifications), and Stravinsky adds a soaring countermelody for first horn. In bars 43–46, Monza's simple I and IV harmonies (outlined by woodwind) invite a tonic pedal – but Stravinsky supplies an entire tonic *chord*, reiterated by the brass and clashing gloriously with chord IV at the start of bar 44 – the first horn is still hanging onto an F♯ in bar 46. After the sequential repetition of this section, Stravinsky injects contrapuntal interest from bar 51 (oboe 2 and bassoon 1 are the added parts) as well as a brief inner pedal on F♯ in bars 57–58.

When reading the score of this variation, remember that while horns in F sound a perfect 5th lower than written when in the treble clef, they sound a *perfect 4th higher* than written when in the bass clef. The brief trumpet part is in C, so its notes sound as printed.

The melody of Variation II is shared between flute and horn, while bubbling bassoons are allocated the Alberti-like accompaniment (which Stravinsky alters to make it less keyboard-like). Bar 69 reveals another way in which he weakened cadences. Monza harmonised this cadence with a conventional Ic–V–I progression in A major; Stravinsky undermines this modulation by retaining G♮ in the first bassoon part.

The **Alberti bass** is named after Monza's contemporary Alberti, who was particularly fond of these busy accompaniment patterns. Its most typical form can be seen on page 255 of NAM, in the left hand of bars 71–80.

At the start of the second section Stravinsky uses the technique of **octave displacement** to change the shape of the original melody:

These scales are like a type of 18th-century ornament called the *tirade*, in which two notes of a melody would be joined by a rapid scale, but Stravinsky's versions are rather more flamboyant.

Stravinsky adds some exuberant ornamentation in the form of upward rushing scales in bars 73, 76 and 78. The second flute and first oboe parts in this section are countermelodies that have been added by Stravinsky, often in a clearly unbaroque style, such as the chain of unprepared dissonances generated by the second flute in bar 77 and the barely disguised consecutive 5ths of bar 79. Both reveal that this is a work of re-composition, not pastiche.

Vivo

Stravinsky's source for the Vivo is the last movement from a work for solo cello by Pergolesi. Typical of such baroque music, it also includes a bass part, from which the player of an instrument such as a harpischord or lute could improvise an accompaniment.

The movement is another **rounded binary** structure, with a first section ending at bar 21. It is in F major and doesn't modulate to the dominant (C major) until the very last moment, in bars 20–21.

The second section begins with a 'false start' described below, and then at bar 25 the opening of the first section is heard in the key of C major. Bars 38–45 are a re-scored repeat of bars 6–13, back in F major. At bar 46 the music plunges into the **tonic minor** key (F minor) for four bars (the sudden switch from major to parallel minor key being a fingerprint of Pergolesi's style).

Melody-dominated homophony can also be described as 'melody and accompaniment'.

Finally, to round off the binary form, a re-scored and abbreviated version of the first section returns at bar 53. It omits bars 5–13 of the opening section, and concludes with a cadence figure (bar 65) that inverts the motif first heard in bar 2. The texture throughout most of the movement is **melody-dominated homophony**.

Stravinsky assigns Pergolesi's cello line to solo double bass until bar 52. After bar 52 the melody is shared with the trombone – that most unbaroque of solo timbres.

The original bass part is allocated to the orchestral double basses (except in bars 30–37, where it is taken by the trombone) but, as we shall see, it is often much altered. Following baroque practice, Stravinsky supplies accompanying harmonies, but often in a way that no 18th-century musician would recognise!

Stravinsky's doubling of the first phrase with trombone glissandi immediately sets the slap-stick tone of this movement. Rather more subtle is the way that the bass part in bar 4 is changed to weaken the perfect cadence by omitting the dominant (C) – see *left*. Notice how Stravinsky then knocks the cadence into shape with a good clout from a syncopated accent on the second quaver of bar 5. The detailed performing directions underline Stravinsky's humourous intentions – sudden changes in dynamics, exaggerated accents and special effects such as the trombone glissandi and the instruction for lower strings to play 'du talon' (at the heel of the bow) in order to produce a rough and rasping quality in this context.

Another technique employed by Stravinsky could be described as 'melodic smudging'. Sometimes rather crudely referred to as 'neo-classical wrong notes', the brassy effect in the following passage is actually one of extreme brilliance. Upward swoops in the second horn part (shown by diagonal lines) and plummeting octaves in the lower strings emphasise the semiquaver slides of the melody:

Pergolesi ended the A section of his rounded binary form in a rather perfunctory fashion by repeating bars 14–17 to form bars 18–21. This is far too predictable for Stravinsky, who abandons the expected sequential repetition in bars 20–21 in favour of a tumbling glissando and a rushing semiquaver ascent that could be another *tirade* (see the margin note *opposite*) although accents on every note ensure that it sounds far from simply ornamental.

What happens after the repeat is a musical joke worthy of Haydn. The rushing strings have withered away to a solo double bass, whose solitary ascending scale of F major leads us back to the opening theme in the tonic for a *third* time (bars 22–23)! The bass, realising its ghastly mistake, then projects the scale up to the dominant (C) in its most stratospheric register, allowing Stravinsky to pick up the threads of Pergolesi's B section at bar 25. (In other words, to achieve this bit of fun, he has interpolated three extra bars, 22–24, into his source material.) But even though the solo bass is now in C major, the orchestral basses have been so won over by the idea of returning to the tonic, that they subvert the implied C-major cadence of the tune by sticking on F (see *right*).

Stravinsky's treatment of bars 30–37 can only be described as re-composition. Here is Pergolesi's original phrase for the first four of these bars – it ends in G minor and is then repeated sequentially a tone lower to end in F major:

Look at these bars in *NAM 7* and you will see that Stravinsky:

- Overlays bars 30–32 with repetitions of a C-major chord
- Cadences in G major, not G minor, in bar 33
- Employs a total silence on the first quaver of bar 33 to create a cheeky syncopated cadence on the next two quavers
- Smudges both chords of that cadence by including the tonic (G) in the D^7 chord, and then leaving the second oboe stuck on F♯ while everyone else is playing G major for the second chord (the result is as topsy-turvy as the plot of the ballet).

The rhythmic equivalent of the 'melodic smudging' noted earlier occurs in bars 38–45. The flutes double the bass melody three octaves higher, but in rhythmically different versions, producing a **heterophonic texture** (which is easier to see in the score than to hear on the *NAM* recording). The weak-beat tonic pedal accompanying this section is also pure Stravinsky – at this point Pergolesi's bass replicates that starting in bar 6 (shown in the first example on page 53).

In the brief excursion to F minor in bars 46–49, Stravinsky's very high **tessitura** for the double bass has the effect of de-focusing the intonation, making the flat 3rd sound very blue. And, while the orchestral basses faithfully outline the original F–F–E–E bass line, the solo cello stays put on a tonic F, adding yet more to the bleary-eyed quality of this tantalisingly short interlude.

Cadences mark out the territory in tonal music and, as we have seen, Stravinsky ruthlessly undermines many of them in this movement. In bars 54–55 he omits both V and I in the bass and then even removes the key note from the tune in bar 55, leaving the ear to imagine the missing notes of the now non-existant cadence.

By changing Pergolesi's sequential bass in bar 59 (marked * *below*) Stravinsky anticipates the tonic and so weakens the perfect cadence in bars 60–61; he also removes the dominant from that cadence, and rewrites the bass of bar 61 to make it less tonic-centred, thus de-stabilising the entire cadential progression:

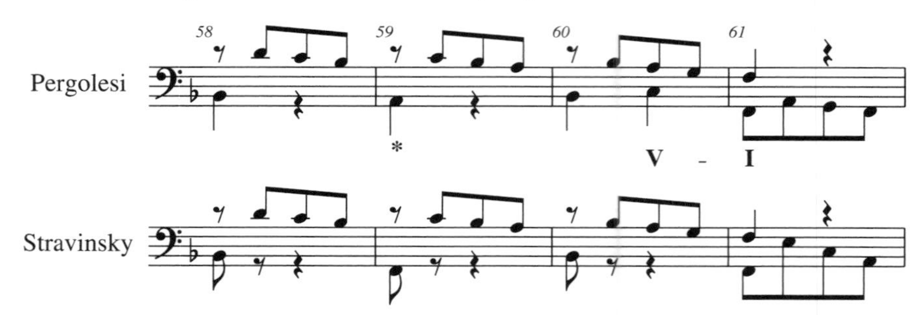

And the final cadence of the movement is singled-out for special treatment. By changing the penultimate bass note from C to A, Stravinsky transforms a standard baroque perfect cadence into a much weaker (and very skeletal) III–I progression. The Vivo simply stops, rather than coming to a convincing tonal conclusion.

? Private study

1. Which aspects of Stravinsky's instrumentation reflect 18th-century practice, and which do not?
2. Show how rounded binary form differs from ternary form.
3. Explain the following two terms **and** give examples of each in *NAM 7*: (i) octave displacement (ii) heterophonic texture.
4. In bars 33–34 of the Sinfonia, show how Stravinsky divides the melody between two different soloists.
5. (a) Compare bars 29–32 of the Gavotta with bars 25–28.

   (b) What is the **sounding pitch** of the first bass note in Variation I (bar 31, beat 1)?

Sample questions

In the exam there will be three questions on the special focus work, from which you must answer **two**.

1. Show how the Gavotta is treated in Variazione I.
2. Describe the features of *NAM 7* which reveal that it is a work of the 20th century.
3. Discuss Stravinsky's treatment of cadences in the Vivo.

Continuity and change in melody, structure and tonality

For examination in summer 2008 and 2009

You do not need to study this topic unless *20th-century art music* is the Area of Study that you undertook for AS Music and which you are now extending for A2.

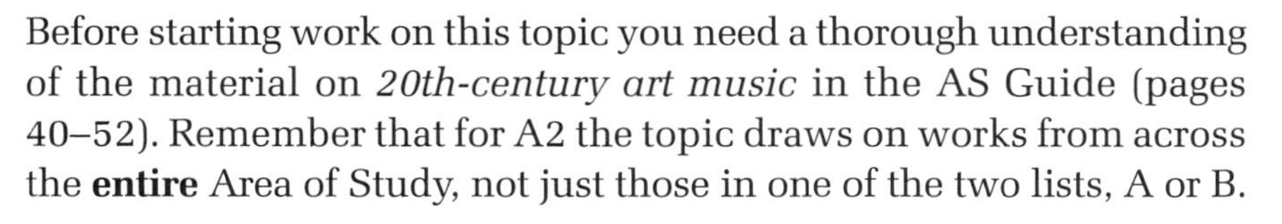

Before starting work on this topic you need a thorough understanding of the material on *20th-century art music* in the AS Guide (pages 40–52). Remember that for A2 the topic draws on works from across the **entire** Area of Study, not just those in one of the two lists, A or B.

Tonality refers to the use of (and relationship between) major and minor keys in music – it is nothing to do with the tone colour of musical sounds. In tonal music, keys are established by cadences, particularly perfect cadence patterns such as V^7–I.

Stravinsky

NAM 7 (page 139) CD1 Tracks 7–9
Academy of St. Martin-in-the-Fields
Conducted by Neville Marriner

The melodies in these three movements from the *Pulcinella* suite are taken from 18th-century works. They are thus tonal and mainly diatonic, using traditional techniques such as sequence. However, as we saw in the previous section, Stravinsky undermines their obvious tonality by weakening bass lines, especially at cadences, and by adding dissonances to create harmonic ambiguity.

Stravinsky sometimes allocates the sub-sections of a phrase to different instruments (as in bars 33–34 of the Sinfonia) and also uses extremes of the range to create unusual tone colours. He highlights individual notes with accents and sometimes adds extra bars or beats to produce unexpected phrase lengths. Techniques such as melodic smudging, octave displacement, the deliberate omission of an obvious note (as at the start of bar 55 of the Vivo), and the use of hetereophonic textures, all play an important role in his neo-classical treatment of melodic material. Also, Stravinsky often adds his own countermelodies to increase the contrapuntal interest of his basically simple source material.

All of these points are explored in much more detail in the preceding section. Make sure that you can illustrate each of them with an appropriate example, giving both the name(s) of the instrument involved and the relevant bar number(s).

Finally, the structures of the three movements all replicate the simple forms of their baroque originals:

- Rounded binary form for the Sinfonia and Vivo
- theme-and-variations form for the Gavotte and two variations (in which the theme, and each of the variations, is in simple binary form).

However, as we saw in the first half of this chapter, Stravinsky often deliberately obscures the neat outlines of these tonally-based forms by weakening the cadences that delineate sections of the structure, or by starting recapitulations in unexpected ways.

Webern

NAM 8 (page 160) CD1 Track 10
Jacqueline Ross (violin),
Ruth MacDowell (clarinet),
Jan Steele (saxophone),
Mark Racz (piano)

Bars	*Structure*
1–5	* Introduction
6–15	A Exposition
16–23	B Development
24–27	* Link
28–39	A Recapitulation
39–43	* Coda

Read pages 43–44 of the AS Guide for the background to serial music. Although written only ten years after *Pulcinella*, the atonal style of *NAM 8* is in total contrast to the tonal idiom of Stravinsky's neo-classical ballet. Unlike tonal music, serialism places equal importance on all 12 pitches of the octave – no particular notes have special importance, such as the tonic and dominant in tonal music. The consistent use of a note row ensures this equality and also gives unity and structure to the music.

But Webern goes beyond this, superimposing on his serial structure mirror canons around a **cantus firmus** and an overall **ternary form**. The latter is summarised *left* (the three sections marked * all use related material). But it is a ternary form without the slightest hint of tonality.

Webern's melodic material is extremely fragmentary and nothing like the flowing four-bar oboe tune heard at the start of the Gavotte in *NAM 7*. Webern presents his note row in tiny two- and three-note cells, with little obvious sense of regular metre at this slow speed. These cells involve wide leaps that sometimes reach the extreme parts of each instrument's range. The slow tempo and sparse texture allow the listener to focus in detail on the tone colour of individual notes rather than complete melodies, especially since almost every note is given its own individual dynamic and articulation. As Webern's teacher Schoenberg noted, in music of this concentration and intensity the slightest nuance conveys an almost unbearable significance.

In early music a **cantus firmus** was a melody around which composers would construct a contrapuntal composition. Here we use the term to refer to the saxophone's presentation of the complete prime order of the note row in bars 6–10, followed immediately with its transposition by a tritone (to start on G) in bars 11–14. It returns in bars 28–32 (thus linking the A sections) but here it is shared with the clarinet and violin, as shown on page 45 of the AS Guide.

The four instruments mainly play one at a time with little overlap, apart from bars 22–23 where the central climax is delineated by a thicker texture, wider range and louder dynamic level. Webern's sparse melodic style in *NAM 8* is largely a result of his **pointillist** texture and use of **Klangfarbenmelodie** (both terms are explained on page 45 of the AS Guide). The nearest thing to a complete melody in this movement is the saxophone's cantus firmus, but even that needs intense concentration if the listener is to consciously spot its relationship to the mirror canons that weave around it.

As to tonality, we can sum up this movement in a single word: it is **atonal** – it does not make use of tonal principles.

Shostakovich

NAM 9 (page 163) CD1 Track 11
Coull Quartet

A	B	C	B^1	A^1
bars 0^2–27	*bars* 28–50	*bars* 50–86	*bars* 87–104^1	*bars* 104^2–126

This movement is an extended ternary structure known as **arch form** which can be represented as ABCB^{1}A^1. In other words, the last two sections are modified repeats of the first two sections, with their order reversed, as shown *below left*.

However, these sections are not differentiated by key, as they are in music of previous centuries. In fact, section B^1 is the only extended passage in the movement to completely break free from the key of C minor. There is some melodic difference between the sections, although even that is compromised by the persistent use of the DSCH motto throughout the movement. The main difference between the sections is one of texture.

Section A is concerned with contrapuntal explorations of DSCH, heard first in the cello (C minor), answered by the viola (G minor), restated by the second violin (C minor) and answered by the first violin (F minor). Although the harmony is dissonant, this choice of keys (I–V–I–IV in C minor) reveals how Shostakovich's style is essentially tonal. However, the harmony allows for no simple cadences to define tonality – new dissonances always move the music on. In fact, Shostakovich has used all 12 semitones of the octave by bar 6 and the shifting triadic harmony of bars 13–14 (E minor, E major, E♭ augmented) leaves a sense of tonal ambiguity. However, the statement of DSCH by the first violin in bars 23–27 is supported by **functional harmony** in C minor that leads to the section ending with its first (and only) definitive perfect cadence (V^{9-8}–I) in bars 25–27.

Section B is differentiated by a new texture – a solo violin melody which, while being chromatic, is pinned to C minor by a **double pedal** (on I and V) lasting more than 17 bars. A further reference to DSCH in the cello (bars 46–49) combines with the first violin's countermelody to end in an inverted perfect cadence in C minor (bar 48–50) that overlaps with the start of the next section.

Section C consists of two-part counterpoint for the violins above sustained pedals on I, V and I in the lower strings. These anchor the tonality to C minor, although the first violin's E♮ in bars 55 and 63 allow brief hints of C major to penetrate the gloom. Various manipulations of DSCH continue in the first violin melody (bar 67) and the second violin countermelody (bars 68–69), and it is then heard in **augmentation**, starting at bar 79. The tonality here is again ambiguous – the chords are G major (bar 79), E♭ minor (bar 80) and F major (bar 81). But the dissonances above the dominant in bar 82 resolve to V^7–I in bars 83^2–85, ending the section with a perfect cadence in the tonic key of C minor.

Thus, each of the first three sections has ended with a clear reference to DSCH at its original pitch, followed by a perfect cadence in C minor.

Section B^1, starting at bar 87, differs from section B in that the chromatic melody is now in the cello, accompanied by upper parts in A minor and then F♯ minor. In fact, this is the only extended passage in the movement to completely break free of C minor. The tonic major briefly emerges at bar 95, but the first violin's variation on DSCH in C major (bars 96–99^1) is pulled towards A minor by the viola's parallel 3rds. The cello E♭ in bar 97 impinges on both keys and leads to the chromatic bass line of bars 99–104.

Finally, **section A^1** begins in the second half of bar 104, with the return of music from bars 11^2–21^1, leading to a final appearance of DSCH at its original pitch (violin 2, bars 118^2–121). As at the end of three of the previous four sections, this is the signal for a perfect cadence in the tonic (bars 120–124). The final G♯ is a link to the next movement and doesn't alter the fact that *NAM 9* is, despite its dissonances and harmonic ambiguities, profoundly tonal.

The sombre mood of the movement is created not only by its intensely minor tonality and long pedal points, but also by slow-moving melodies of narrow range that lie in a low tessitura for all four instruments. Many are built around manipulations of the DSCH motif (sometimes referred to as a 'cipher'), developed into long, legato phrases, while the B section introduces a new idea based on a gloomily descending chromatic scale.

Cage

NAM 10 (page 166) CD1 Tracks 12–14
Joanna MacGregor

Superficially there are features in the sonatas that resemble those of tonal music, such as the triadic-looking chords in Sonata I, or the pedal point in the first eight bars of Sonata III. But listening to CD1 immediately reveals that these are **atonal**, not tonal pieces. Cage's 'mutes' not only change the timbre of the piano but also radically affect its tuning, creating some notes of indeterminate pitch and others in which the relationship between notes is quite different from that of the tempered scales of western music. In any case Cage's focus is not on tonality (he once dismissed harmony as 'the tool of western commercialism') but on units of duration, rhythm and timbre.

Cage's approach to structure might at first sight seem to be more conventional. Each sonata in *NAM 10* is in **binary form** (like some of the single-movement keyboard sonatas of the baroque period). However, as we saw in *NAM 7*, 18th-century musical structures use contrasts in tonality to define their sections and this is not an option with the complex, often indeterminate pitches produced by the prepared piano. Only the division of each binary-form sonata into two repeated sections is a reminder of their baroque ancestry.

In the absence of both tonality and conventional melody, Cage adopts duration as his main structural element, in particular using what he described as a 'micro-macrocosmic' structure. Today we would recognise this as the formation known in mathematics as a fractal, seen in nature in structures such as snowflakes and ferns.

On page 49 of the AS Guide we showed how the first sonata is built on a seven-bar unit whose 28 crotchets are arranged in the pattern 4:1:3 + 4:1:3 + 4:2 + 4:2. The whole sonata mimics this pattern by using seven-crotchet units in the multiples 4, 1, 3 (repeated) and 4, 2 (repeated). The other two sonatas are structured in a similar way, although their proportions are more complex.

This careful attention to proportionality makes its impact in a subconscious way. Aurally more obvious is the fact that, because the two sections of the macrocosmic binary form are repeated, the microcosmic structures of the individual sections also create paired units (this is particularly evident at the start of Sonata I, where bars 3–4 form a varied repeat of bars 1–2).

There are many other internal repetitions that serve to strengthen the structure of each sonata. For example, in Sonata I, bars 20–21 are subjected to varied repetition in the next two bars. The entire progression of parallel chords creates a conclusion (although not a cadence) that is strengthened by a tiny codetta, in which the right hand of bar 24 is subjected to varied repetition in bars 25–26.

Repetition of a different kind occurs in Sonata II. When the four-note figure in the left hand of bar 2 is repeated in bar 3 it begins after a crotchet rest and so it begins on a weak beat rather than a strong beat – a device known as **metrical displacement**. Such jazz-like rhythms permeate much of this sonata. For example, the metrical displacement of the repeated figure in bars 7–8 is essentially the early-jazz device of 'secondary rag', in which a three-beat figure is repeated across the four-fold beat of quadruple time. A cascade of rag-like syncopation follows in the rhythmic repetitions of bars 10–14.

Repetition is just one of many traditional devices that contribute to the structure of the third sonata. The first section consists of three statements of the opening right-hand figure, in the second of which the final note is truncated to a crotchet. The initial three demi-semiquavers of this motif are augmented to eight times their value in bar 13. These crotchets are heard in retrograde order in bar 14, extended into bar 15 by means of a sequence. The left-hand of bars 14–15 repeats the ostinato accompaniment first heard in bars 11–12, but in bar 14 (only) it is transposed up a semitone.

Note that accidentals in *NAM 10* apply only to the notes they directly precede, so the demi-semiquaver F in bar 5 is an F♮.

The left-hand motif in bar 9 is subtly transformed into a rising chromatic scale in bar 17, truncated to two notes in bar 18, and then greatly extended in bars 19–21. The last F of bar 21 is also the first note of a retrograde repetition of the previous 14 pitches, so the two-note chord in bar 24 is the same chord with which the pattern began in bar 19. A further variant appears in bars 25–26 and versions of the two-note chord (a 4th) are heard until the end of the work. Meanwhile the right hand picks up the chromatic scale figure in bar 22. It begins in octaves with the left hand, but the tied A causes it to lag by a beat, producing minor 9ths in bar 23. This right-hand pattern is inverted in bars 27–28, and is subsequently joined with variants of the motif from bar 2 in the final system of the sonata to round off the binary structure.

Despite being atonal, lacking in conventional melodic phrases and bearing only superficial resemblance to binary form, we can see that Cage's sonatas are nevertheless tightly structured works. But this structure arises from internal repetitions of short ideas that are then mirrored in the overall form by Cage's innovative 'micro-macrocosmic' technique.

Berio

NAM 11 (page 171) CD1 Track 15
Cathy Berberian

If Cage's Sonatas seem to show little continuity with earlier music, Berio's Sequenza III might appear to be a total break with the past. Pitch is largely indeterminate – even when intervals are precisely notated, their pitches are not absolute – and so the work is **atonal**. And while the composer gives occasional indications of rhythm by means of headless notes, there is no sense of regular pulse or metre – the music is governed by the ten-second lengths of its 52 units, rather than by barlines.

Neither does Berio use the voice melodically, despite a few intervallic patterns. The work has an improvisatory quality in which extended vocal techniques are used to explore the border between speech and song.

The structure of *NAM 11* is equally unconventional. There is no set form as such. Instead Berio selects phonetic ideas from the text which he repeats, mixes and matches into a patchwork of rapidly changing moods. These broadly fall into five categories:

A **tense** (urgent, nervous, apprehensive, intense)
B **anxious** (bewildered, desperate, whimpering, whining, relieved)
C **hyperactive** (witty, giddy, ecstatic, excited, coy)
D **dreamy** (distant, impassive, wistful, langourous, faintly)
E **serene** (noble, calm, joyful, tender)

Berio weaves these into a fast-changing **episodic** structure. For example, the first minute swings between emotions from groups A and D. Both are then combined ('dreamy and tense') at 1'10". A brief element from group C ('giddy', just before 1'30") is sandwiched between more of the tense group A emotions, to be followed by the first group B state ('relieved') at about 1'43". These mood swings provide contrast but they mostly happen too rapidly and randomly to provide a conventional musical structure. Nevertheless, in the final 50 seconds, it is obvious that the tense and anxious emotions of groups A and B, have all disappeared, and the piece eventually ends with dreamy and serene moods of groups D and E.

Reich

NAM 12 (page 176) CD1 Track 16
Roger Heaton

The atonality and avoidance of traditional metre, melody and form in *Sequenza III*, which was written in 1966, is typical of much post-war modernist music. The reaction to such abstract techniques came in the form of post-modernism, of which the second movement of Reich's *New York Counterpoint* (1985) is a typical example.

The music is entirely **diatonic** – every note belongs to the key of B major (heard as A major, since the clarinets sound a tone lower than written). The melodic ostinati are centred on hypnotic alternations of chords IV and V, but their canonic entries cause the chords to overlap and change at different times in different parts:

For clarity, pairs of parts that are a 10th apart have here been printed a 3rd apart.

These melodic parts come from the pitches of a **hexatonic** (six-note) scale, B–C♯–E–F♯–G♯–A♯. The remaining note of B major (D♯) occurs only in the pulsating homophonic textures that add a harder edge. Even when these hint at a tonic chord there is always an added diatonic dissonance to cloud the issue, such as the C♯ below a B-major triad which introduces these textures in bar 27.

Although the movement is entirely diatonic, the blurring of its chords with dissonances and the lack of progression towards the tonic means that the harmony is **non-functional** – it is colouristic, and there is no contrast of sections by use of modulation. Thus there is continuity with the tonal traditions of the past, but there is also change in that this is a minimalist interpretation of tonality.

Bar numbers given here are those in the score. In performance, many of the two-bar units are of course repeated.

Given the absence of different keys or different themes to delineate sections of the movement, Reich structures his music through the careful control of texture.The first section (bars 1–26) is characterised by a steady build-up of contrapuntal complexity with most parts entering in pairs:

- Two parts in the first two bars
- Four parts in bars 3–8
- Two more parts enter in bar 9, but because they double existing strands for four bars, a six-part texture only emerges at bar 13
- A seventh part is added from bar 21.

In the second section (bars 27–65), clarinets 1–6 continue with various permutations of this contrapuntal texture, but the live clarinettist breaks free to take on a more soloistic role. This section is also distinguished by the addition of six dissonant four-part chords, each played as repeated semiquavers. These fade in and out on clarinets 7 and 8 plus two bass clarinets. The first two last for six bars and the third for eight, after which the pattern repeats. Finally the chords disappear, leaving six more bars of fading counterpoint, followed by a cheeky three-note fragment of the opening motif in the final two clarinet parts.

An important part of Reich's melodic treatment involves the technique of **phasing** which can be most clearly seen in the opening bars. For clarity, the example *below* shows only the upper of each pair of parts and omits the repeat signs. When the live clarinet enters in bar 3 it plays the same motif as clarinet 7, but half a beat later. When heard against the original motif (which continues in clarinet 7) it is therefore a half-beat out of phase (shown by the arrows), creating a **canon**:

Only four notes are imitated at this point – the grey notes in bar 4 *above* are replaced by rests. But look at bar 5 and you will see that the canon continues out of phase despite the missing notes. Reich fills in one more note (A♯) in bar 6 – and from bar 7 onwards the live clarinet gets the entire 11-note melody, still half a beat out of phase. This **additive** process of gradually completing a melody by replacing rests with notes is a common technique in minimalist music, and one of the fingerprints of Reich's style.

Next look at the live clarinet entry in bar 13 of the score. Do you see that it has now moved one whole beat out of phase? (At this point a subtractive process of replacing some notes of the melody with rests begins.) The importance of the phasing process is that it causes expected rhythmic accents to be thrown 'out of sync', giving rise to complex new contrapuntal patterns as metrically different versions of the same idea are heard simultaneously.

Reich's basic melodic material is **triadic** (based on the chords of E and F♯ major) and minimal – the opening two-bar motif is heard in one form or other throughout the entire movement. This melody is also limited in range to just one octave, but Reich's treatment of it includes transposing the motif to different octaves, enabling the distinctive timbres of the clarinet's low, middle and upper registers to be exploited. In addition, the bottom note of the bass clarinet (sounding D below the bass stave) adds to the depth of the overall texture in bars 33–38 and 53–58.

The live clarinet gradually takes on a more soloistic role from bar 25 onwards, developing ideas from the opening over a wider range of two and a half octaves, although it continues to present its melody in repeated two-bar patterns, just like the canonic ostinati.

Private study

1. Explain what is meant by tonality, using the expression 'functional harmony' in your answer.
2. What is the difference between simple binary form and rounded binary form? In which work that you have studied can both be found?
3. Explain the meaning of arch form and name a work from this area of study in which it is used.
4. What is a *Klangfarbenmelodie*?
5. Explain the following five terms and give an example of each from the works you have studied:

   countermelody — phasing — canon
   metrical displacement — micro-macrocosmic structure

6. 20th-century music is often divided into tonal and atonal styles. Is *NAM 12* tonal? Give a reason for your answer.

Sample questions

In the exam there will be two questions on this topic, from which you must answer **one**.

(a) Contrast the melodic writing in the works you have studied by Stravinsky and Webern.

(b) Comment on the different approaches to tonality seen in the works you have studied by Shostakovich and Reich.

(c) Show how 20th-century composers have structured atonal music by comparing the forms used by Webern in *NAM 8* and Cage in *NAM 10*.

Music for small ensemble

There are *two* Special Focus works, *NAM 15* and *NAM 19*, both of which must be studied for the exam in 2008 or 2009.

Corelli: Trio Sonata in D, Op. 3, No. 2: movement IV

Special Focus Work 1 for 2008 and 2009	
NAM 15 (page 200) Fitzwilliam Ensemble	CD2 Track 4

Before starting on this section you should work through (or revise) the information about the context and structure of this music given on pages 57–58 of the AS Guide. Make sure that you understand all of the terminology used on those pages.

Context

Given that this movement is from a 'church sonata' and bears no title, how can we be certain that *NAM 15* is a gigue? Is it likely that people danced jigs in churches? They probably didn't, but in the baroque period much music (whether for performance in church or the home) reflected dance styles of the age. This extract has all the characteristics of a gigue, including:

- A **fast tempo** (*Allegro*)
- **Compound time** and
- **Binary form** (like most baroque dance movements).

Rhythm and metre

NAM 15 is a gigue in tempo and metre, but there are a couple of rhythmic features in bars 26–27 to enliven the regular dotted-crotchet pulse. The first is **cross rhythm** in bar 26, where the tie across the middle of the bar results in the first violin sounding as though it is in $\frac{3}{4}$ while the lower parts remain in $\frac{6}{8}$. The second is the **hemiola** in bar 27 that results in all three parts appearing to be in $\frac{3}{4}$ time. An added delight is the **syncopation** caused by the first violin's tie that joins these two bars:

Now compare the rhythm and metre in this cadence with the same elements in bars 31–32 and 42–43.

Texture

The movement has a **contrapuntal** texture with **fugal** elements (as explained in the AS Guide). **Imitative entries** are shared among all three parts, although the bass takes on a more **functional** role after bar 23 (especially in bars 35–38). The wide gap between the two high violin parts and the much lower bass (which is filled in by the continuo) is known as a **polarised texture**, and is a feature of much baroque music.

Harmony and tonality

The harmonic rhythm in bars 26–27 reinforces the cross rhythm and hemiola. At this point the music is in B minor. The chord progression is shown by Roman numerals beneath the example, and the harmonic rhythm they generate is shown below them. Note that in 6/8 time the first change of chord is on the *fourth* quaver, whereas the first chord change in 3/4 time comes on the *third* quaver.

This passage illustrates Corelli's mastery of tonal harmony – the music has a sense of purpose, an exciting drive towards this, the first cadence in a minor key. The suspensions in the first violin part (marked 'S' in the example) are given extra rhythmic impetus by their decorated resolutions (marked 'R'). The F♯ in bar 26 clashes with the G♯ in the cello part but, before it resolves to E, a couple of decorative semiquavers are introduced. Similarly the tied E clashes with the F♯ below, and the resolution to D is decorated with another pair of semiquavers. Notice, too, that in both cases the resolutions coincide with a change of chord, thus adding a further element of urgency to the drive toward the cadence.

The same is true in the lead in to the cadence at the end of the first section. The **inverted pedal** (bars 15–17) clashes with cello part on the second beat of each bar creating tension that leads us to expect the resolution that comes when the key of A major is at last confirmed by the cadence (IIb–V–I) in bars 18–19.

If we now stand back from the detail and focus on the tonality of the whole gigue we will find this tonal structure:

Bar	9	20	26	29	32	33	43
‖: **D major**	**A major** :‖	‖: **D major**	**B minor**	**E minor**	**A major**	**D major** :‖	

Nothing could be simpler than this outward and return journey through closely related keys. It was precisely such assured handling of tonality – with no suggestion of the modality that persisted in the compositions of his contemporaries – that made Corelli's music so famous throughout the western world soon after his 48 trio sonatas were published in Rome between 1681 and 1694. Their influence on later composers, such as Vivaldi, Bach and Handel, cannot be overestimated.

Private study

1. Why are four people usually needed to play a trio sonata?
2. Explain the purpose of the figures printed below the bass part.
3. In which bar does the first suspension in this music occur?
4. What is a polarised texture?
5. Complete the blanks in the following sentences:

   The first violin part in bar 20 is an .... of the melody in bar 1. It is .... by the second violin in bar 21 and by the violone in bar 22.

Special Focus Work 2 for 2008 and 2009

NAM 19 (page 242) CD2 Track 8
Nash Ensemble

Poulenc: Sonata for Horn, Trumpet and Trombone, movement 1

Before starting on this section you should work through (or revise) the information about the context and structure of this music given on pages 64–66 of the AS Guide. Make sure that you understand all of the terminology used on those pages.

Classical parody

Poulenc once said 'Above all do not analyse my music – love it!' At the risk of ignoring this advice, we will start by seeking out the objects of Poulenc's good-humoured parodies. Who do you think wrote this melody?

If you gave the name of one composer you are wrong, for the first 11 notes come from *NAM 19* (trumpet, bars 2–3) but the remainder come from the first movement of Haydn's String Quartet Op. 71, No.1 (first violin, bars 8–10, transposed from B♭ to G major).

It is of course Haydn who is the first target for Poulenc's wit. Now compare the first violin part *below* (which comes from the same movement by Haydn) with Poulenc's trumpet part in bars 0–2^3:

Can you see that they begin with the same descending triad (D–B–G) and that they both leap an octave? Of course such triadic melodies are two-a-penny in classical music, which is why the whole four-bar trumpet melody at the start of *NAM 19* sounds so familiar.

So in what sense is Poulenc's music a parody of classical style? The answer lies in the deliberate banality of Poulenc's three statements of exactly the same motif. Like a bad-tempered teacher Poulenc's music seems to say 'If I've told you once, I've told you *three times* that the first five notes make a motif that you will jolly well remember for the rest of the movement'. And at the end of the whole phrase (***f*** *très sec*) the brutal detached crotchets proclaim 'this is a cadence at the end of a four-bar phrase – *and don't you forget it*'.

Now look at Haydn's four-bar phrase *above*. The descending triad is heard only once, and the phrase ends with a simple but highly effective manipulation of it, so the end gracefully mirrors the beginning (also compare the second violin part in bar 1 with the first violin part in bar 4). The parallel 6ths in bars 2–4 of the same extract are typical, not just of Haydn's music, but of classical styles in general. The trumpet and horn parts in bars 9–17 of *NAM 19* are also in parallel 6ths, but they go on far too long to have come from the pen of a classical composer.

Remember that a horn in F sounds a pefect 5th lower than written. So its first note in bar 9 is E, a 6th below the trumpet's C.

In the AS Guide, we described the modified recapitulation that starts on the last quaver of bar 39 as 'hiccuping'. The object of Poulenc's satire is something like the following passage, which comes from the same Haydn string quartet as the previous example (now shown in its original key). In this example the 'hiccuping' first violin interpolates short off-beat notes in the silences between the on-beat notes of the lower instruments. See if you can describe the similarities and differences between this passage by Haydn and the passage in bars 40–45 in *NAM 19*.

'Wrong' notes and romantic harmony

Early 20th-century neo-classical music like *NAM 19* or *NAM 7* (Stravinsky's *Pulcinella* was first performed in Paris two years before Poulenc wrote this work) is sometimes described as 'Bach with wrong notes'.

In fact, there are only half a dozen 'wrong notes' in the first 25 bars (listen to the recording and you will soon find them), and the same is true of the central section (bars 26–39) of the ternary form. Here we enter the scented world of Gabriel Fauré, as a comparison with this extract from Fauré's song *La Rose* (1890) will reveal:

The accompaniment figures (left-hand piano part in *La Rose* and horn part in the sonata) and the crotchet bass part are almost identical, as is Poulenc's mix of romantic and modal harmony – although on beat 2 of bar 27 Poulenc cannot resist the temptation to lay out the B♭^{13} chord in such a way that the trumpet's E♭ sounds more like a wrong note than the 11th of the chord – and more 'wrong notes' follow in bar 29.

Texture and form

The texture of *NAM 19* is mainly **homophonic**, with some **exchange of parts** (compare trumpet in bars 34–35 with horn in bars 30–31). Other points, including structure, are covered in the AS Guide, which you should revise before attempting the questions *below*.

Private study

1. What is a cadenza, and where does one occur in this work?
2. Name the form of *NAM 19* and state the key(s) of each section.
3. (a) Name the texture heard in bars 22–25.

   (b) How do the broken chords in bars 22–25 prepare for the new key that starts in bar 26?
4. In bar 40, what is the *sounding* pitch of the triad played by the horn in F?
5. Name the type of scale played by the trombone in bars 86–87.

Sample questions

In the exam there will be three questions on the two special focus works, from which you must answer **two**.

(a) Comment on Corelli's writing for strings in *NAM 15*, showing the extent to which each instrument shares in the development of the movement's melodic material.

(b) Describe the harmonic language of Poulenc's Sonata for Horn, Trumpet and Trombone, movement I.

(c) Contrast the ways in which tonality is used to define structure in the special focus works by Corelli **and** Poulenc.

Continuity and change in texture

For examination in summer 2008 and 2009

You do not need to study this topic unless *Music for small ensemble* is the Area of Study that you undertook for AS Music and which you are now extending for A2.

Before starting work on this topic you need a thorough understanding of the material on *Music for small ensemble* in the AS Guide (pages 53–66). Remember that for A2 the topic draws on works from across the **entire** Area of Study, not just those in one of the two lists, A or B.

Texture refers primarily to the number of simultaneous parts in a passage of music and the way in which they relate. At A2 you need to use precise terminology and should avoid vague descriptions of texture as 'thick', 'thin' or 'open'. For instance, you may need to describe a texture not only as contrapuntal but more specifically as two-, three- or four-part counterpoint, and you may need to indicate whether the type of counterpoint is fugal, canonic or just freely imitative. Similarly, you may need to describe a texture as not just homophonic but as melody-dominated homophony (or 'melody and accompaniment') or homorhythmic (all parts moving in the same rhythm to form a series of block chords).

Holborne

NAM 13 (page 191) CD2 Tracks 1–2
Rose Consort of Viols

All five string parts are employed throughout both dances in a largely **contrapuntal** five-part texture. Because there are so few rests, the **imitative entries** are not always obvious. For instance, at the start of the galliard the descending scale figure in the first viol is imitated at one minim-beat intervals by the third viol, bass viol and the second viol. But it is hard to hear because the scale figures are masked by the minims that precede them, and these notes also mask the clever **inversion** of the scale figure entering off the beat in viol 4. Notice that viols 3 and 5 play the imitative figure twice in melodic sequence, thus further clogging the texture. This is just one example of contrapuntal density – see if you find others.

Why did Holborne do it? The answer must be that this music was not composed for a passive audience, but for the delight of the performers themselves. They would derive extra pleasure every time they discovered a new link between their own part and those that their friends were playing below, around or above them.

Holborne's dances date from a time when music for an instrumental consort was little different from multi-part vocal music. For example, the compass of the two top parts in *NAM 13* is a 9th, the same as the two soprano parts in *NAM 34* (published a year earlier in 1598) – and the compass of the bass part in both works is a 12th.

Although all five parts are employed throughout, they don't always have an equal share in the counterpoint. For example, in bars 34–39 of the pavane, the upper four parts engage in imitation based on a rising scale figure but the bass remains on a **tonic pedal** (and it has a **dominant pedal** in bars 54–57, just before the final cadence). Also, counterpoint disappears briefly in bars 9–16 of the galliard, where a **homophonic** texture offers contrast with the intense imitative polyphony of the first strain (bars 1–8).

Many of the features mentioned *left* also feature in *NAM 34*. For instance, bars 34–43 of 'Sing we at pleasure' have a contrapuntal texture in which the fifth part (the alto) is allocated a subsidiary, non-imitative role. And, like Holborne, Weelkes varies his texture by introducing homophonic passages, such as 'All shepherds in a ring' in bars 32–35.

Gabrieli

NAM 14 (page 194) CD2 Track 3
His Majesty's Sagbutts and Cornetts
Directed by Timothy Roberts

While *NAM 13* was probably intended for amateurs to play at home, Gabrieli's *Sonata pian' e forte* was designed to stun a large congregation in the opulent surroundings of St Mark's in Venice. To that end the most obvious textural element is the **antiphony** between two four-part 'choirs' of instruments, the one distinguished from the other by (almost certainly) being spatially separated and by the different timbres and ranges of their soprano instruments.

The cornett part has a relatively high range (D above middle C to F a 10th above) while the part marked 'violin' has a range that is mainly an octave lower (it is too low for a modern violin, the compass being more like that of a viola).

This contrast in range of the two choirs is apparent at many points in the score, but nowhere is it more obvious than in bars 45–46 where the descending scale figure in choir 2 is heard an octave higher when it is passed to choir 1 – and a similar effect occurs with the dotted four-note figure in bars 47–48.

But Gabrieli was well aware that an extended composition like this could not achieve its effect by exploiting just one textural device, so he begins with 13 bars of **free four-part counterpoint** for choir 1 (with a tiny point of imitation for trombones 2 and 3). The entry of choir 2 overlaps the cadence of choir 1, and they begin with similar free counterpoint. But a contrasting **imitative texture** begins on the second crotchet of bar 17 where trombone 5 plays a figure of four crotchets and a minim (all of the imitative subjects are similarly concise). A second point of imitation begins at the second beat of bar 21 – see if you can spot the other three statements of this subject.

The novel idea of marking such dynamic contrasts in the score was, of course, the reason for the sonata's title.

Suddenly (at bar 26) the first choir enters above the continuing counterpoint of the second choir 2, the effect of the majestic **eight-part texture** being reinforced by the first change from *piano* to *forte*.

Gabrieli uses **homophonic** textures for contrast, although they are mostly short-lived and coincide with moments of antiphony, as in bars 45–49 where one choir answers the other.

We have now dealt with all of the most important types of texture apart from those in the grand climax (bars 71–80). It begins with a five-note figure in trombone 6 that is imitated at quaver or crotchet intervals by all other instruments except trombones 5 and 1. In bars 71–74 there are no fewer than 17 statements of this figure: see if you can find them. In the last six bars there are two more points of imitation, the first beginning in trombone 4 at bar 75, the second in the 'violin' part at bar 77, and the whole sonata ends on a tremendously vibrant seven-part chord.

Corelli

NAM 15 (page 200) CD2 Track 4
Fitzwilliam Ensemble

There could hardly be a greater contrast between Gabrieli's dense eight-part texture and Corelli's polarised three-part texture. The main points about the texture of *NAM 15* were discussed earlier, but now we can see how this work differs from the two earlier ones we have studied in its variety of texture. *NAM 13* uses five parts throughout and *NAM 14* uses either four parts or all eight. Corelli, in contrast, starts with a **monophonic** texture, which becomes **two-part** with the entry of the second violin and then **three-part** from bar 6 (the same is true at the start of the second section). And, unlike Holborne, Corelli allows his listeners to hear the imitation by retreating to just one or two parts immediately before each entry (bars 11, 22, 23, 28–29 and 32–33).

It would be possible to sing *NAM 13* or *14*, but it would be very difficult to sing this gigue. For the first time we encounter a type of texture that has been customised for the intended instruments – it is idiomatic string music.

Haydn

NAM 16 (page 202) CD2 Track 5
The Lindsays

All three pieces so far discussed are mainly contrapuntal and include substantial passages in five-, eight- and three-part imitative textures. Look through the first violin part of *NAM 16* and you will see that the first violin carries most of the melodic burden leaving the other three parts to provide a homophonic accompaniment.

This is particularly evident in the first four bars where the lower string parts are **homorhythmic** (an extreme type of homophony in which the instruments play exactly the same rhythms to produce block chords). A much longer homophonic passage occurs in the lower strings in bars 41–58. Passages such as these are often described by the useful term **melody-dominated homophony**. Even when there is some degree of independent movement in the lower parts, this term still applies. For example, in bars 5–6 the cello's dotted minim with slurred notes above contrasts with the previous detached chords, but the homophonic accompaniment remains dominated by the first-violin melody.

One of the most common textures of the period consists of **parallel 3rds, 6ths or 10ths** supported by a simple accompaniment. In bars 8–12, for instance, the second violin plays in parallel 3rds, then parallel 10ths, with the first violin's melody and both are supported by a dominant, then a tonic, **pedal**. This is an absolutely typical classical texture so you ought to see how many more examples you can find.

Then – much more difficult – see how many passages you can find where any of the lower parts have fragments of melody that are *not* tied to the first violin part by such parallelism. In fact, the only passage where the first violin part ceases to be the envy of the rest of the quartet is to be found in bars 111–115 where there is an **inverted pedal** (the repeated B♭s). This is also the only passage where there is a quasi-**imitative** texture, but significantly the parts are coupled in 3rds (second violin and viola from bar 111, and viola and cello from bar 113).

Haydn's use of silence is more pronounced than it is in Corelli's gigue, and it is used to clarify the symmetrical rondo structure (ABACABA starting in bars 0, 8, 28, 36, 71, 79 and 99 respectively) rather than to highlight imitative entries. And, without the use of silence, the joke of the quartet's nickname would have been a lead balloon (bars 132–172).

Beethoven

NAM 17 (page 207) CD2 Track 6
Berlin Philharmonic Octet

By now you should have had sufficient experience of a wide range of textures to be able to describe the textural contrasts of this much larger movement. But remember that the timbre of the six different instruments plays a more significant role in the textures here than it did in the earlier works we have discussed. Remember, too, that

- The clarinet sounds a tone lower than printed
- The horn sounds a major 6th lower and
- The double bass an octave lower.

As you study the music, notice how Beethoven exploits a much wider range in all instrumental parts than was the case in any of the earlier music we have studied.

If you are asked in an exam question to comment on a variety of textures in the works you have studied, it is better to select clearly contrasted passages (as here) rather than to attempt to list every texture you can find on a bar-by-basis.

Let's just choose some of the most diverse passages and describe them as concisely as possible.

- Bar 1: Five-part chord of E♭ major – root doubled in octaves, 3rd doubled once (violin and viola double-stopping), but no 5th.
- Bar 2: **Monophonic texture** (crotchets with acciaccaturas).
- Bars 8–11: Alternation of three-part strings and tutti chords.
- Bars 12–14: **Melody-dominated homophony** (tune in violin accompanied by wind and cello, with melodic fragments in the viola).
- Bars 19–28: **Melody-dominated homophony** (tune in violin, broken chords in viola and detached bass notes in cello).
- Bars 29–39: **Melody-dominated homophony** (tune in clarinet, sustained bassoon and horn, syncopated violin and viola, and staccato arpeggios in the cello (supported by double bass).
- Bars 47–49: **Antiphonal exchange** between wind and strings.
- Bars 111–115: **Melody in octaves** with harmony sketched in by horn and double bass.
- Bars 221^3–231^1: A **homorhythmic** texture in which three-part strings alternate with tutti chord.
- Bars 254–257: **Two-part counterpoint** (clarinet and horn in octaves against lower strings in octaves) plus **tonic pedal** in bassoon and second violin.
- Bars 258–264: **Imitation** (the part for cello and bass is imitated by oboe and bassoon in bar 260, which in turn is imitated by cello and bass in bar 262) plus a **countermelody** for violin. The violin and bass parts in bars 258–261 form a **contrapuntal inversion** of the clarinet and bass parts in the previous four bars.
- Bars 274–277: **Duet** for clarinet and bassoon above sustained string chords.

Romantic fusion

NAM 18 (page 231) CD2 Track 7
Guarneri Quartet with
Peter Serkin (piano)

The textures of *NAM 18* are at least as varied as those in *NAM 17*, but rather than the changes occurring as part of the general unfolding of sonata form, Brahms uses sudden changes in texture to highlight the complex structure of the movement. This particularly applies to the terrific change from the **homorhythmic** texture in bars 57–67 to the intensely contrapuntal **fugato** that follows it. Equally abrupt is the change from the repeated piano chords with hammered string appogiaturas in bars 190–193 to the piano solo over the cello's **tonic pedal** at the start of the trio.

One of the most important textural features is the interplay between piano and strings. Here are a few examples:

- Bars 1–13: Piano supplies an inner part between the syncopated melody and tonic pedal with **canonic imitation** of the sequential string melody from bar 9.
- Bars 22–29: Piano doubles and thickens string chords.
- Bars 30–34: Imitation between the string melody in octaves and the piano chords pitched a 10th higher.

- Bars 67–99: Piano provides two contrapuntal strands to a **fugal** texture that grows from two to five real parts.
- Bars 100–109: Piano provides syncopated urgency to what had previously been a **homorhythmic** texture in bars 57–67.
- Bars 210–225: Piano provides arpeggio then chordal accompaniment to the melody-dominated string parts.

Poulenc

NAM 19 (page 242) CD2 Track 8
Nash Ensemble

Poulenc's sonata is written for a trio of instruments, but it is far removed from the polarised texture of Corelli's trio sonata. Its texture is nearer to the **melody-dominated homophony** of Haydn's quartet movement in that one instrument usually has the tune while the other two accompany.

However, lacking a fourth part and given the impossibility of double stopping on wind instruments, one of the two accompanying instruments is obliged to supply something in the nature of a broken-chord accompaniment to fill out the harmony. This is most obvious in bars 26–29 where the gap between the trumpet melody and trombone bass is filled, not by continuo harmony, but by horn arpeggios. When the roles are reversed at bar 30 the horn melody keeps bumping into the trumpet filling, and the trombone is given the other chord notes in a grotesque send-up of the horn's arpeggios. Other aspects of the texture of this movement were discussed earlier in the chapter.

Private study

1. State the meaning of 'polarised texture' and name a work from this area of study in which such a texture is found.
2. On page 74 we used the expression 'antiphonal exchange'. What does this mean?
3. Which of the works you have studied begins with a monophonic texture?
4. (i) Identify the texture used in bars 13–18^1 of *NAM 18*.

   (ii) How does this texture change in bars 18^2–21?
5. Choose one of the expressions below to complete this sentence: In bars 197–200 of *NAM 17* the clarinet and cello play in ...

   octaves unison parallel 6ths parallel 9ths

Sample questions

In the exam there will be two questions on this topic, from which you must answer **one**.

(a) Compare and contrast the musical textures used by Holborne in *NAM 13* with those used by Corelli in *NAM 15*.

(b) How do the textures of Haydn's quartet movement (*NAM 16*) differ from those of Gabrieli's *Sonata pian' e forte* (*NAM 14*)?

(c) Comment on the variety of textures used by Beethoven in *NAM 17* **and** Brahms in *NAM 18*.

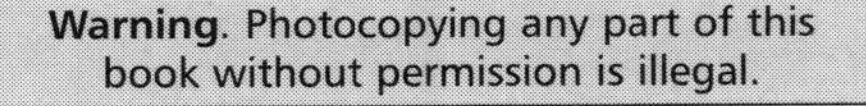

Keyboard music

There are *two* Special Focus works, the Sarabande (only) from *NAM 21* and Debussy's Sarabande (*NAM 24*), both of which must be studied if you are taking the exam in 2008 or 2009.

Bach, Sarabande from Partita in D

Special Focus Work 1 for 2008 and 2009
NAM 21 (page 249) CD2 Track 10 András Schiff (piano)

Before starting on this section you should work through (or revise) the information about the context and structure of this music given on pages 69–70 of the AS Guide. Make sure that you understand all of the terminology used on those pages.

Structure

‖: D (I) – A (V) :‖: Bm (vi) – Em (ii) – D (I) :‖

You have already studied the overall **rounded binary form** of this dance and you will have noticed how, with the exception of the repetition of passages from the first section in bars 29–38, the form is largely determined by Bach's key scheme (see *left*). Now we must look more closely at the way Bach's harmony defines the tonal structure and the very slow triple metre of this stately dance.

Harmony and tonality

An accent on the second beat of the bar – sometimes regarded as one of the most important features of baroque sarabande style – occurs in bars 1, 13 and 29. At these points it is the change of harmony and the dissonance that are chiefly responsible for the rhythmic effect (notice that Schiff does not tie the two As in the right hand of bar 13, so the clash of a 7th is as strong in this bar as in the other two).

Functional harmony refers to the use of chord progressions, particularly cadences, that establish the main key(s) of the work, and which thus help to give it structure.

Do you think that the minim (the longest note value in the melody) on the second beat in bars 2, 14 and 30 also creates a sarabande rhythm? Only to a limited extent, because the chromatic secondary dominant implied by the unaccompanied melody lasts for the whole bar. But Bach's functional harmony – clearly implied by the two-part counterpoint – *does* emphasise the triple metre by using a new chord on the first beat of every bar.

For instance, the chord outlined in bar 2 is chord VII of G major (the notes G and B are passing notes). When this resolves to a chord of G major in bar 3, the new chord emphasises the first beat of that bar. The perfect cadence in bars 3–4 creates another first-beat accent in bar 4 and also re-establishes the tonic key after the chromatic C♮ in bar 2 (notice that chord I of D major continues right through bar 4). This cadence marks the end of the **first four-bar phrase**.

Although the rapidly modulating harmony of the **second four-bar phrase** is more complicated, its final chord lasts throughout bar 8, thus balancing the long-held chord of bar 4. It is V^7 of A major, and it creates a feeling of tension that is only dispelled when it resolves to the tonic chord of the new key at the start of the **third four-bar phrase** (bars 9–12). With the sole exception of the decorative F♮ in bar 12, this third phrase is diatonic and the chord changes continue to emphasise triple metre.

As is so often the case, the **harmonic rhythm** speeds up just before the cadence with VIIb–I (in A major) on the first beat of bar 11, chord Ib on the second beat, and Ic–V on the third. resolving to a decorated tonic chord of A major in bar 12.

So, the whole of the first section consists of three four-bar phrases, the first in the tonic key of D major, the second modulating to V^7 of A major, and third in the dominant key of A major. This is one of the most common tonal structures for the first section of a movement in binary or rounded binary form.

This regular phrasing reflects the origin of the sarabande as a dance which needed clear-cut phrase lengths to match the dance steps. However, *NAM 21* merely reflects this style and was never intended to accompany an actual dance.

Four-bar phrasing is less evident in bars 13–28, but the tonal structure gives it an underlying shape. The modified repeat of the first bar of the sarabande in bar 13 seems to be heading back to the tonic key of D major, but is interrupted by V^7b of B minor in the next bar (B and D are passing notes). This is to be the principal key of bars 14–20, with perfect cadences in bars 16–17 and 19–20. The obvious cadential harmony in the latter (see *right*) confirms B minor as the first important goal of the section.

The chords in bar 19 are, in the key of B minor, Vb–I, IIb–IVb and Ic–V^7, followed by chord I in bar 20.

The structural importance of this cadence is further emphasised by the melody ending on the tonic of B minor, given further emphasis by an appoggiatura. The only other cadences ending on the tonic in both right- and left-hand parts come at the end of section A (bars 11–12) and section B (bars 37–38).

The next eight-bar phrase (bars 21–28) moves more rapidly through a series of related keys confirmed by the perfect cadences at bars 23–24 (E minor), 25–26 (G major), 26–27 (D major) and 27–28 (A major). The last three of these cadences are part of a **harmonic sequence** that can easily be detected by playing the bass part. It finishes on an implied chord of A major in bar 28 which, with the addition of G♮, becomes V^7 of D major leading without break into the return of the first two bars (bars 29–30). This 'rounding' of the binary form also includes slightly modified and transposed versions of bars 6–7 (in bars 31–32) and bars 10–12 (in bars 36–38). Notice that, after the tonal turbulence of the middle section, these last ten bars never leave the tonic key and contain only one chromatic note.

Melody

As in most baroque movements Bach's melodic line seems to grow and develop organically with no contrasting themes. Just as the shape of a sapling largely determines the shape of the mature tree, so melodic ideas heard in the first few bars of the sarabande seem to determine the contours of the rest of the melody. This is because Bach consistently manipulates a few melodic fragments (motifs) and characteristic rhythms throughout the dance. Let's trace the evolution of the very first motif, the descending slide heard on the first beat of the first bar (motif *x* in the example, *right*).

What two changes are made to *x* when Bach reuses this motif at the start of bar 5? How does bar 6 relate to bar 5? What new change is made to the motif on the first beat of bar 7?

All of these variants move by step, but, provided the rhythm remains unchanged, it is possible to change the pitches of a motif (e.g. to fit different chords) without altering its relationship to a version heard earlier. If you compare our motif *x* in the *last* beat of bar 7 with the version in the first beat of bar 5 you will see that Bach has maintained the same rhythm but augmented the interval between the last two notes from a descending 2nd to a descending 6th. Pitch changes become more radical at the start of bars 9 and 10, but the connection with *x* in bar 5 is still clear.

We have discussed all but one of the appearances of motif *x* in the first part of the sarabande. Find and describe the missing one.

One way in which baroque composers 'grew' their melodies was to repeat an established motif in a **sequence**. In bar 17 Bach inverts the variant of motif *x* heard at the start of bar 7 then repeats it in a rising sequence. See if you can find another such sequence in the second part of the sarabande.

Understanding chromatic colour

Accidentals can signify modulation, as we saw in the section on harmony and tonality, but sometimes they just add chromatic colour. For example, we noted earlier that the C♮ in bar 2 is part of chord VII of G major which resolves to a chord of G in bar 3. But this is not a modulation – the C♮ is cancelled by the C♯ in bar 3 and so the music continues in the key of D major. The C♮ is purely chromatic colour.

The type of chord heard on the last beat of bar 6 is known as a **secondary dominant** – it is the dominant of one of the *chords* in the current key, but it doesn't generate a modulation because it is not a cadence chord – it merely adds chromatic colour.

Similar chromaticism occurs on the last beat of bar 6, where every note of V^7 in E major is sounded. But when this chord resolves to E-major on the first beat of the next bar Bach immediately cancels the effect of the D♯ with D♮ in the bass, turning the chord into E^7, the dominant 7th of A major, thus introducing the second main key of the movement.

Two other types of chromaticism occur in the sarabande. The first is a note borrowed from the tonic minor (F♮ in bar 12) for decorative effect. The other is a chromatic chord known as the 'Neapolitan 6th' (the notes A, C and F♮ in E minor) which occurs on the third quaver of bar 23 to add to the expressiveness of the melody at this point.

Ornamentation

The melodic lines of baroque slow movements for harpsichord tend to be highly ornamented, partly because of the instrument's limited ability to sustain long notes. Ornaments in baroque music may be indicated by symbols or written out in full. In this sarabande (as in many of his other works) Bach preferred to write out most of the ornamentation. This is true of motif *x*, which in England was an ornament known as a slide; the French (who had a variety of symbols for it) called it a *coulé sur une tierce* (a slur over a third).

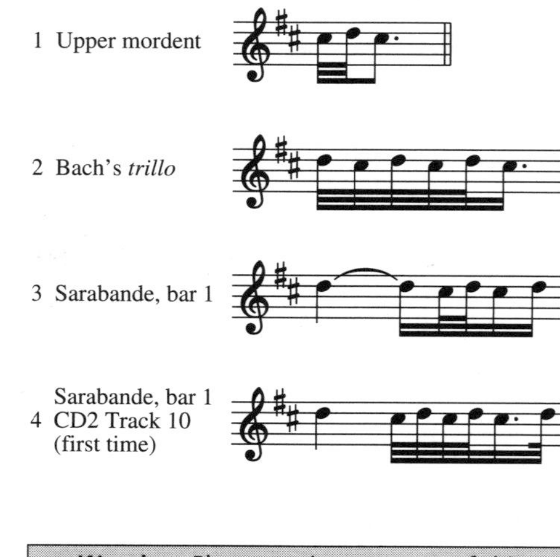

The only symbol for an ornament Bach uses in this movement is a wiggly line (bars 1, 13 and 29). Most people call this an upper mordent, often played as shown on stave 1 *left*, but Bach called it a *trillo* and wrote out an example of it for one of his sons in the manner shown on stave 2. You will see that it begins on the beat with the upper note and that it is extended into a sort of trill. However, the precise interpretation of this symbol depends upon its context and the good taste of the performer. For instance, if the sign appears above a note that is slurred to the previous note (as it is in bar 1) a common interpretation in a piece in moderate tempo and in French style (like this sarabande) could be that shown on stave 3. In fact, because of his very slow tempo, András Schiff on CD2 chooses to interpret the *trillo* in the manner shown on stave 4, and in the repeat he turns the ornament into an extended trill.

Listen to the same ornament in bars 13 and 29. Is Schiff consistent in his interpretation of this ornament?

We know from books printed in the 18th century that it was usual for baroque performers to add extra ornamentation, according to the known and understood conventions of the time, especially when a section was repeated. Listen to the repeats on CD2, paying particular attention to Schiff's added ornaments. The first of these is an ascending slide inserted between the sixth and seventh semiquavers of bar 3, which mirrors Bach's descending slide in bar 1. There are many more of them for you to identify, and they are all in keeping with the French style of Bach's sarabande.

J. S. Bach's second son, C. P. E. Bach, wrote about ornamentation in his *Essay on the proper method of playing keyboard instruments* (published 1753): 'It is not likely that anybody could question the necessity of ornaments. They are found everywhere in music, and are not only useful, but indispensable. They connect the notes; they give them life. They emphasise them ... when there are few or no signs, the piece must be ornamented according to its proper style.'

Texture

On paper the texture looks thin – it is mainly in **two parts** with the melodic interest in the right hand and a supportive bass in the left hand. In addition, Bach highlights important structural moments (the starts and ends of the two main sections plus the return of the first section at bar 29) with some short-lived inner parts.

However, when heard it sounds much richer than it appears. This is because the melody is **harmonically charged**. At its simplest this means that Bach outlines chords in triadic melodic lines such as that in bar 9, where a triad of A major emerges from the figuration (with passing notes between C♯ and A). We can tell that this is chord I of A major because Bach outlines V^7 in this key in the melody of the previous bar and because the leading note (G♯) appears as a lower auxiliary three times in bar 9. Can you work out which chord in A major is outlined by the melody in bar 10?

Private study

?

1. What are the characteristics of a baroque sarabande in terms of tempo, metre, rhythm and form?
2. Read the margin note on page 49 of this book, and then explain why the structure of Bach's sarabande is rounded binary form rather than ternary form.
3. On CD2 the sarabande is played on the piano. On what instrument might it have been played in Bach's day?
4. Which of the three ties in bars 23–24 indicates the use of a suspension?
5. (i) How are the first three right-hand notes in bar 32 related to the opening of the sarabande?

   (ii) In the same bar, describe how the music in both hands of beat 1 is treated in beats 2 and 3.

   (iii) Describe the harmonic function of the G♯ in bar 32.

Debussy, Sarabande from *Pour le piano*

Special Focus Work 2 for 2008 and 2009

NAM 24 (page 260) CD2 Track 16
Zoltán Kocsis (piano)

Before starting on this section you should work through (or revise) the information about the context and structure of this music given on pages 74–75 of the AS Guide. Make sure that you understand all of the terminology used on those pages.

Rhythm and metre

As you would expect the sarabande is in triple time, and Debussy ensures that it will be performed slowly and with elegant solemnity by his performance direction above the first bar. He emphasises the second beat accent so characteristic of many baroque sarabandes by stopping the flow of the music on a minim in 13 of the 72 bars (2, 4, 8 etc.). In the first 18 bars these have the effect of dividing the music into two-bar and four-bar phrases starting at bars 1, 3, 5, 9, 11, 15 and 17 (bars 9–10 are divided from the following four-bar phrase by a change of register).

A subtler rhythm – also characteristic of the baroque sarabande – can be heard in bars 50, 52 and 53 where a dotted crotchet on the second beat hardly interrupts the rhythmic flow (compare the marks of articulation here with those in the first eight bars). The same effect occurs in bars 56, 57, 60 and 61, where the change of chord on the third beat results in the dotted crotchet becoming a crotchet tied to a quaver. Notice that Debussy makes his intentions clear by tenuto marks. These horizontal dashes indicate a degree of separation and a slight emphasis on the second beat.

Yet more subtle are the instances where the second beat is singled out for special attention solely by tenuto marks. This is most noticeable in bar 21, but there are many less obvious examples. Tenuto marks also occur in bars 67–68, but here they emphasise a **hemiola** rhythm – again characteristic of the baroque sarabande – in which three two-beat notes cut across the $\frac{3}{4}$ metre, giving the impression that the music has temporarily moved into $\frac{3}{2}$ time (an effect supported by the phrasing of the bass part).

Despite these references to the rhythms of the baroque sarabande, there are many instances of **cross phrasing** where the melody and harmony, as well as the phrase marks, run against the triple-time pulse. The most obvious example occurs in bars 38–41, where repeated groups of quavers cross the bar lines, briefly obscuring the basic metre of this stylised dance.

Melody and harmony

The aeolian mode transposed to C♯:

Despite the key signature of C♯ minor the melody in the first section (bars 1–22) is entirely in the **aeolian mode** transposed to C♯, shown *left*. Notice the lack of B♯ (the leading note of C♯ minor). However, Debussy keeps us waiting until bar 22 for a cadence on the final ('tonic') of the mode.

The harmony in the first eight bars is equally modal, with cadences on a minor triad on the fifth degree (G♯) in bars 2 and 4, and a major triad on the seventh degree (B) in bar 8. But the streams of gentle discords in bars 1 and 3 draw a misty veil over the modality. Debussy is using both concords and discords as **non-functional** sound events.

The one-bar melodic fragment in bars 9–10 is accompanied by root position triads containing a false relation effect (A♮/A♯) typical of much 16th and early 17th-century music. But when this melodic fragment is repeated at a lower pitch in bars 11–12, it is accompanied by **parallel 7th chords**, characteristic of impressionist music, that have no tonal function. They blur the modality of the melody all the more effectively because they are based on six of the seven pitches of a **whole-tone scale** (D–E–F♯–G♯ in bars 11–12 and A♯ in bar 13).

The central section (bars 23–41) begins with **quartal harmony** (chords consisting of superimposed 4ths). Then, initially as a result of the sequence in bars 25–28, **chromaticism** invades both melody and harmony.

When the original melody returns in bar 42 it is re-harmonised with unrelated and chromatic root-position chords, but the second phrase (bars 46–49) returns to the chaste modal harmonies that characterised the first eight bars. The mock-medieval **parallel 5ths** in the bass of bars 50–53 cover all but one of the modal pitches, but the dissonances formed with the chromatic chords above them help generate the climax of the whole piece – the D♯-major chord in bar 55. This is the only truly tonal moment in the whole piece: with the ***ff*** chord in the next bar it forms a perfect cadence in G♯ minor, the dominant of the home key (or mode) of C♯ minor. But when V of G♯ minor returns in the cadence at bar 59 it fails to resolve, simply slumping on to a chord of C♯ minor at the start of bar 60.

In the last six bars, 4th-based chords ascend above a bass that traces the most important notes of the mode (C♯–E–G♯–B–C♯) and the whole piece finishes with a modal cadence (B rising to C♯ in the melody). The sarabande ends on a chord of C♯ minor, but without any sense of a perfect cadence in that key.

Structure

The form of the sarabande is almost as elusive as its tonality. The double bar line between bars 22 and 23, the clear cadence on the final of the mode before it, and the new melody and harmony after it invite us to regard it as an example of the sort of binary form that was so common in the baroque dances. But the first section is in ternary form:

A (bars 1–8) **B** (bars 9–14) **A¹** (bars 15–22)

in which the central chromatic section is flanked by entirely modal sections with common thematic material. This, of course, is unheard of in baroque binary structures. There are other quotations from the first section that could be regarded as 'roundings' of binary form (like those in *NAM 21*). But they are too substantial, too much altered and in the wrong place – the first quotation comes as early as bar 42, not much more than half way through the whole piece, whereas Bach's comes just 10 bars from the end.

Some have suggested that the whole piece could be regarded as ternary form, with a modified repeat of the first section starting in bar 42. But this 'repeat' starts in the wrong 'key' and there is as much new as there is repeated music. What emerges from Debussy's deliberately elusive structure when it is heard is a rondo-like patchwork of repeated sections (all of them significantly varied) that can be represented like this:

Bars 1–8	*9–14*	*15–22*	*23–41*	*42–49*	*50–55*	*56–62*	*63–72*
A	**B**	**A¹**	**C**	**A²**	**D**	**B¹**	**coda**

The first four bars of the coda are centred round the 'dominant' of the mode, the rest leads up to the final modal cadence. What holds this patchwork together is not so much the varied repetitions of sections A and B, but the sarabande rhythm and repetitions of the little figure of two semiquavers and a quaver first heard in bar 9.

Private study

1. What term describes the harmony in bars 67–70 of *NAM 24*?
2. Define the terms hemiola and cross-phrasing, and give an example of each from Debussy's sarabande.
3. Explain what is meant by parallel chords and give an example of their use in this sarabande.
4. What is unusual about the final cadence of *NAM 24*?
5. What are the similarities between the two sarabandes you have studied?

Sample questions

In the exam there will be three questions on the special focus works, from which you must answer **two**.

(a) Show how Bach used the melodic motif from bar 1 of *NAM 21* in the rest of the movement.

(b) Comment on the differences in harmonic style between Bach and Debussy, as revealed in their respective sarabandes.

(c) Explain the structure of Debussy's sarabande.

Continuity and change in structure and tonality

For examination in summer 2008 and 2009

You do not need to study this topic unless *Keyboard music* is the Area of Study that you undertook for AS Music and which you are now extending for A2.

Before starting work on this topic you need a thorough understanding of the material on *Keyboard music* in the AS Guide (pages 67–77). Remember that for A2 the topic draws on works from across the **entire** Area of Study, not just those in one of the two lists, A or B.

Tonality refers to the use of (and the relationship between) major and minor keys in music – it is nothing to do with the tone colour of musical sounds. In tonal music, keys are established by cadences, particularly perfect cadence patterns such as V^7–I.

Sweelinck

NAM 20 (page 245) CD2 Track 9
Peter Seymour (harpsichord)

Bars		
1–16	A	Dowland bars 1–8
17–32	A^1	Variation on A
33–48	B	Dowland bars 9–16
49–64	B^1	Variation on B
65–81	C	Dowland bars 17–24
82–98	C^1	Variation on C

This set of variations on Dowland's ayre (*NAM 33*) can be represented as AA^1 BB^1 CC^1, in which A, B and C are free transcriptions of the three strains of the song, each followed by a variation (A^1, B^1 and C^1) – see *below left*. Almost every note of Dowland's three strains are retained in the variations, often buried in elaborate figuration. The use of this technique is the reason why works such as this are sometimes described as **figural variations**.

NAM 20 was written at a time when renaissance **modality** was giving way to the **tonal system** of major and minor keys. Look at bars 1–16. There are cadences at the end of each four-bar phrase, all in the key of A minor, and every chord derives from the harmonic or melodic minor scales of this key. Chords I, IVb and V dominate the harmony. These primary triads (plus chords II and VI) are said to be functional because they define the tonality. Yet despite this **functional harmony** and clear **tonal cadences** the music still has a decidedly modal feel. Why? There are several answers:

- The first three phrases each end with a **phrygian cadence** (a type of minor-key imperfect cadence that uses the progression IVb–I) which gives a somewhat archaic, modal tinge.
- In bar 6 the leading note (G♯) is replaced with G♮ (from the descending melodic minor scale but also from the aeolian mode).
- The only sort of modulation is a brief visit to G major in bars 9–10. This again sounds much more like a modal relationship than the modulations to the dominant or relative major that are common in later tonal styles.
- In the G-major chord at the start of bar 10, the G♮s in the bass and alto parts are immediately contradicted in the second half of the bar by the G♯s in the melody – such **false relations** are one of the most characteristic sounds of modal polyphony.

The most pungent example of this device is the **simultaneous false relation** in bar 96 where the treble G♮ (the highest note in the pavan) sounds against the sustained G♯ on the bass stave.

Even when Sweelinck uses a device particularly associated with tonality – the four bars of **dominant pedal** starting in bar 65 – it underpins another false relation in which G♮ (bar 67) undermines the expected G♯ of tonal harmony. And this pedal cadences to a version of chord I in bar 69 which is neither major nor minor – its **bare 5th** harks back to earlier times. Elsewhere, most noticeably at the end, perfect cadences end with a tonic major chord (A major).

A major 3rd in the final tonic chord of a passage in a minor key is known as a **tierce de Picardie**. It is another throwback to renaissance modality, although very common at the time. It was not until the 18th century that most composers felt that a minor tonic chord could produce a satisfactory ending for a work in a minor key.

So, while we can see glimmerings of tonality in this work, the influence of modal harmony remained strong in 1615.

Bach

NAM 21 (page 249) CD2 Tracks 10–11
András Schiff (piano)

The clear tonal scheme of Bach's sarabande in **rounded binary form** was discussed earlier in this chapter and is summarised in the diagram on page 72.

The gigue is in **simple binary form** (‖: A :‖: B :‖) and has a **fugal** texture. The fugal subject in bars 1–6 is in D major (the C♮ in bar 2 unifies the gigue with the previous movement, but is purely chromatic, as it was in the sarabande). This subject is answered by the left hand in bar 7, where the transposition to the dominant emphasises that there is a hierarchy of keys in tonal harmony, with the tonic (D major) at its head. Although the A section briefly refers to other related keys, it ends with a decisive cadence in the dominant.

A new fugal subject is stated in the left hand at the beginning of section B. When this is answered in the right hand it is combined with the original subject in the left (bars 55–60). This is the start of a short **double fugue**. See how many more entries of the two subjects you can find. All of this is achieved as the B section passes through related keys before ending unequivocally in the tonic.

This assured handling of tonality, in which related keys not only help structure the movement but also serve to underline the pre-eminence of the tonic, distinguishes Bach's dance from Sweelinck's variations, written more than a century earlier and which remain in a modal A minor almost throughout.

Mozart

NAM 22 (page 253) CD2 Track 12
Alfred Brendel (piano)

Bars	
1–63	An **exposition** of the main themes, grouped into two contrasting tonal centres (tonic and dominant: B♭ and F)
63–93	A **development** of these themes passing through several keys (notably F minor, C minor and G minor in bars 63–86)
93–165	A **recapitulation** of the principal themes in the tonic

There is a direct connection between the rounded binary form of Bach's sarabande and Mozart's **sonata form**. Both start with a section that modulates to the dominant, and both return to the tonic by way of a tonal journey through several related keys. Both also include restatements of some (Bach) or all (Mozart) of the first section with modifications and transpositions to ensure that the recapitulation remains in the tonic key. But there are two obvious differences. Firstly, Mozart's sonata movement is much longer than either of Bach's dances. Secondly Bach's **monothematic** elaboration of a few pervasive motifs is replaced by a number of clearly differentiated and self-contained themes in Mozart's sonata.

Movements in sonata form have three main sections (shown *left*), yet a comparison of Bach's sarabande with Mozart's sonata movement reveals the historical truth that sonata form developed from baroque rounded binary form.

Kinderscenen

NAM 23 (page 258) CD2 Tracks 13–15
Alfred Brendel (piano)

'Von fremden Ländern und Menschen' is a miniature example of **rounded binary form** – ‖:A:‖:BA:‖ – and is thus related to Bach's sarabande in terms of structure, but there are significant differences:

- The periodic phrasing (2+2+4 in the first section) is typical not only of classical music (such as *NAM 22*), but also of Schumann's early romantic style
- Unlike Bach's sarabande, the first section ends in the tonic and there is no modulation (only a chromatic chord) in the B section
- Schumann's final section (bars 15–22) is an exact repeat of the whole of his first A section, whereas Bach repeats only some of his opening material, modifying it to end in the tonic key.

Because bars 1–8 form a self-contained section that begins and ends in the tonic, and because this music is then repeated exactly in bars 15–22, you could describe 'Von fremden Ländern und Menschen' as **ternary form**. However, the division into two repeated sections is a characteristic of binary rather than ternary form.

'Hasche-Mann' is another **rounded binary form** movement, but it contains tell-tale signs of romanticism, such as the sudden intrusion of an unrelated key (C major in bars 13–15) and the abrupt shift (there is no modulation) from this C major chord to the dominant 7th chord of the home key (B minor) in bar 15.

'Fürchtenmachen' is in **symmetrical rondo form** (ABACABA). The periodic phrasing is also similar to many classical phrase structures and, as we have already seen, it is also a characteristic feature of Schumann's style. But the rondo theme is less integrated with the episodes (B in bars 9–12, repeated in bars 37–40, and C in bars 21–28) than the much longer and more complex sonata-rondo structures of classical music.

These cadences consist of chord I on the first beat of the bar and chord V on the second. This 'strong-weak' pattern (rather than the more usual 'weak-strong' rhythm) is known as a **feminine cadence**.

Although the rondo begins in a clearly romantic style with both melodic and harmonic **chromaticism**, the key of G major is firmly established in the imperfect cadences of bars 4 and 8. The first episode consists of two bars in E minor, repeated sequentially in C major (such 3rd-related keys being more a feature of the romantic style than the classical). The start of the central C episode contrasts with all the other sections through the use of a new rhythm pattern, a loud dynamic and off-beat accents. Despite the chromatic chords, bars 21–24 are in G major. Bars 25–28 then restore the tranquil mood with a two-bar melodic (but not harmonic) sequence that leads back to the rondo refrain.

Debussy

NAM 24 (page 260) CD2 Track 16
Zoltán Kocsis (piano)

The structure and tonality of this work were discussed on pages 75–77, which you should revise now. The structure doesn't adopt a conventional plan, although it contains elements of both ternary and rondo form. Most importantly, its modal melodies and ambiguous harmonies do not permit clear-cut cadences in well-defined keys to define its sections. So, although the music pays homage to baroque music, the clear tonal structures of that period are blurred by modal and chromatic harmonies, and by themes and modes that lack the presence of a key-defining leading note.

Shostakovich

NAM 25 (page 262) CD2 Track 17
Tatiana Nikolayeva (piano)

Although larded with discords and modulations to unrelated keys the tonal structures of these **neoclassical** pieces are much less ambiguous than Debussy's sarabande. The prelude is an improvisatory movement based, like Bach's dances, on a limited number of motifs that are heard in a variety of guises throughout most of the piece. In this case there are just two, and both are heard in the first bar (the semiquaver figure and a three-note leaping quaver figure).

The **ternary form** of the prelude is determined by its key scheme. In the first section A major is firmly established by pedals that form the simple progression I (bars 1–3), VI (bars 4–5) and V (bars 8–9). The central section is based on a series of unrelated chords – for example, C major in bar 10, C♯ major in bar 13, A♭ major in bar 19 and D♭ major in bars 21–22. D♭ is the same pitch as C♯, which is the third of chord I in the home key of A major. It is through this common note that Shostakovich banishes tonal uncertainty with a short closing section (bars 23–28) that remains in A major to the end of the prelude.

Bach's sarabande is followed by a gigue in fugal style (it uses *some* elements of fugue) but Shostakovich followed his prelude with a complete three-voice fugue. The three important elements are:

- A fugal exposition in the tonic key of A major (bars 1–14). It starts with a subject (bars 1–4) which is answered a 4th lower in the left-hand part of bars 5–8. As the left hand plays the answer a regular countersubject is heard in the right hand. Bars 9–10 form a codetta, and finally the subject is combined with regular and new countersubjects (bars 11–14, bass, middle and upper parts respectively).
- A set of episodes in which motifs from the exposition are manipulated in a variety of keys, such as A major in bars 15–20, and D and F major in bars 41–46. These alternate with middle entries of the fugue subject in a variety of keys, such as F♯ minor in bars 21–24 (middle part) and B♭ major in bars 51–54 (bass)
- A closing section (bars 70–99) which, despite some colourful chromatic triads, remains throughout in the tonic key of A major and includes stretto entries (bars 70–75) and a return of the pedals that dominated the prelude.

The most important aspect of Shostakovich's approach to tonality is his **non-functional** use of harmony. Both movements begin and end in A major but keys are suggested by chords and pedal points rather than being confirmed by conventional cadences.

Private study

1. (a) What determines the structure of *NAM 20*?

   (b) Explain what is meant by a phrygian cadence and identify an example of one on page 247 of the *New Anthology*.

   (c) *NAM 20* ends with a tierce de Picardie. What is this?

2. Why can Bach's sarabande be described as monothematic?
3. Why is sonata form described as a development of rounded binary form rather than an extension of ternary form?
4. If a rondo form can be described as ABACA, what name is given to (i) the recurring A sections and (ii) the intervening sections?
5. What is a feminine cadence?
6. How does Debussy's use of modality and quartal harmony weaken the sense of tonality in his sarabande?
7. Explain the difference between functional and non-functional harmony. Which is better at creating a sense of tonality in music and why?

Sample questions

In the exam there will be two questions on this topic, from which you must answer **one**.

(a) What are the similarities and differences in both structure **and** tonality between bars 1–19 of Bach's gigue and bars 1–14 of Shostakovich's fugue?

(b) Contrast Sweelinck's approach to tonality in *NAM 20* with Schumann's approach to tonality in *NAM 23*.

(c) Show the relationship of sonata form to rounded binary form by comparing the structure of *NAM 22* with the structure of Bach's sarabande in *NAM 21*.

Sacred vocal music

There are three Special Focus works – John Taverner's *O Wilhelme, pastor bone* (*NAM 26*), Bruckner's *Locus iste* (*NAM 30*) and John Tavener's 'The Lamb' (*NAM 32*) – all of which must be studied if you are taking the exam in 2008 or 2009.

Genesis

All three special focus works were written to be sung **a cappella** (that is, unaccompanied) by small choirs. *O Wilheme* and *Locus iste* have texts in Latin because that was the language used for Roman Catholic services at the time they were composed. They were also both written for all-male choirs, in which boys sang the top part(s) and men sang the lower ones.

Although the words of *The Lamb* focus on the image of Christ as the Lamb of God, the text is not taken from any Christian liturgy. However, the work is suitable for use as an anthem or motet in church, and is sometimes sung in Christmas carol services.

Taverner, *O Wilhelme, pastor bone*

Special Focus Work 1 for 2008 and 2009
NAM 26 (page 266) CD3 Track 1 Christ Church Cathedral Choir Oxford Conducted by Stephen Darlington

Before starting on this section you should work through (or revise) the information about the context and structure of this music given on pages 78–79 of the AS Guide. Make sure that you understand all of the terminology used on those pages.

Introduction

When Cardinal Thomas Wolsey founded Cardinal College (now called Christ Church College) at the University of Oxford in 1526, he decreed that after the last service of the day, one of the pieces of music to be sung should honour the memory of the 12th-century Saint William, one of his predecessors as Archbishop of York, and he also expressed the hope of prayers for his own salvation. Both of these requests are met by *NAM 26*, with its opening plea to William of York ('*O Wilheme*') and its reference to Cardinal Thomas in the second stanza ('*Thomam Cardinalem*' in bars 36–37).

However, like many pieces from long ago, the original setting has been lost and *NAM 26* has been reconstructed from a later version of the work, made after Wolsey's fall from power, which has totally different words that make no mention of the Cardinal or Saint William.

A further complication results from the fact that vocal music in the 16th century was not normally written as a full score, like that seen in *NAM 26*. Instead, pieces would normally be collected into a series of part books – one volume with all the treble parts for various works, another with all the alto parts, and so on. Unfortunately no tenor part has survived for even the later adaptation of this work, and so the one printed in the *New Anthology* has been reconstructed by a modern musicologist, based on a knowledge of the style and the clues provided by the other parts. As explained on page 266 of the *New Anthology*, it is possible to reconstruct the missing tenor part in other ways, one of which can be heard on the anthology recording. Remember, though, that it is the printed version of *NAM 26* that you are required to study.

The recording on the anthology CD is by the choir of Christ Church Oxford (now a cathedral as well as a college chapel). They are the successors of the choir for whom Taverner wrote this work nearly five centuries ago. In their performance on CD3 only the treble part is sung by boys – the part for means is sung by adult male altos.

Melody The mean has a compass of an 11th, the bass a 10th and the other three parts encompass only a 9th. Phrase lengths are determined by the text and are not governed by a preference for two, four and eight bar units found in later styles of music – for example, bars 33–47 contain three clearly separated five-bar phrases.

Taverner combines **conjunct** movement with generally **small leaps** to create phrases that often have an elegant arch shape, as in the opening treble melody. If the leap is wider than a 3rd, Taverner usually prefers to return to a note within the leap, as in bar 2 of the opening treble melody. However, there are some notable exceptions to this in the mean part of bar 22 and 31, where the angular line is rare in 16th-century polyphony. Also, it is important to note that leaps are of necessity more frequent (and less strictly treated) in the bass part, because it sometimes consists of roots of chords that are a 5th apart (as in bars 23^4–27).

Totally stepwise movement is infrequent, but when it does occur it is particularly expressive. In the treble part of bars 13–16, for instance, the conjunct ascent and descent throws the modal flat 7th (E♭) into relief, vividly expressing the word *agone* (strife). Whenever this note occurs it draws attention to the text since the melodic lines basically conform to F major at the beginning and end of the work, and G minor from the last beat of bar 22 to bar 52. Thus, in the treble part of bars 33–37 an almost complete ascending scale and a conjunct descent (both with E♮) is followed by an E♭ on the first syllable of *Thomam Cardinalem*.

The setting is largely **syllabic** (one note per syllable) with longer notes for stressed syllables. Short **melismas** occur in the mean and countertenor to illustrate the word *gloriam* (glory) in bars 31–32 as well as in the mean part at bars 51–52 and bar 55. But the main section of melismatic writing occurs in all parts (except bass) during the closing bars where the text refers to 'the life eternal'.

Harmony One of the most remarkable features of *NAM 26* is the total lack of on-beat discords (ties across barlines might look like suspensions, but none of the tied notes is dissonant). In fact the only chords used are major and minor triads in either root position or first inversion (plus an occasional bare 5th, octave and unison).

Instead, Taverner makes use of a particularly English device – a 6th resolving to a 5th above a static bass. An expressive example occurs in conjunction with the modal flat 7th discussed earlier. In bars 15–16 the treble E♭ (a 6th above the bass G) falls a semitone to complete a G-minor triad then, in the next bar, this pitch is tied over to form a 6th resolving a tone to complete an F-major chord in root position.

A **tierce de Picardie** is a major 3rd in the final tonic chord of a passage in a minor key. Here, the prevailing key is G minor, but the tierce de Picardie (B♮) results in a chord of G major in bar 32.

The most startling example occurs in bar 32 where the 6th-5th melodic line (E–D in the mean) is combined with a **tierce de Picardie** (B♮ in the treble) to form a totally unexpected chord of E minor in first inversion resolving to a triad of G major in root position.

The **false relation** is a more familiar effect. Since it is formed between the outer parts it is particularly obvious in bars 40–41 where the countertenor's E♮ at the end of bar 40 is immediately followed by an E♭ in the bass at the start of bar 41. The same notes are implicated in the less obvious false relation between treble and countertenor parts in bars 50–51. See if you can spot other false relations in bars 28–29 and bar 53.

Tonality

To our ears the music sounds like a fusion of tonal and modal harmony. Looking at the bass part in bars 10–13, for instance, we might be forgiven for thinking that it traces a progression in F major. But notice that the treble E in bar 11 does not not rise to F, as a well-behaved leading note would. And at the end of the phrase the chord of B♭ major (bar 12^4) is not followed by a chord of F major to form a plagal cadence, but by a chord of A minor (decorated with the 6th-5th formula in the treble part). Similarly the phrases that end in bars 15–16 and 19–20 are harmonised with by the progression Gm–F, producing a very modal-sounding cadence.

The reason is simple. This music pre-dates the tonal system, and is essentially modal, even though its first section sounds similar to F major, because six of the seven cadences in the first 22 bars end on a chord of F. This key is so strongly entrenched that the E♭ in bar 15 sounds like a modal intruder.

With the introduction of F♯s and more E♭s, the music gives the impression of shifting to G minor in the central section (bars 22^4–52). This is apparent in the first phrase (bars 22^4–27) which begins with chords that we (but not a 16th-century musician) might regard as alternating tonic and dominant chords of G minor, and ends with the first 'perfect cadence' of the motet (bars 26–27) and the first 'imperfect cadence' (bar 28). However, Taverner did not think in those terms, as is apparent in the modal F♮s and E♮s that precede those cadences as well as in the decidedly modal cadence of bars 31–32 and bar 52, where there is no F♯ before the chord of G.

A decisive return to F major is marked by the perfect cadence in bars 55–56 where the mean's E rises to F in the manner of a leading note rising to the tonic. The work ends with another perfect cadence with rising E–F (treble, bar 65) followed by a plagal cadence (bars 66–67) in what may now be regarded as the tonic key of F major.

Texture

Until the final section, most of the motet is **homophonic**. So, although it begins with **two-part counterpoint** for upper voices, this is answered by **three-part homophony** for lower voices – the first of many examples of **antiphony** in *NAM 26*. Taverner then proceeds to a full **five-part** texture in bar 10. This establishes a pattern that is only slightly varied during the next few sections. At bar 16^3 the lower voices start first and the upper pair answer, but the original order is restored at bar 33. In bars 43–48 Taverner answers the three-part lower voices of the previous phrase with three-part upper voices, achieved by dividing the trebles into two parts (a device known as **gymel** – early English for 'twin').

Because many of these passages begin with parts that are out of step with each other (treble in bar 1, bass in bar 4, and so on) Taverner gives an *impression* of contra-puntal activity, but there is noactual imitative counterpoint until much later in the work.

Bars 36–49 are almost entirely **homorhythmic** (or 'chordal') – i.e. except for two bars, all parts have the same rhythm. But finally Taverner introduces **imitative counterpoint** for the last line of the text, starting with the setting of *Aeternae* in bar 56.

Structure

Structure is largely governed by the text – one musical phrase to each line of the rhyming verse. The effect is emphasised by melodic repetition. Thus the treble phrase of bars 1–4 is repeated in the countertenor part (with newly-composed lower parts), and the mean part of bars 7–10 is repeated as a bass part in the next phrase (with newly-composed upper parts). The beginning and end of the countertenor and bass parts in bars 16–20 are repeated by the upper parts in bars 20–24, and these repetitions throw into relief the change of tonality/modality (a cadence on F in bar 20 contrasting with a cadence on V of G minor in bar 24). Most of the phrases in bars 1–32 are overlapped, but at bar 32 the 6th-5th formula extends the cadence and creates a sense of repose at the point where the first stanza ends.

Taverner marks out the start of the second section (bar 33) with the sort of melodic repetition presented in antiphonal exchanges with which the first section began – although key, melody and texture are all different. From *Et utrisque concedatur* this technique gives way to imitation which, as mentioned earlier, becomes pervasive in the setting of the last line of text (*Aeterna vitae praemium*).

Private study

1. Explain the meaning of *a cappella* singing.
2. What type of voice is meant by a 'mean'?
3. Explain what is meant by the following statement:
   Bars 1–10 of *NAM 26* consist of antiphonal exchanges.
4. What is the difference between syllabic and melismatic word setting?
5. Why could the treble melody in bars 43–47 be described as 'arch shaped'?
6. Explain the terms 'tierce de Picardie' and 'false relation'.
7. What is remarkable about the harmony of *NAM 26*?

Bruckner, *Locus iste*

Special Focus Work 2 for 2008 and 2009

NAM 30 (page 305) CD3 Track 8
Christ Church Cathedral Choir Oxford
Conducted by Stephen Darlington

Before starting on this section you should work through (or revise) the information about the context and structure of this music given on pages 85–86 of the AS Guide. Make sure that you understand all of the terminology used on those pages.

Context, word setting and texture

Locus iste is a text originally sung to plainsong between biblical readings in a Mass to celebrate the dedication of a church. Like *O Wilhelme*, this setting was originally composed for a particular church – the Cathedral of Linz in Austria, where Bruckner served as organist from 1856 to 1870. Begun in 1855 (and not finished until 1924) it is thought that *Locus iste* was first sung at the opening of one of the chapels in the gigantic new cathedral.

Bruckner ensures that the words can be heard clearly, even in the echoing vaults of a large cathedral, by using a mainly **homophonic** texture in which each phrase of the text is repeated. For the same reason, the word-setting is **syllabic**, apart from bars 40–42 where a **melisma** in all parts highlights the word God (*Deo*).

Bruckner also takes account of the effect of reverberant acoustics by the judicious use of silence – short at the end of bars 4 and 33, longer at the end of bars 20 and 29, and extended to a full five beats after the reference to God in bar 40.

Variety comes from contrasting the **four-part** texture of most of the setting with the **three-part** texture of bars 21–29, where the basses get a well-earned rest after starting four phrases before the rest of the choir enters. The last two of these are imitated (rather freely) by the sopranos and Bruckner also includes **imitation by inversion** between the tenors and sopranos in bars 21–26.

Melody

Many of Bruckner's melodic ideas stem from the descending scalic melody in the soprano part of bars 1–2, and are dominated by **sequential repetition**. The inexact sequence of the first four bars in bars 5–8 allows the sopranos to soar to their highest note while the return to a descending scale pattern in bars 10–12 carries them to their lowest note. Up to this point the melody is entirely diatonic, but the next phrase (bars 12–20) starts with a *rising* scale pattern in D minor, repeated in sequence a tone higher in E minor.

Compared with these soaring melodies the **chromatic** link back to the tonic key (bars 21–29) is almost static, the tenor's semitonal descent being imitated by the soprano's semitonal ascent in yet another sequence (six bars long in the tenor part, four in the soprano part). With the exception of the few short imitative passages, the melody is in the soprano throughout.

Harmony, tonality and structure

It is likely that the very first time you heard this motet, you were struck by the fact that Bruckner's style is much more emotionally charged than the austere, devotional music of Taverner. This is a by-product of the romantic age in which Bruckner lived, but it is important to understand why *Locus iste* has such an effect.

Some obvious reasons are the wide-ranging melodies, concentrated in the soprano and bass parts, the vivid dynamic contrasts and the exciting chromatic harmonies. But the motet has links with the past, and not just in its use of an *a cappella* choir. Its subtle appeal also depends on a fusion of modal, diatonic and chromatic harmony.

The work opens with three bars of tonic chord in C major, leading to chord II in bar 4 – such a progression would sound modal were it not for the romanticly sighing **appoggiatura** on G in the soprano part above the D-minor harmony of bar 4. In fact, the soprano's A–G above the bass C in bar 2 might remind you of the 6th-5th formula we saw in *O Wilheme*.

In bar 5 the second phrase starts as a sequence of the first, a tone higher. However, although it uses the same rhythm, both harmony and melody are varied after the first few notes. It begins with a bright **secondary dominant** chord (D major, which is V of V in the key of C major) that leads to V itself in bar 6 (the soprano and alto forming a double suspension over the bass G at the start of bar 6). This formula is then repeated in varied form in bar 8 (G^7 over C in the bass, resolving to chord I on beat 3) – here the soprano's F is an accented passing note rather than a suspension. All of these melodic dissonances are typical of earlier church music from the classical period, such as Mozart's motet *Ave Verum Corpus* that Bruckner knew and loved.

A third four-bar phrase starts in bar 9 with a rhythmic variant of bar 8 (*a Deo*). This is varied again in bar 10, now an octave lower in the sopranos – but this time they project the F–E pattern down the scale to a low B (*Deo factus est*). The melody of bars 10–12 is a rhythmically varied transposition of bars 1–2, extended to end on chord V in bar 12, thus neatly rounding off the first section of this **ternary form** motet with an **imperfect cadence**.

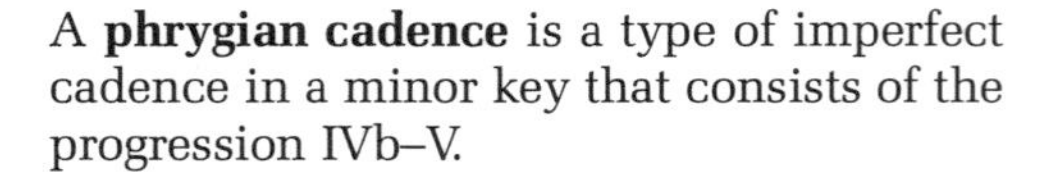

A **phrygian cadence** is a type of imperfect cadence in a minor key that consists of the progression IVb–V.

As the G-major chord of bar 12 gives way to G minor in bar 13^3 a **false relation** is formed between the soprano B♮ of bar 12 and the B♭ in the bass of bar 13. It is at this point that the key begins to change from C major to D minor, confirmed by the **phrygian cadence** (IVb–V in D minor) in bars 15^4–16^2.

We saw false relations in *O Wilhelme* and phrygian cadences are the stock-in-trade of 16th- and 17th-century composers – although Bruckner spices his up with an anticipation (the soprano E in bar 15) and a suspension (the tenor D in bar 16).

Bars 12^2–16^1 do not include a tonic chord of D minor – the key is only suggested by the imperfect cadence. Instead of confirming the key of D minor, Bruckner immediately embarks on a sequence a tone higher in E minor (bars 16^2–20^1). This reflects all of the features of the previous phrase:

- The A-major chord of bar 16^2 gives way to A minor in bar 17,
- This again involves false relations (between C# and C♮), and
- The new key of E minor is only suggested by the chord V of its imperfect (phrygian) cadence.

At the end of the first half of the middle section (bar 20), Bruckner leaves us poised on a chord of B-major – almost as far distant from the key of C major as it is possible to get. And yet in the next bar unaccompanied tenors must remember the original tonic (or pitch the tricky interval of an augmented 2nd from D# down to C) to launch a very chromatic passage.

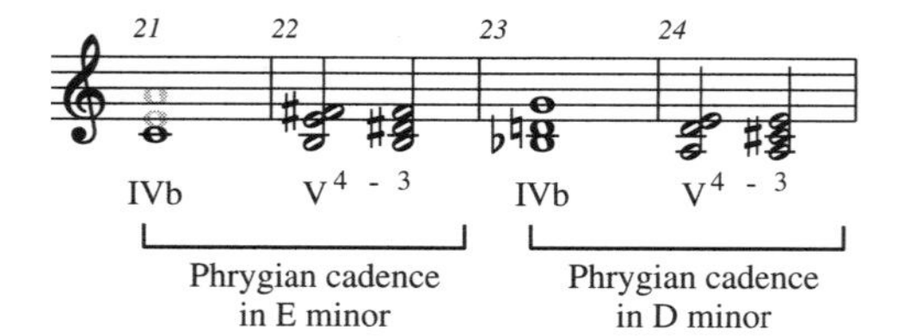

What actually happens is another example of Bruckner's ability to combine ancient and modern by re-working phrygian cadences in the context of romantic harmony. The chord of B major in bar 20 proves to be the dominant of E minor, the key of bars 21–22. But again there is no tonic chord, just a phrygian cadence (IVb–V^{4-3}) in that key. Even more elusive is the fact that the first of these chords is represented only by its bass note (the rest of its notes are shown in grey in the example *left*).

When this progression is repeated in sequence a tone lower in bars 23–24, the entire first chord of the phrygian cadence is now present – but this G-minor chord comes straight after the totally unrelated B-major triad at the end of bar 22. And there is no more sign of chord I in D minor than there was of a tonic chord in E minor.

The absence of tonic chords in these bars, combined with chromatic movement in all of the voice parts, gives this section a sense of tonal instability. But as the tenors complete one more iteration of their chromatically descending two-bar sequence, they arrive on G in bar 26 and the upper parts combine with them in the simplest diatonic harmony in C major, coming to a close with an **imperfect cadence** decorated with a Mozart-like cadential 6/4 (chords Ic–V in bar 29).

This prepares the way for a repeat of the first section of this **ternary structure** (bars 30–39 = bars 1–10). In bars 40–42, the word 'God' (*Deo*) is expressed through a typically romantic progression of chromatic harmony. Diminished-7th chords on the last beats of bars 40 and 41 act like secondary 7ths dominants, resolving to chords II and III of C major in bars 41^2 and 42^3 respectively.

Bars		
$1–12^1$	**A**	C major
$12^2–29$	**B**	Sequences suggest D minor, E minor, and D minor, ending on V of C major
30–48	**A**^{1}	Repeat of **A** with extended ending.

After a dramatic silence, diatonic simplicity again returns in the last phrase, with a chromatic passing note (C♯) supplying a farewell touch of colour in the solemn procession towards the final perfect cadence.

Private study

1. Explain the meaning of 'imitation by inversion', giving an example from bars 21–26.
2. Where on page 306 of the *New Anthology* is there an example of a feminine cadence?
3. Complete the blanks in the following statement:

   A phrygian cadence is a type of .... cadence that consists of chord .... followed by chord .... in a minor key.
4. What is the total range of the soprano part in *NAM 30*? How does this compare with the range of Taverner's treble part in *NAM 26*?
5. Make a list of the the ways in which *Locus iste* differs from renaissance motets such as *NAM 26*.

Tavener, The Lamb

Special Focus Work 3 for 2008 and 2009

NAM 32 (page 344) CD3 Track 10
Westminster Abbey Choir
Directed by Martin Neary

Before starting on this section you should work through (or revise) the information about the context and structure of this music given on pages 88–90 of the AS Guide. Make sure that you understand all of the terminology used on those pages.

Context and word setting

In 2004 John Tavener wrote the following short programme note for this work:

> The Lamb was written twenty-two years ago [in 1982] for my then three-year old nephew, Simon. It was composed from seven notes in an afternoon. Blake's child-like vision perhaps explains The Lamb's great popularity in a world that is starved of this precious and sacred dimension in almost every aspect of life.

The text of *The Lamb* comes from *Songs of Innocence*, a collection of poetry by William Blake, first published in 1789. Blake appears to speak as a child ('I a child' in bar 17), but in reality the poem deals with the destiny of the human spirit. The subject of the setting is Jesus (referred to in the Bible as 'the lamb of God') who 'became a little child' (bar 16). Because of this reference to the birth of Christ, Tavener's setting was first sung at a carol service in Winchester

Cathedral on 22 December 1982 and was broadcast two days later as part of the famous Christmas Eve carol service from King's College, Cambridge. *The Lamb* is also sometimes sung as an anthem at the end of the Anglican service of Evensong.

The setting is largely **syllabic**, although occasionally two notes are slurred together to draw attention to important words. Tavener's combination of outward simplicity and underlying sophistication reflects the dual nature of the text – an innocent little lamb, but a lamb that is a symbol of God incarnate who was to be slain as a sacrifice for the sins of the world. This explains the bitter-sweet dissonances, particularly the Am^9 chord that appears at the words *such, all, Lamb* and *know* in bars 7–10 (and all four chords with a tenuto dash in bars 17–20). Tavener himself refers to it as his 'joy–sorrow' chord, and it certainly adds pathos to these passages.

Rhythm

The initial performance direction, lack of time signature and the variable number of quavers in each bar make it clear that there is **no regular metre** (even though some bars equate to four crotchet beats). The text reigns supreme and the barlines simply mark the ends of lines in the poem, being given as reference points for rehearsals (and for exams!).

Melody

The thematic material for the whole piece derives from the first bar (**A** in the example *left*). Like phrase A itself, all derivatives revolve around a fixed pitch with leaps of no more than a 3rd. Here are the permutations of phrase A:

- The repetition of A in bar 2 is accompanied by its **inversion** (**AI**) in the alto. It replicates every interval exactly – a rising major 3rd becoming a falling major 3rd, and so on. The result is a **bitonal** combination of two melodies – one in G major (or E minor), the other in E♭ major (or C minor) – that are reconciled by beginning and ending on the same pitch (G).
- The melody in bar 3 is made from the four pitches of motif *x* in the example plus the three pitches of motif *y*. (These are the 'seven notes' mentioned by John Tavener in the quotation on page 89.) Bar 4 is the **retrograde** of bar 3 (sing or play bar 3 backwards and you will have the melody of bar 4). The result is a melody that seems to begin and end in G major with a central passage in E♭ major (though these keys are not firmly established because only three or four pitches of the respective scales are used).
- In bars 5–6 the long melody of bars 3–4 is accompanied by its **mirror inversion** (see *left*), again with bitonal clashes that are reconciled by the unison G at the beginning and end. Notice how this manipulation allows soprano and alto to exchange three-note cells of the pitches between the surrounding Gs.
- Phrase A is stated three times in bars 7–9 then sung in rhythmic **augmentation** in bar 10 (all of the notes are exactly twice as long as they were before).

The same processes are used in the second verse, where the fuller texture arises from the doubling of parts in octaves. The devotional style of the music arises in part from the very restricted range of the soprano's melody (an augmented 5th, from E♭ to B♮) as well as from the limited dynamic range (***pp*** to ***mp***).

Texture

Although *The Lamb* is short, the work includes a good deal of variety, for example:

- Bar 1 is **monophonic**
- Bar 2 contains **note-against-note two-part counterpoint**
- Bars 7–10 contain **four-part homophonic** writing
- Bar 11 is sung **in octaves**
- Bar 12 has a two-part texture in which each part is **doubled in octaves** (tenors double sopranos, basses double altos).

Harmony and modality

The intervals formed in bars 2 and 12 are governed by the technique of mirror inversion, but the apparently simple melody has been so cunningly contrived that only three of the eight harmonic intervals are dissonant. The level of dissonance is greater in bars 5–6 and 13–14, but by now the ear has come to accept it.

What is particularly satisfying is the way phrase A is transformed by modal harmonisation in bars 7–10 and 17–20. This phrase originally suggested the key of G major, but in these passages it is harmonised in the **aeolian mode on E** (E–F♯–G–A–B–C–D–E). Every note of this mode is contained in these passages – there is no sharpening of the 7th degree in the dominant chords (the penultimate chord in every bar of these two passages) nor is there a tierce de Picardie to dispel the modality.

Structure

The song is in **modified strophic form**. This means that the same music is used for both verses, but a fuller texture is achieved in bars 11–16 by the doubling of parts mentioned earlier. Although the verses are tightly integrated by their use of material from the opening bar, the ear tends to notice that the melody of bar 1–2 returns in bars 7–10, giving the impression that verse one is a **ternary** structure (ABA^1) in which section B is formed by bars 3–6. This is then repeated in verse 2 (A=bars 11–12, B=bars 13–16, A^1=bars 17–20).

Private study

?

1. (a) What is the range of the soprano part and how many different pitches does it use?

   (b) On what pitch does every two-bar phrase in the soprano part begin and end?

2. Explain the following terms: (i) bitonal, (ii) mirror inversion, (iii) monophonic texture, (iv) modified strophic form.

3. How does Tavener ensure that the words are heard clearly?

4. (a) In what sense can the final cadence of this work be described as a modal cadence?

   (b) Name the mode in which the *The Lamb* ends.

Sample questions

In the exam there will be three questions on the special focus works, from which you must answer **two**.

(a) Comment on the variety of textures in *O Wilheme*.

(b) To what extent does modal harmony play a part in the motets by Taverner and Tavener?

(c) Compare and contrast the ways in which both *Locus iste* and *The Lamb* are based on material from their opening bar(s).

Continuity and change in texture

For examination in summer 2008 and 2009

You do not need to study this topic unless *Sacred vocal music* is the Area of Study that you undertook for AS Music and which you are now extending for A2.

Before starting work on this topic you need a thorough understanding of the material on *Sacred vocal music* in the AS Guide (pages 78–90). Remember that for A2 the topic draws on works from across the **entire** Area of Study, not just those in one of the two lists, A or B. It is important to be aware that tonality refers to the relationship of keys in music (and for exam purposes that also includes modes) – it is nothing to do with the tone of musical sounds.

Texture refers primarily to the number of simultaneous parts in a passage of music and the way in which they relate. At A2 you need to use precise terminology and should avoid vague descriptions of texture as 'thick', 'thin' or 'open'. For instance, you may need to describe a texture not only as contrapuntal but more specifically as two-, three- or four-part counterpoint, and you may need to indicate whether the type of counterpoint is fugal, canonic or just freely imitative. Similarly, you may need to describe a texture as not just homophonic but as melody-dominated homophony (or 'melody and accompaniment') or homorhythmic (all parts moving in the same rhythm to form a series of block chords).

Taverner

NAM 26 (page 266) CD3 Track 1
Christ Church Cathedral Choir Oxford
Conducted by Stephen Darlington

The textures in *O Wilheme* were discussed on page 85 and you should re-read this section before continuing. The restricted use of imitative counterpoint in this work was unusual for Taverner, but the largely syllabic and homophonic setting allowed him to get through a long text in a relatively short setting. Also, the homorhythmic texture of its central section allowed Taverner to give special (and politically important) prominence to the reference to his patron 'Cardinal Thomas our founder'.

NAM 26 was written for an all-male choir that required both high (treble) and low (mean) boys' voices. The part labelled 'countertenor' is not as high as this term often suggests – it is of normal tenor, rather than male alto, range. Similarly, the tenor part is relatively low, corresponding with a baritone range. Three of the five voice parts span a modest pitch range of a 9th, while the bass part has a compass of a 10th and the mean encompasses an 11th. The whole antiphon can therefore be sung in a relaxed manner with the most characteristic timbre of each type of voice contributing colour to the varying textures.

On CD3, adult male altos sing the mean part, leaving all 16 boys to take the treble line – something which Dr Hugh Benham, a leading authority on Taverner, suggests may give undue prominence to the top part within the overall texture.

There could hardly be a greater contrast between the *a cappella* choral textures of *O Wilhelme* and the opening of *In ecclesiis*. In the latter, a solo voice is poised high above a functional bass part, creating a **polarised texture** – a common feature of baroque music – with the gap between the two poles being filled with an improvised organ accompaniment.

This opening (and similar passages, such as bars 13–24) can also be described as **monody** – a term used for early-17th century music for solo voice accompanied by continuo. However, it is only the first of the wide variety of textures that form such an important feature of this **polychoral motet**. In the list below we have used the following abbreviations:

- CT, A, Ten, Bar are the vocal soloists
- AI, AII, T, B are the chorus parts
- C1, C2, C3, Vla, Tbn I, Tbn II refer to the solo instruments (cornetti, viola and trombones)
- *basso* is the *basso continuo* ('Basso per l'organo') part.

For reference, the rondo structure of the work is summarised in the box *right*. Here are the principal textures found within its sections:

1. Bars 1–5: monodic texture for CT and *basso*
2. Bars 6–12: choral **homophony** in $\frac{3}{4}$ section, **two-part imitation** (AII and T) overlaid with CT solo in $\frac{4}{2}$ section
3. Bars 13–24: monodic texture for Bar and *basso*, with some clever imitation in the realisation of the *basso*
4. Bars 25–31: as 2 above, except that Bar replaces CT
5. Bars 31–39: instrumental symphony begins **homophonically** followed by four **points of imitation** (bars 32^3–34^1, 34^2–35^2 which overlaps with 35^1–36^2, and 36^3–39^1)
6. Bars 39–61: A+T duet (echo effects and imitation) integrated with **contrapuntal** and often imitative instrumental parts
7. Bars 62–68: **antiphonal exchanges** in $\frac{3}{4}$ section between chorus on the one hand and A+T with instruments on the other; two-part imitation between AI and T, doubled at the octave above by C1 and C2, in $\frac{4}{2}$ section
8. Bars 68–94: CT+Bar duet (echo effects and imitation) with continuo only
9. Bars 95–101: as 2 above, plus Bar
10. Bars 102–114: **14-part homophony** contrasting with lighter textures and the beginnings of a **contrapuntal** texture in the instrumental parts of bars 111–114
11. Bars 114–118: **canon 8 in 3** (described below)
12. Bars 119–127: 14-part version of 2 above (last phrase repeated)
13. Bars 127–129: 14-part homophony

The most complex texture of the work is the **triple canon** in bars 114–118. The first of the three simultaneous canons occurs in the solo vocal parts and can be described as a **canon 4 in 1** (four voices

Gabrieli

NAM 27 (page 269) CD3 Track 2
Gabrieli Consort and Players
Directed by Paul McCreesh

Bars		
1–5	A	First vocal solo
6–12	B^1	*Alleluja* refrain
13–24	C	Second vocal solo
25–31	B^2	*Alleluja* refrain
31–39	Instrumental *Sinfonia*	
39–61	D	First vocal duet
62–68	B^3	*Alleluja* refrain
68–94	E	Second vocal duet
95–101	B^4	*Alleluja* refrain
102–118	F	*Tutti* (everyone)
119–129	B^5	*Alleluja* refrain

entering in turn with the same overlapping melody). It begins in the countertenor part on the last beat of bar 114, Two beats later the baritone sings exactly the same melody (except that the length of the penultimate note has been halved so that both voices can end together). Two beats after the baritone has started, the tenor sings the same melody until the group of four quavers (which have to be pitched a 4th lower than expected to allow for dominant harmony at the perfect cadence). The fourth voice (alto) enters six beats after the countertenor, so it follows that the melody has to be curtailed by omitting the quaver group altogether.

The same process is evident in the **canon 2 in 1** that starts with the chorus tenors (bar 114^3) imitated two beats later by the second altos (who omit the two quavers and semibreve of the tenor part in bar 117 so that, again, the parts can end together).

The third canon is also **2 in 1** and begins with the entry of the first cornetto at bar 115^4. In it the semiquaver figures of the first canon are inverted. Two beats later the second cornetto enters with the same melody (slightly modified and curtailed at the end).

Together these parts form a staggering **canon 8 in 3** (eight contrapuntal strands simultaneously combining three canonic subjects). As if this were not enough there is a pre-echo of the first canon by the violas in bars 114^2–115^3 and a reference to the second canon in Cornetto III (bar 117). But notice that this intensely contrapuntal texture grows out of the simplest harmonic progression (alternating I and V chords over a **dominant pedal**), whereas the chords at the end of *O Wilhelme* emerge from the imitative counterpoint.

Bach

NAM 28 (page 288) CD3 Tracks 3–6
Yorkshire Bach Choir, Fitzwilliam Ensemble, Clare Mathias (alto)
Conducted by Peter Seymour

There are several different textures in this piece, but unlike *NAM 27* they are separated into independent movements, each having its own distinct texture. All of them, however, are firmly based on a *basso continuo* (like the *basso per l'organo* in *NAM 27*) which is usually played on a cello with chords realised on an organ.

Movement 1

There are three components contributing to a variety of textures in this opening movement:

1. A ritornello for strings with a texture of **melody-dominated homophony** (tune in the first violins, accompanied by chords in the parts). First heard in bars 1–12, the ritornello sometimes reappears complete (e.g. bars 19–31 and 44–56) and sometimes incomplete (e.g. bars 40^3–44^1 are a transposition of bars 8^3–11^1).

2. Freely **canonic** vocal parts that vary in density. For example, bars 88–96 build up to four-part counterpoint with the voices entering in order from high to low (SATB). This is followed by two different combinations of three parts in bars 97–100^2.

3. A strict **canon at the 4th below** based on the chorale melody of the last movement of this cantata (not shown in *NAM*). The canon in bars 14–20, for instance, begins with a trumpet melody that is exactly replicated by unison oboes six beats later and a perfect 4th lower. There are another six identical or similar canons for trumpet and oboe. See if you can spot them all.

Movement 2

This alto recitative has a **homophonic** accompaniment for strings and continuo.

Movement 3

An anonymous chorale melody harmonised by Bach. The first seven bars are largely **homophonic**, but in the setting of the last word the texture becomes **contrapuntal** with expressive suspensions. Notice that the vocal parts are **doubled** by the orchetsra.

Movement 4

This *da capo* aria with obbligato oboe starts with a 16-bar ritornello in which a florid oboe melody is accompanied by a simple **walking bass**. Together they form a **two-part polarised texture** which, as at the start of *NAM 27*, is infilled by the continuo's chords. The vocal phrases are separated by passages from the ritornello, although both are unified by the walking bass, which paces throughout the entire aria. When all three parts (alto, oboe and bass) perform together the texture is like that of the late-baroque trio sonata (see *NAM 15*), particularly in passages such as bars 30–34, where **two-part counterpoint** is accompanied by the ubiquitous walking bass.

Haydn

NAM 29 (page 299) CD3 Track 7
Barbara Bonney (soprano)
London Symphony Chorus
City of London Sinfonia
Conducted by Richard Hickox

This is an excerpt from a symphonic Mass – not in the sense that a symphony orchestra accompanies the singers (Haydn scored it for the small orchestra shown *below right*), but in that the orchestra carries the burden of the musical argument. This is particularly true of bars 9–61, a long passage that would make complete musical sense were it to be played by the orchestra without singers. Notice particularly bars 9–15 where the soprano part is nothing more than a simplification of the ornate first violin part – together they form a **heterophonic** texture.

Haydn's original instrumentation was for trumpets, timpani, strings and organ. The woodwind parts shown in *NAM 29* are a later addition.

Bars 1–21 are essentially **homophonic**, opening with **antiphonal exchanges** between the soprano soloist and the choir. In bars 9–15 the choral writing is, with the exception of only a few beats, **homorhythmic** – that is, all the choir parts have the same rhythm. As mentioned above, the lively orchestral embellishment of the vocal parts provides much of the impetus in this passage. Even in bars 15–21, the simple choral phrases above a tonic pedal are enlivened by a syncopated orchestral accompaniment, which also supports the melody in the viola part (follow the minims in the orchestral reduction).

A **fugal texture** (or **fugato**) begins on the first beat of bar 22, the start of the subject (basses, bars 22–24^1) overlapping with the cadence of the previous section. This subject forms **two-part counterpoint** with the countersubject in the orchestral bass part. As this is a regular countersubject (it accompanies the subject at every entry) there is a constant rhythmic interplay between its quavers and the more distinctive rhythms of the subject.

This two-part counterpoint continues with the entry of the answer (an adaptation of the subject) in the tenor part at bar 24. In bars 26–42 there are a variety of **three-part textures** involving the subject or the answer, the countersubject and melodic fragments derived from the last four notes of the countersubject. For instance, three low voices in bars 26–27 are contrasted with three high voices in bars 28–29.

In bars 43–44 the texture briefly reduces to two parts in preparation for a **stretto** in which statements of the subject come tumbling in ahead of schedule – tenors two beats after basses, altos six beats after tenors and sopranos four beats after altos. This builds to the first substantial passage of **four-part counterpoint** (bars 47–52) which, after a brief reduction to two parts, leads to a **dominant pedal** and the perfect cadence that marks the end of the fugato (bars 60-61).

We have described the fugal textures in terms of the vocal parts because they are on separate staves, making it possible to follow the contrapuntal detail more easily than in the orchestral reduction. However it is important to realise that almost every note in the choral parts is doubled by an instrumental part – in other words, the texture continues to be symphonic. See if you can spot one beat where this generalisation does not hold true and, while you are at it, see if you can find a passage in which the orchestral part is an elaboration of the vocal parts.

The final section begins with a **tonic pedal** (bars 61–68) over which bass and tenor soloists sing a **canonic duet**, with triadic embellishments from the violins and soprano soloist. A repeat of bars 62–68 begins in bar 71, after which the choir re-enters for the closing bars.

Bruckner

NAM 30 (page 305) CD3 Track 8
Christ Church Cathedral Choir Oxford
Conducted by Stephen Darlington

We have already discussed the textures of *Locus iste* so all we need do now is summarise our findings and draw comparisons with the earlier pieces you have studied.

- Like *NAM 26*, *Locus iste* is unaccompanied, but the largely homophonic four-part textures are simpler than the five-part textures of *O Wilhelme* and much simpler than the massive accompanied textures of *NAM 27*.

- The contrast between homophonic and polyphonic textures has been important in all of the pieces studied so far. *NAM 26* ends in counterpoint despite much of the work being homophonic – the same applies to the chorale in *NAM 28*. *NAM 27*, on the other hand, rounds off some intense counterpoint with three final bars of homophony, just as the fugal texture of *NAM 29* culminates in a short homophonic coda. Such contrasts in *Locus iste* are more modest – some brief points of imitative counterpoint are confined mainly to the central sections of the motet, and its final phrase is virtually homorhythmic.

- Similarly, Bruckner makes only limited changes to the density of his texture – apart from a few beats where a single voice part is heard alone, the only substantial deviation from four-part writing occurs in the three-part texture of bars 22–29. In contrast, Taverner's textures vary from two to five parts (including two totally distinct three-part groups in bars 38–47), Gabrieli's vary from two to 14 parts, and the works by Bach and Haydn include a variety of textures.

- Unlike any of the earlier pieces, *Locus iste* includes the use of silence as a textural element.

Stravinsky

NAM 31 (page 307) CD3 Track 9
Choir of Westminster Cathedral
City of London Sinfonia
Conducted by James O'Donnell

Whereas Haydn's Mass is symphonic in the sense that it is rooted in the style and forms of a classical symphony, the title of Stravinsky's *Symphony of Psalms* reflects an older usage of the word symphony, meaning a 'sounding together'. It is a usage that Gabrieli would have understood, since *In ecclesiis* was first published as part of a collection of his *Symphoniae sacrae* ('sacred symphonies').

Stravinsky's work is scored for a large orchestra *excluding* clarinet, violins and violas, but *including* two pianos used to give a percussive edge to bass **ostinatos**. Despite the layering of these ostinatos with choral melodies and orchestral chords the texture has the hard-edged clarity that is a hallmark of Stravinsky's style. He was familiar with late renaissance and early baroque music (he completed the missing parts from three motets by Gesualdo) so it should not surprise us that **layered textures** and sudden textural changes should remind us of Gabrieli's techniques in *NAM 27*. For instance, compare the change from monody to vocal homophony in bars 1–10 of the latter with the change from **choral homophony** to **unison** chant in bars 2–5 of *NAM 31*. Also compare the layered texture of bars 114–118 in *NAM 27* (where three canons are combined) with similar layering in bars 12–20 of *NAM 31* (where three ostinato patterns are combined). Textural changes usually coincide with structural ones (e.g. new, modified or repeated thematic material), and Stravinsky often reworks previous textures when thematic material returns. In the table below such recurring textures are shown by letters while numbers signify completely new textures.

Bars		*Texture*
1–2	**1a**	Widely spaced wind chords
2–3	**2**	Choral homophony, unaccompanied apart from the strings' tonic and dominant notes
4–6	**3a**	Chorus ostinato plus harp/piano ostinato, both in octaves
7–8	**1b**	Tutti chord spread over more than five octaves. In context it sounds like the tonic chord of C major, but its crystal clear sonority can be attributed to the omission of the fifth and the doubling of the third at the top of the chord (flutes, oboe 1 and pianos). A cello/bass ostinato figure begins in these bars
9–11	**4**	Outer chorus parts in octaves, inner parts alternate between the major and minor 3rds of the C-major chord outlined by the continuing bass ostinato.
12–20	**3b**	As **3a** plus soprano/alto parts in 3rds, two-note horn ostinato and doubling of bass ostinato by five flutes. A typical example of Stravinsky's layered textures
21–23	**1c**	Tutti chord as **1b** but with flat 7th (B♭ in second cello part)
24–39	**5a**	Rapidly repeated bassoon and horn chords alternate with ostinato (strings) overlaid with second ostinato (trumpet and harp, transferred to piano and low brass in bars 38–39)
40–52	**6**	New diatonic versions of previous bass ostinato (timpani, piano 2 and strings) plus the motif of repeated chords overlaid with woodwind triplet figures. These build to a homophonic climax (bars 48–49) followed by a loud tonic chord of C major (bar 51, beat 4).
53–64	**3c**	Two ostinatos (left hand parts of pianos 1 and 2, doubled on – or transferred to – other instruments) plus soprano chant with alto countermelody
65–98	**5b**	Repeated chords of **5a** (strings plus altos and tenors) above ostinato (piano, harp, timp) then cantabile choral melodies with repeated chords and homorhythmic scales leading to a second climax (bar 98)

Bars 99–149 contain a varied repeat of earlier material, so you should be able to spot and describe the return of textures **1d** (bars 99–102), **2** (bars 102–103) and **3d** (bars 104–149).

At bar 150 a canon between soprano and bass is heard above a simple triadic ostinato for double bassoon and bass trombone (after bar 156 the choral parts are imitative but no longer canonic). In bars 163–198 a new version of the choral chant is accompanied by a four-note ostinato stated 31 times (harp and pianos). It cuts across the barlines – three statements of the ostinato to four bars of the choral chant – but the tempo is slow so this rhythmic layering has the effect of a solemn processional that eventually leads back (bar 205) to a second repeat of bars 2–8.

Taverner

NAM 32 (page 344) CD3 Track 10
Westminster Abbey Choir
Directed by Martin Neary

We have already discussed the textures of this piece but now we must compare and contrast it with the earlier works studied. None of these include the monophony of bar 1 or the unaccompanied octaves in bar 11 (Stravinsky's vocal textures of this sort are always accompanied by instruments). The two-part counterpoint of bar 2 echoes that in the soprano-mean duets of *NAM 26*, but there is no precedent for the octave doubling of these two contrapuntal strands in bar 12. You should be able to find plenty of examples of the chordal textures of the remaining sections, but you also need to recognise the differences. For instance the unaccompanied homorhythmic settings of *Et ecclesiam piorum* on page 268 are scored for three, then five, voices – and the four-part homophony that occurs in *NAM 27*, *28* and *29* is accompanied by instruments. The nearest parallel, both in the spirit and in the letter, is between the final phrase of *Locus iste* and the last bar of *The Lamb*.

Private study

1. Explain each of the following terms and give an example of its use in *NAM 27*: monodic texture, antiphony, canon.
2. Why can the term homorhythmic be applied to *The Lamb*?
3. Describe the opening texture of *NAM 28* (movement I).
4. Define the term polarised texture, showing how it refers to the opening of movement IV of *NAM 28*.
5. Explain what is meant by a fugal texture and give examples of a subject, answer, countersubject and stretto from *NAM 29*.

Sample questions

In the exam there will be two questions on this topic, from which you must answer **one**.

(a) Compare and contrast Bach's canonic writing in the first movement of *NAM 28* with Gabrieli's canonic writing, seen on pages 284–285 of the *New Anthology*.

(b) Comment on the difference in approach to accompanied vocal textures you have seen in the works by Haydn and Stravinsky.

(c) Compare the variety of textures used by Gabrieli in *In ecclesiis* with the range of textures used by Bruckner in *Locus iste*.

Secular vocal music

There are *three* Special Focus works, Weelkes' *Sing we at pleasure* (*NAM 34*), Monteverdi's *Ohimè, se tanto amate* (*NAM 35*) and Gershwin's 'Summertime' from *Porgy and Bess* (*NAM 41*), all of which must be studied if you are taking the exam in 2008 or 2009.

Weelkes, Sing we at pleasure

Special Focus Work 1 for 2008 and 2009

NAM 34 (page 349) CD3 Track 12
Purcell Consort of Voices
Directed by Grayston Burgess

Before starting on this section you should work through (or revise) the information about madrigals, and the context and structure of this work, given on pages 91–93 of the AS Guide. Make sure that you understand all of the terminology used on those pages.

Context

Madrigals were hugely popular among the educated classes of late-Elizabethan England, where they might be sung by family and guests as after-dinner entertainment. In fact, they could be performed by any combination of voices and instruments that could cover the required ranges (many published collections were subtitled 'apt for voices or viols'). As explained in the AS Guide, *NAM 34* is a lighter type of madrigal, known as a **ballett**, characterised by syllabic word setting, dancing rhythms and 'fa-la-la' refrains.

Rhythm and metre

Even were it not mentioned in the text (see bars 31–43) we should know that Weelkes intends to summon the spirit of the dance by his lively **triple-time rhythms**. Most of them are **dotted** (|♩. ♪♩|) and immediately repeated in another voice part. The rhythm is given added spice with **syncopation** (e.g. alto bars 7 and 12, tenor bar 9) and with the use of **hemiola** (e.g. bars 20–21). A hemiola is created when six beats in triple time are articulated as three groups of two, instead of the expected two groups of three. In other words, it sounds as if the music has briefly gone into duple metre, as shown in the example *right*, where bars 20–21 have been barred in $\frac{2}{4}$ time to illustrate the effect.

Melody, harmony and tonality

Although there is no key signature it is obvious that the home key of the whole ballett is G major. This is not only evident in the principal cadences (bars 21–22, 30–31, 52–53, 61–62 and 83–84) but also in the first soprano part on page 349 of *NAM*, which begins with an ascent from dominant to tonic via the crucial leading note (F♯) of G major. The only note in the first soprano part on this page that is foreign to G major is the F(♮) in bar 16. Weelkes would have thought of this as the 7th degree of the mixolydian mode (G–G on the white notes of a keyboard), but to our ears it seems as though the melody in bars 13–18 has modulated into C major.

Now look at the harmony on page 349, being careful to note that the real bass (the lowest-sounding part) is sometimes in the tenor. The harmonic rhythm is | 𝅗𝅥 ♩ | (emphasising triple time) in all bars except bar 21 where a change of chord on the second beat (shown in the example *above*) emphasises the hemiola. In the first eight bars the progression is | I–V | I–V | I–IV | Ib–IV | Ib–II | Ib–II | Ib–VIIb | I |. Remembering that VIIb–I functions in the same way as V–I, you will see that all but two of the 15 chords are key-defining primary triads and the phrase ends with a perfect cadence.

The *fa-la-la* refrain begins with a modulation to D major (bars 8–11) and a return to G major (bars 12–14^1). It is not until bars 14–15 that we encounter a truly modal progression consisting of adjacent chords of F major (a chord on the flat leading note is very common in English madrigal style) and E minor (the only minor chord on this page). These chords initiate a passage in C major (bars 15^3–18^2) and a modulation back to G major with amazingly tonal harmony (all tonics and dominants in bars 19–22).

All of the chords in this first section are root-position or first-inversion triads, and the only on-beat discords are the half-beat suspensions where syncopations occur in the alto and tenor parts. Strictly speaking the last suspension (bar 21) is not prepared – the alto G simply crashes into the minim A in the first soprano to form a **consonant 4th** with the bass.

A 4th above the bass was long regarded as a dissonance that normally needed to be prepared. However, in a cadential position such as this, approaching the dissonance by step was widely regarded as acceptable, hence the term **consonant 4th**.

All we have said about the first 22 bars applies equally to the rest of the madrigal – there's no need to check the truth of this statement beyond bar 53 because bars 53^3–85 are a written-out repeat of bars 22^3–53^2 with the two sopranos exchanging parts.

Texture

The texture consists mainly of **five-part counterpoint**. Short rests are used primarily to draw attention to the **imitative entries** that follow them, rather than to offer contrasting two- or three-part textures. However, contrast is provided by **homophonic** (bars 22^3–25^1) and **homorhythmic** (bars 31^3–34^1) sections, although these are very short.

In a **homorhythmic** (or 'chordal') texture all parts have the same rhythm.

On page 349 there are three points of imitation:

1. *Sing we at pleasure* (sopranos 1 and 2 only)
2. *Content is our treasure* (paired imitation in which the parts sung together by soprano 2 and tenor are imitated one bar later by soprano 1 and bass)
3. *Fa-la-la-la-la* (bass, then soprano 2 and then soprano 1, followed by another nine entries in these parts).

In the setting of the next two couplets of the text (bars 22–43) there are two points of imitation:

1. *Whilst we his praises sound* is particularly joyful because the entries come on successive beats of the bar to create **cross rhythms** that threaten to disrupt the triple metre
2. *Shall, dancing, ever sing* contains more paired imitation – tenor and soprano 1 enter together at bars 34^3 and 38^3 and are imitated by soprano 2 and bass together two bars later in both cases.

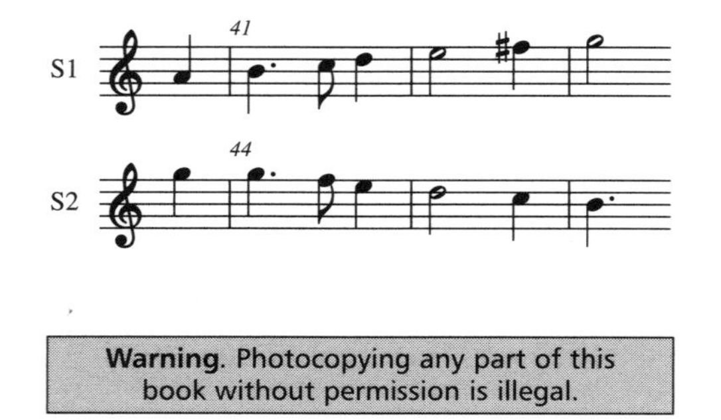

In the second *Fa-la-la* refrain (bars 43^3–53) the descending melody at the beginning of the **canon** between soprano 1 and soprano 2 (starting at bars 43^3 and 44^3 respectively) is an **inversion** of the ascending melody of the previous section – see *left* (the inversion differs only in that it starts with a repeated note). The tenor and bass parts begin imitatively (bars 43^2–44^3) but continue with **free counterpoint**, the bass having a jagged line as it chases round supplying the roots of chords V and I in C major (and the roots of the same chords in G major in bars 52–53).

You may have noticed that the alto part has not been mentioned in this list of imitative entries. In fact, the alto has only two brief points of imitation, at bars 26^3 and 44^3 (repeated at bars 57^3 and 75^3), and is often confined to an **inner pedal** (D in bars 28–31 and G in bars 46–52). But Weelkes does allow the alto some independence in bars 8^3–22 (which contains the syncopations and hemiola we have already noticed).

Structure

Like most balletts, *Sing we at pleasure* is a **binary** structure. Both sections end with a *fa-la-la* refrain and both are repeated, though, as we have already noticed, the second section has a written-out repeat in which the two sopranos exchange parts.

Although the music in both sections modulates from the home key of G major to the relative keys of D major and C major, passages in these keys are short-lived and serve no structural purpose (as they do in 18th-century binary forms). Sometimes these changes of key are a by-product of a **sequence** (as in bars 25^2–29 where the first phrase is in C major and the second is in G major).

In bars 34^3–43^2 the key is G major because of the sharpening of the 7th degree (F♯) in the ascending melody, but when the melody is inverted (bars 43^3–46^2) this note is flattened (F♮). The result is a change of key from G major to C major.

All of this is summarised in the following table (in which I and II are the two sections of the binary structure while capital letters refer to sub-sections within them):

Section		Bars	Text	Texture	Keys (all major)
I	A	1–8	First couplet	Imitative counterpoint	G
	B	8–22	First refrain	Imitative counterpoint	D G C G
Repeat of section I					
II	C	22–31	Second couplet	Homophony / imitation	G D C G
	D	31–43	Third couplet	Homophony / imitation	G
	E	43–53	Second refrain	Canon + free parts	C G
Repeat of section II with voice exchange (i.e. the sopranos exchange parts)					

Private study

1. What is (i) a hemiola, and (ii) a ballett?
2. Explain what is meant by syllabic word setting.
3. How does *NAM 34* reflect the idea of dancing?
4. What evidence can you find in *Sing we at pleasure* to suggest that tonality was becoming an important element in secular vocal music by the end of the 16th century?
5. Explain the difference between free counterpoint, imitative counterpoint and canon, giving an example of each of these types of texture from *NAM 34.*
6. What is the form of *Sing we at pleasure*?

Special Focus Work 2 for 2008 and 2009

NAM 35 (page 353) CD3 Track 13
The Consort of Musicke
Directed by Anthony Rooley

Monteverdi, *Ohimè, se tanto amate*

Before starting on this section you should work through (or revise) the information about the context and structure of this work given on pages 94–95 of the AS Guide. Make sure that you understand all of the terminology used on those pages.

Context

NAM 35 is representative of the serious style of madrigal and has a sophisticated text by Guarini, one of the major Italian lyric poets of the period and father of a famous virtuoso soprano. In fact, the vocal technique needed for this madrigal is one of the many features that distinguishes it from Weelkes' ballett – *Ohimè, se tanto amate* is written for highly trained singers to perform in private concerts for aristocratic audiences, not for amateurs to sing at home.

Words and music

It was Monteverdi's aim to express every nuance of the texts he set through what was called the 'representational style', many elements of which are apparent in this madrigal. It follows that we need to know the meaning of the text so turn to the translation on page 539 of *NAM*. The poem depends on the realisation that *Ohimè* in this context can mean the same as the Shakespearean 'alas!' but it can also refer to the sigh of a lover. It is also important that in both Italy and England in this period the verb to die (Italian *morire*) was also used as a euphemism for sexual release. So the poet might die of love withheld or, if his lady chooses, she might accede to his requests and hear ten thousand ecstatic sighs.

This translation was originally written for the London Anthology of Music (1985) by Walter Shewring. In it he comes as near as possible to Guarini's punning text by a rhyming paraphrase which, of its nature, cannot be a line-by-line, let alone a word-by-word, translation.

The music is almost entirely governed by the text, so in what follows we will examine some of the more important relationships between them (in the score notes with stems up belong to the canto or tenor parts and notes with stems down refer to the quinto or bass parts).

Bars 1–4

An exchange of sighs represented as a dialogue between male (including male alto) and female voices. Their ardour is evident in **unprepared dissonance** (bar 2^2 and bar 4^2) and a **false relation** between the quinto F♯ in bar 2 and the alto F♮ in bar 3. Every time *Ohimè* occurs it is set as a falling 3rd from a weak to a strong beat. No sooner has G minor (the tonic of the whole madrigal) been established than it is banished in bars 3–4, where B♭ major (the principal subsidiary tonal centre) is muddied by the dissonant E♮.

Bars 5–11

The **homophonic** settings of the first part of the question (cantus, quintus and bass, bars 5–8) and its **imitative** repetitions in the tenor and alto parts are ensemble version of recitative. But the section ends (bars 8–11) with *deh perchè fate* set against ever more ardent repetitions of *ohimè* and a questioning imperfect cadence (IVb–V in D minor) in bars 10–11. Monteverdi was the first great composer of opera and he knew that music can express more than one thing at a time – in this case, a rather exasperated question combined with amorous sighs.

Bars 12–19

A **free sequence** sees bars 10–11 repeated a 3rd higher in bars 12–13, then a 4th higher still in bars 14–15 (follow the bass part as the other parts are rearranged to avoid taking their vocal ranges too high). The question 'why, if you like to hear me sigh, do you condemn me to die?' is completed in a **dissonant** and **chromatic** style leading to a perfect cadence in D minor (with a **tierce de Picardie** in bar 19). Here are some detailed points about the dissonances:

1. Bar 16: The unprepared bass G clashes with all other notes of the F-major chord. Instead of being resolved it is followed by a leap of a 7th.

2. Bars 16–17: Similar effects occur when B♮ in the tenor at bar 16^4, and the canto B♮ and quinto D at bar 17^2, all form acute discords against the prevailing chord of A major and all are quitted by descents of a 5th.

3. Bar 17^{3-4}: The movement of the quinto from G to F forms parallel 7ths with the movement of the bass from A to G, and the sustained E in the canto clashes with both the quinto's F and the alto's D on the fourth beat.

4. Bar 18: The conventional **consonant 4th** at the cadence (canto, minim D) is frustrated by the alto's G above the bass A, which refuses to obey the principle that 7ths should fall.

Faced with this level of dissonance you may be asking the same question as some of Monteverdi's more reactionary critics did when this madrigal was first published in 1603 – is it necessary to flout all the rules of musical beauty that it took generations to develop? His answer would have been that 'music must be the handmaid of the words', and here the lover is in an (ironic) state of frustration which can only be expressed through the most anguished discords.

It would be impossible to deal with the rest of the madrigal in such detail but you should notice:

- The differing textures, ranging from three-part and five-part **homophony** (bars 20–23^3 and 29^4–33^1 respectively, both being strictly homorhythmic) to **imitative** passages in three and five parts (bars 23^4–27 and 33^2–37 respectively). Notice the dissonant start to these imitative phrases and the wilting 3rds in the upper parts at *ohimè*.
- The contrast between these passages and the dancing rhythms and B♭-major tonality of bars 39–43 (where the lover has high hopes of the lady's capitulation).
- The parallel first-inversion triads in bars 49–51 in which the falling 3rds of 'ten thousand "Ah me"s' produce bitter **false relations**.
- The extraordinary alto part in bar 56. Its effect is intensified by a truly awesome false relationship between the first note (F♯) and the F♮ nearly two octaves above in the canto part.
- The **dominant pedal** and **interlocking suspensions** in the closing bars, which lead to a final *ohimè* set to the progression IIIb–I, with a **tierce de Picardie** on the last chord. This unusual variant of a perfect cadence seems to have a weary finality that leaves little doubt about the lover's lack of success.

Ohimè, se tanto amate is **through-composed** – in other words, each phrase of the poem has new music, the structure being determined by the text, although the falling 3rds of *Ohimè* act as a unifying device. As we have seen, the basically minor tonality of the work is spiced with some startling chromaticism as well as with a number of unprepared and unresolved discords.

Private study

1. Is the word setting in *NAM 35* melismatic or syllabic?
2. Give three examples of the way in which Monteverdi's music reflects the meaning of Guarini's poetry.
3. Explain the meaning of tierce de Picardie, and give an example of its use on page 354 of *NAM*.
4. Identify three different textures in bars 47–57^2 of *NAM 35*.
5. How do the probable original performance circumstances of this madrigal differ from those of *NAM 34*?

Special Focus Work 3 for 2008 and 2009

NAM 41 (page 366) CD3 Track 19
Leona Mitchell (soprano)
Cleveland Orchestra and Chorus
Conducted by Lorin Maazel

Gershwin: 'Summertime' from *Porgy and Bess*

Before starting on this section you should work through (or revise) the information about the context and structure of this work given on pages 104–105 of the AS Guide. Make sure that you understand all of the terminology used on those pages.

Context

'Summertime' comes from Gershwin's opera *Porgy and Bess*, a work that is as much at home in a Broadway theatre as an opera house. It is based on the short novel 'Porgy' by DuBose Heyward, written in 1925 and adapted as a stage play two years later. Heyward's story centres on the impoverished lives of a black community living in the tenements of Catfish Row in his hometown of Charleston, South Carolina at the beginning of the 20th century.

The expressive lyrics of 'Summertime', written by Heyward and his wife, were the first part of *Porgy and Bess* that Gershwin set to music in 1934. The shortened syllables and unusual spellings are, of course, meant to represent the dialect of African-Americans of the southern states of the USA.

Gershwin's score is a rich fusion of jazz styles of the 1920s and 30s, blues, folk-influenced melodies and spiritual-like choruses, shaped into an operatic structure and supported by the sound of a lush, full orchestra. But to add realism to the drama, and to ensure idiomatic singing of his vocal parts, Gershwin insisted on an all-black cast for whom jazz idioms would be second nature.

Porgy and Bess had a mixed reception – its tragic finale, in which Bess leaves Porgy for life with a drug dealer, was nothing like the happy endings of Gershwin's earlier musicals, and the work was widely criticised for its negative portrayal of African-Americans. It was not until long after the composer's death in 1937 that it came to be regarded as one of the most brilliant, and possibly unique, works of 20th-century music theatre.

In *Porgy and Bess* the songs are not discrete items separated by spoken dialogue as they often are in musicals. Instead, the dialogue is set to music and each item flows into the next without a break. Thus the introduction in *NAM 41* is actually a continuation from the opening chorus and the rests in bar 46 are, in the stage show, filled by chords that crescendo into the next section.

'Summertime' occurs early in the work, forming part of a long opening number. Initially, the image of Clara, a mother singing a tender lullaby to her baby on a sultry summer evening, seems to be just part of the atmospheric 'scene setting' established during the first few minutes of Act 1. However, later in the opera both of the child's parents perish in a storm, and Bess is left to reprise 'Summertime' to the orphaned baby, adding great poignancy to the final phrase, 'With Daddy an' Mammy standin' by'.

Rhythm and metre

If you play or sing the melody of *NAM 41 precisely* as written, you will find that it sounds very 'square' compared with the recording. True, there are printed **syncopations** such as the one in bar 15, where the crotchet comes just *after* the beat (known as a 'lean' in jazz), and the one in bar 16, where the tied note comes just *before* the beat (called a 'push'). There are also more complex rhythms, such as that of the oboe melody in bar 19 and the **cross rhythm** in bar 25 (formed by triplet crotchets against two ordinary crotchets).

What gives the song life in the recording on CD3 is Leona Mitchell's interpretation of the rhythm. She sings every ♪.♬ pattern as ♩♪ (triplet) and the printed syncopations and cross rhythm we have already noticed are subtly modified in a similar way. She also pushes the first note of bar 31 and the second half of bar 33 becomes 𝄽♪ ♩♪ (triplets) – in fact the only even quavers she sings are those in bars 20 and 38.

These **swung rhythms** are a fundamental part of many jazz and pop styles and, because of the slow tempo, they help create the blues-like mood of 'Summertime's vocal line. The orchestra, though, plays rhythms as notated, with the exception of bars 40 and 44 where cellos and basses turn the dotted rhythms into swung quavers. Gershwin has, however, introduced lazy triplet rhythms into the string parts of bars 12 and 30, and oboe part of bars 19 and 37.

Text and melody

The word setting is **syllabic**, but Leona Mitchell introduces **slides** (known as *portamenti* in art songs) between the two notes in bar 10. She also slides up from the B in bar 40 to an unnotated B an octave higher in bars 41–42 and then slides back to the printed note in bar 43. The wavy lines in bars 20 and 39 indicate microtonal slides through a whole tone, but Mitchell chooses not to observe them.

The melody is in B minor but without a sharpened leading note (A♯) or sixth degree (G or G♯). Indeed, with only one exception (C♯ in bars 14–15, repeated in bars 32–33), the melody uses the pitches of the **minor pentatonic** scale based on B (B–D–E–F♯–A). Despite the expressive modal 7ths (A in bars 20 and 38) the melody, even if sung unaccompanied, is clearly in B minor because:

- A triad of B minor is outlined by the main notes of the melody in bars 7–10 and 15–19
- The first and third phrases end on the dominant (F♯ in bars 10 and 18–19) while the fourth phrase ends on a sustained tonic (B in bars 22–24)
- Every note, including the non-pentatonic C♯ at the end of the second phrase, belongs to the **natural minor** scale on B (B–C♯–D–E–F♯–G–A).

Harmony and tonality

The introduction begins with a falling minor 3rd (F♮–D), one of the most characteristic sounds of the blues. Bar 1 is the end of a link from the previous section in which this interval was heard many times, but the replacement of F♮ by F♯ in bar 2 has the effect of reasserting the dominant and signalling the start of a new number, which is confirmed by the **dominant pedal** on F♯ in bars 3–7. Over this pedal, the clarinet part falls in 3rds through every pitch of the natural minor scale on B. The gentle rocking of the child in Clara's arms is suggested by the continuation of the clarinet part as it oscillates between the sharpened 6th and 7th degrees of the ascending melodic minor on B (G♯–A♯).

Both the dominant pedal and the leading note (A♯) resolve at the double barline to the type of chord that colours the whole song – a bitter-sweet minor triad with an added major 6th. The rocking motion of the lullaby continues with the alternation of Bm^{6} and C♯m^{6} in bars 8–11. These added 6ths on chords I and II of B minor are repeated in bars 16–19^{2} thus supplying the harmony for nearly half of the verse.

The harmony between these two passages seems complex because of **chromaticism** but it is essentially an elaboration of the simple progression IV–V, preparing the way for a return to I^{6} in bar 16. Here it is, stripped of most of its decoration – the chords marked * act as **secondary dominants** (in other words, each sounds like the dominant of the *chord*, not key, that follows it):

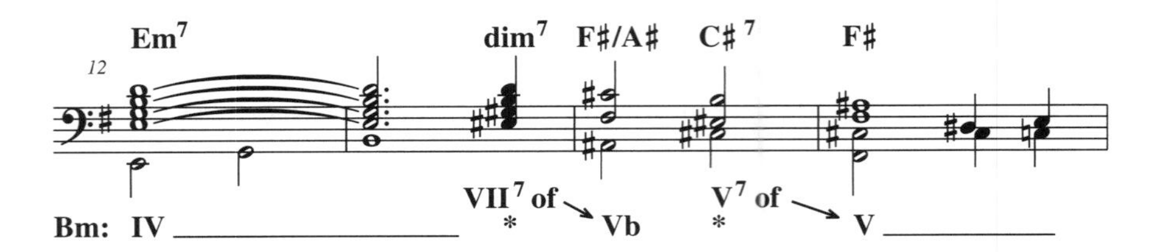

These chords are overlaid with diatonic and chromatic passing notes, a blue note (E♮ clashing against E♯ in bar 14), an appoggiatura (bass D♯ on the second beat of bar 15), plus the accented passing note (another D♯) shown *above* on the third beat of the same bar.

After the return to the bitter-sweet 'rocking' chords in bars 16–19^{2}, Gershwin completes bar 19 with a chord of E^{7} (above which an A♯ resolves to the 5th of the chord on the last beat of the bar). But although the bass moves to A in bar 20, instead of the expected A-major chord, Gershwin irregularly resolves the E^{7} to a second-inversion of D major, providing an unexpected and radiant shift as Clara comforts her child with the words 'hush, little baby'.

At the end of the bar the bass turns the chord of D major into Bm^{7}. A chord of E major (bar 21) is then followed by a modal-sounding cadence (G/A – Bm), producing a wistfully inconclusive return to the tonic key. Fragments of the melody from bar 9 are heard in the treble (bar 22) and bass (bar 23), leading to a return of the 'rocking' chords at bar 24, as this short link leads into the second verse.

If we strip away Gershwin's blue notes, added notes and chromaticism, and identify just one main chord per bar, the 16-bar blues chord pattern in B minor that supports the melody is revealed (it is much easier to hear on CD3 than to analyse from the score):

bars	8	9	10	11	12	13	14	15	16	17	18	19	20	21	22	23
chord	Bm I	Bm I	Bm I	Bm I	Em IV	Em IV	F♯ V	F♯ V	Bm I	Bm I	Bm I	Bm I	D III	E IV	Bm I	Bm I

Verse 2 uses the same harmonic progressions as verse one until bar 40. The B-minor chord in this bar marks the beginning of a **circle of 5ths** heard against the soprano's sustained **tonic pedal**. Each of the bass notes (B–E–A–D–G–C♮–F♯–B) is the root of a triad or 7th chord, except in bar 41^{3} (Em7/A) and bar 43^{3} (V^{13}).

Although this looks complicated, the effect is of a steady march toward the final perfect cadence.

Structure and texture

The song is in **modified strophic form** – in other words, the music of verse 1 is repeated, with adaptations, for verse 2. The main changes in the second verse are a violin **countermelody** (not heard in the recording on CD 3) and a **vocalise** (wordless singing) for two- and then three-part womens' voices. In both verses there are four four-bar phrases, forming the pattern ABAC. Melodic fragments in the accompaniment fill the gaps in the vocal part so the music is continuous. The avoidance of a perfect cadence in the tonic until bars 43–44 has a similar unifying effect, making the resolution at the end of the circle of 5ths particularly satisfying.

The texture of the song is **melody-dominated homophony**, in which the accompaniment has a purely supportive role. The texture is thickened in the second verse by the countermelody and vocalise, although the latter mainly doubles orchestral parts.

Private study

1. Explain the variety of musical influences evident in this song. (Reread the list on page 104 of the AS Guide if you find this question difficult.)
2. What is the only non-pentatonic pitch used in the melody of 'Summertime'?
3. Explain why the chromatic chord in the second half of bar 32 (C♯^{7}) can be described as a secondary 7th in the key of B minor.
4. Name, as precisely as possible, the type of scale sung by the first sopranos of the backing choir in bars 41–43.
5. What is the form of 'Summertime'?
6. Explain how the terms cross-rhythm and swung rhythm relate to *NAM 41*.

?

Sample questions

In the exam there will be three questions on the three songs you have studied, from which you must answer **two**.

(a) What would audiences in Monteverdi's day have found to be surprising in his use of harmony in *NAM 35*?

(b) Compare and contrast the use of rhythm in the works by Weelkes and Gershwin.

(c) Comment on the original performing circumstances and the textures of all three special focus works.

Continuity and change in structure and tonality

For examination in summer 2008 and 2009

You do not need to study this topic unless *Secular vocal music* is the Area of Study that you undertook for AS Music and which you are now extending for A2.

Before starting work on this topic you need a thorough understanding of the material on *Secular vocal music* in the AS Guide (pages 91–

105). Remember that for A2 the topic draws on works from across the **entire** Area of Study, not just those in one of the two lists, A or B.

Tonality refers to the use of (and the relationship between) major and minor keys in music – it is nothing to do with the tone colour of musical sounds. In tonal music, keys are established by cadences, particularly perfect cadence patterns such as V^7–I.

Dowland

NAM 33 (page 347) CD3 Track 11
James Bowman (countertenor) with David Miller (lute) and bass viol.

Flow my tears is an adaptation by Dowland of a lute solo that he had written in the early 1590s and which rapidly achieved fame throughout Europe. *NAM 33* is representative of the English ayre, a genre that flourished for only some 25 years, between 1597 and about 1622.

The song is in three strains (phrases or sections), each eight bars long and each repeated. The words, which were presumably written to fit the earlier lute tune, integrate with this structure as follows:

Strain 1	bars 1–8	Stanza 1 of the text
	repeated	Stanza 2 of the text
Strain 2	bars 9–16	Stanza 3 of the text
	repeated	Stanza 4 of the text
Strain 3	bars 17–24	Stanza 5 of the text
	repeated	Stanza 5 of the text repeated

We could therefore say that the first two verses are set **strophically** (the same music to different words) as are verses 3 and 4, although to a different melody. Dowland also intended that the last verse should be repeated to maintain the overall form of repeated eight-bar strains, but this final repeat is not observed on CD3.

Although published two years after Weelkes' ballett, in which we saw strong indications of major-key tonality, *NAM 33* harks back to the modality of earlier generations, despite cadences that point towards the tonal concept of the key of A minor.

Thus, the aeolian mode (A–B–C–D–E–F–G–A) on which the song is based is given a sharpened seventh degree (G♯) to form the cadences at the end of each strain:

- Perfect in bars 7^3–8
- **Phrygian** in bars 15^4–16 (a type of imperfect cadence that consists of the specific progression IVb–V in a minor key)
- Perfect in bars 23^3–24

In addition, the two perfect cadences include a **tierce de Picardie** (C♯) in their final chord. None of these chromatic inflections of the mode would have surprised previous generations of renaissance composers any more than the **false relations** that arise from the juxtaposition of the natural and sharpened seventh degrees of the mode (bar 5, beats 3 and 4) and the sharpened and natural third degrees (bar 8, lute, and bar 9, voice).

Equally important to the structural cohesion of the three strains is the interval of a descending 4th. It is outlined or stated explicitely three times in the first three bars. At the beginning (*Flow my teares*) it appears as a descent through the upper four notes of the aeolian mode (outlining a perfect 4th). Then (*fall from your springs*) it falls from the third degree to the sharpened seventh degree of the mode (outlining a diminished 4th). Finally (*Exilde*) it appears as a direct fall of a perfect 4th from the tonic to dominant.

The first version appears again in C major at the start of the second strain (bar 9). The third version comes at the end of bar 10, and later it is treated in sequence (*Happie, happie* in bars 20–21). But the most fruitful source for motivic integration (and for the expression of melancholia for which Dowland was so famous) is the phrase descending a diminished 4th from C to G♯ first heard in bar 2. Its imagery comes again in bar 6 (*infamy sings*) and bars 21–22 (*they that in hell*); it is inverted in bar 17 (*hark you shadowes*) and appears in varied form in bar 5 (*night's black bird ...*) and bars 15–16 (*joyes have deprived*).

Weelkes

NAM 34 (page 349) CD3 Track 12
Purcell Consort of Voices
Directed by Grayston Burgess

We discussed the structure and tonality of *Sing we at pleasure* in the first part of this chapter, so it just remains to compare these elements with the structure and tonality of *Flow my tears*.

Both works are based on repeated sections (three in the Dowland, two in the Weelkes), that each end with a tonal cadence. In *Flow my tears* different words occur in the first two repeats, while in *Sing we at pleasure* both text and music are repeated. However, the repeat of its second section is written out in full to allow for the voice exchange between first and second soprano parts.

Sing we at pleasure is in G major. The occasional use of the unsharpened leading note suggests a modal legacy. However, the music is given a distinctly tonal direction by Weelkes' preference for key-defining primary triads (such as the I and V chords of bars 19–22) and scale-based figures (such as the soprano 1 and 2 parts in bars 1–3 and 34^3–42^2).

Thus the use of the flattened seventh often sounds more like part of a modulation to C major (as in bars 13–18) than a remnant of modality. Similarly, the raised fourth degree (C♯ in bars 9–10) is followed by a chord of D major, suggesting a brief transition to the dominant, and thus reinforcing the feeling that G major is the tonal focus of the ballett. The use of inner pedals in the alto part (D in bars 28–31 and G in bars 46–53) further strengthen the tonality of the music.

In contrast, modal influences are much stronger in *Flow my tears*. This is partly because minor keys tend to be less stable than major keys – hence the reason for the different forms of minor scale that we still use today, which reflect the various ways in which the sixth and seventh degrees of of the minor mode can be inflected. These inflections frequently result in false relations in *Flow my tears*, as in bar 5 where G♮ in the lute part of beat 3 is followed by G♯ in the vocal part on the very next beat. The editor of *NAM 33* has suggested a further inflexion (the F♯ indicated by the small sharp sign above the stave in bar 7) to avoid an inelegant augmented 2nd in the vocal line at this point. Other accidentals, such as the bass C♯ in bar 11 or the lute F♯ in bar 19, also sound more like modal inflections than modulations because they are cancelled within a few beats. However, perfect cadences at the end of the first and third strains (both with a tierce de Picardie), and the phrygian cadence that concludes the second strain, all help assert A-minor tonality.

Monteverdi

NAM 35 (page 353) CD3 Track 13
The Consort of Musicke
Directed by Anthony Rooley

The dorian mode on G consists of the notes G–A–B♭–C–D–E–F–G.

As in Dowland's ayre, so in this Italian madrigal, minor tonality prevails with only brief glimpses of major keys. But where the lute song is rooted in A minor, this piece is tonally restless and often ambiguous. Thus the first two bars form an imperfect cadence in G minor, and the next two would be a sequence in B♭ major were it not for Monteverdi's use of E♮, the sixth degree of the dorian mode on G (see *right*), that lurks behind most of the setting. Play bars 3–4 with an E♭ instead of E♮ to hear how a conventional tonal sequence would sound.

In bar 6 Monteverdi raises the third degree of the mode to B♮ and for the first time introduces an E♭, resulting in what amounts to a modulation to C minor. Then in bars 10–13 the phrygian cadence in D minor (shades of Dowland) is immediately cancelled by a perfect cadence in what seems to be C major (VIIb–I in bars 12^4–13).

We have already noticed (page 103) the intense dissonance and chromaticism of bars 16–17, but in bars 18–19 this is followed by a conventional consonant 4th cadence in D minor with an equally conventional tierce de Picardie in the last chord.

D minor becomes the prevailing key in bars 20–29^1. It is seasoned with a modal triad on the flat seventh (the C-major chord in bar 21), but the phrase ends with the simplest possible perfect cadence (bars 28–29). In the second setting of this text (bars 29–38) almost the same progression is repeated in G minor. The tierce de Picardie in bar 38 results in a chord of G major, the 3rd (B♮) forming a false relation with the tenor B♭ in bar 39. There is no modulation; the music simply shifts up a 3rd to the relative major (B♭) in bars 39–43.

Monteverdi returns to G minor (bars 44–45^3), samples C major in a **harmonic sequence** (bars 45^4–46) and then what appears to be B♭ major – until the fearsome progression of false relations (bars 49^4–51^3) leads to a strange perfect cadence (IIIb–I in the tonic major) in bars 51–52.

The same tonal ambiguities prevail in the rest of the madrigal, where the F♯s of G minor are contradicted by the F♮s of B♭ major. Here, however, **tonic and dominant pedals** of G minor act as tonal anchors, so the last two chords – a repeat of the IIIb–I perfect cadence, now with a tierce de Picardie – just about convince us that the madrigal has ended in the tonic.

It is obvious from this account that tonality (or modality) is not being used as a structural agent. As explained earlier, the work is **through-composed**, its form being dictated by the text. The use of a falling 3rd acts as a unifying motif, but since this is always associated with *Ohimè* it is not so pervasive as Dowland's systematic exploitation of perfect and diminished 4ths.

Purcell

NAM 36 (page 356) CD3 Track 14
Carolyn Watkinson (soprano)
with the English Baroque Soloists
Directed by John Eliot Gardiner

A similar sort of tonal instability reflects Dido's mental instability as she contemplates suicide in the recitative (bars 1–9). But before we explore this you should first note that the following comments relate to the printed pitches in the anthology, not to the baroque pitch used in the accompanying recording. Secondly, the figuring of the bass part is incomplete (in fact, Purcell's original manuscript of *Dido and Aeneas* has not survived). Beneath the continuo bass part there ought to be a natural signs under the semibreve in bar 2, the first G in bar 5 and the second G in bar 6, and sharp signs under the first note of bars 8 and 9 (all of these accidentals indicating major chords). There are other smaller discrepancies between the figuring and the recording on CD 3, but without these essential additions the printed harmony makes little sense or appears to fail to follow the conventions of the period.

So with these in mind we see that the recitative starts with a triad of C minor then modulates to F minor (with a **tierce de Picardie** at the start of bar 3). The original key is re-established by the **phrygian cadence** (IVb–V in C minor) in bars 4–5. The perfect cadence in C major (bars 6–7) only serves to highlight the gathering shadows of death as the music plunges into G minor in bars 8–9, and the recitative ends with a phrygian cadence in this key. Like almost all recitative, the structure of these nine bars is dictated by the text (in other words, it is **through-composed**). And while rapid modulation is often a feature of recitative, Purcell has underpinned the descending chromaticism of the vocal melody with a clearly tonal harmonic progression, signposted by cadences.

The form of the main part of *NAM 36* (bars 1^3–56^1) is, of course, a **ground bass aria** with concluding ritornello. It is entirely locked into just one key – G minor – despite the chromatic descent from tonic to dominant of its ground bass and the chromatic B♮ in the vocal part of bar 7. A small and very boring book would be needed to describe the incredibly resourceful and dissonant harmony with which Purcell clothes the repeating ground. Suffice to say that there is hardly a bar without a **suspension** (see how many you can find).

The ground is exactly five bars long and is stated 11 times. Sometimes the cadence at the end of the ground coincides with a vocal cadence (bars 35–36 for instance), but more often their cadence points are out of synch (magnificently so in bars 31–32). Perhaps the most amazing avoidance of a perfect cadence at the end of the ground-bass pattern is in bars 49–55, where the complete tonic-dominant chromatic descent of the ground is imitated twice in the first violin part (bars 49–52 and 52–55). But though the music is chromatic it is the unwavering G minor tonality of the air that most remorselessly expresses the inevitability of the heroine's death.

Haydn

NAM 37 (page 359) CD3 Track 15
Elly Ameling (soprano)
Jörg Demus (piano)

This song comes from *VI Original Canzonettas* (little songs) that Haydn wrote in 1794. They are all settings of verses by the London society hostess and poet, Anne Hunter. Her original text for this song consisted of four stanzas, of which this is the first:

My mother bids me bind my hair,
With bands of rosy hue,
Tie up my sleeves with ribands rare
And lace my bodice blue.

Haydn combined stanzas 1 and 2 of her poem for the first verse of his **strophic** setting, and stanzas 3 and 4 as his second verse, freely repeating phrases of the text in stanzas 2 and 4 – thus the structure of the poem does not synchronise with the musical structure.

Given the date, we might expect Haydn to write **balanced four-bar phrases** with **antecedent-consequent** pairings – and that is exactly what he does in the first 16 bars:

A (bars 1–8): A major
A four-bar antecedent, ending with an imperfect cadence (Ic–V) in bars 3–4. It is answered by a four-bar consequent ending with a perfect cadence (Ic–V–I) in bars 7–8.

A^1 (bars 9–16): A major modulating to E major.
The antecedent is formed from a slightly varied repeat of the first four bars of the piano introduction, ending with the same imperfect cadence (bars 11–12). This is followed by a consequent that begins with a repeat of the start of the original antecedent and then modulates to a perfect cadence in E major (IIb–Ic–V–I in bars 15–16).

B (bars 17–27): E major
Although Haydn now repeats the second line of the poem, he does so to a new melody and in a new key (the dominant). To avoid the predictability of constant four-bar phrasing, a short piano link (bars 16^4–17^1) delays the vocal entry by half a bar, and the repetition of *and lace* adds a futher half bar, thus creating a five-bar antecedent that ends with a perfect cadence in E major (Ic–V^7–I) in bars 20–21.

The consequent is a four-bar vocal phrase (extended to six bars by piano links before and after) which, like the antecedent, begins with a scalic descent from E, but differs in being chromatic and punctuated with rests, perhaps expressing the mother's exasperation. Meanwhile the harmony of these bars consists of **dominant preparation** for the return of A major. Regular four-bar phrasing then returns in the closing section:

C (bars 27^6–39): A major
The rests of the previous vocal phrase are retained, but in a diatonic melody (bars 27^6–31^5) that includes a dramatic pause on the word *creep*. The varied repeat of this phrase in bars 31^6–35^5 makes its relationship to the last phrase of section B clearer by starting with a descending scale, although it too is now entirely diatonic. In the final phrase (bars 35^6–39^5) the thought of Lubin's absence provokes melodic fragmentation. All three phrases in this section end with perfect cadences in the tonic key.

So the tonal structure is ternary: A major – E major – A major, but the three distinct melodies (beginning in bars 0, 17 and 27) form the pattern ABC.

Schubert

NAM 38 (page 361) CD3 Track 16
Peter Schreier (tenor)
András Schiff (piano)

Haydn's canzonetta is a strophic song in which the same music serves for both verses. Heine's three verses are treated by the teenage Schubert to a **through-composed** setting that mirrors the mounting horror of every word of the text.

From a tonal point of view *Der Doppelgänger* is similar to Purcell's air, but with an intermittent four-bar ostinato instead of a persistent five-bar ground. The first two verses are built on the ostinato and, like Purcell's ground, this locks the music into the tonic (in this case B minor).

However, from bar 43 the music is wrenched up a 3rd to D♯ minor, returning to B minor in bars 51–52. The modulations to and from this distant key would not have such a devastating effect had Schubert not kept us waiting so long for a change from the tonic key and the ostinato. Since his three-part structure follows Heine's three verses so precisely we will analyse it in terms of the text, so make sure you read the translation on page 539 of the *New Anthology* and that you understand the meaning of key German words before continuing.

Verse 1 (bars 1–24): B minor

The piano states the **four-bar ostinato** on its own just as Purcell's five-bar ground is played on its own. As in Dowland's lute song the most prominent interval is the **diminished 4th** between A♯ in bar 2 and D in bar 3. The first and last chords of the ostinato are empty bare 5ths. The fragmented vocal part in its lower register is heard against the ostinato, the continuation of which in bars 9–14 contains two modal chords that include the flat 7th of B minor (A♮) – chord $V^{\flat 3}b$ in bar 10 and chord III in bar 11. The last two bars of the eight-bar vocal melody are echoed by the piano in bars 13–14 over chord V^7c.

The whole progression is then repeated for the last two lines of Heine's first verse. Together they emphasise the end rhymes (*Schatz* and *Platz*) and the eight-bar phrases of the vocal part, the second being a slightly varied repeat of the first (including an expressive appoggiatura on *längst* in bar 16).

Verse 2 (bars 25–42): B minor

The ostinato begins again, but the voice rises via another appoggiatura (bar 28) to a high F♯ in bars 31–32. Here chord V^7c of the first verse is replaced by an unexpected chromatic discord – the **French augmented 6th chord** in bars 32–33 (see *right*).

The ostinato returns again in bar 34 but this time the singer rises to the highest note in the vocal part, accompanied by a **German augmented 6th chord** in bar 42 (see right). Verses 1 and 2 are unified by a dominant pedal (F♯) that is contained within every chord of bars 1–40.

An **augmented 6th chord** is usually based on the flattened sixth degree of the scale, although in bars 32, 41 and 51 it is on the flattened second degree (C♮). It always includes a 3rd and an augmented 6th above the root (E and A♯ above C♮ in the examples *below*). A French augmented 6th also includes an augmented 4th above the root (F♯ in bar 32) while a German augmented 6th includes a perfect 5th above the root (G in bar 41). This discord is resolved by both notes of the augmented 6th interval moving apart by a semitone (here to the tonic, B):

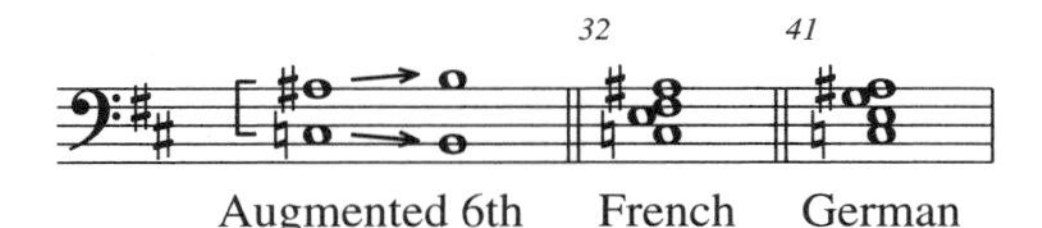

Verse 3 (bars 43–63): B minor modulating to and from D♯ minor

The chords in bars 43–47 embrace a rising **chromatic scale**, doubled over three octaves, that reaches a chord of D♯ minor in bar 47. These chords are related to each other only by the F♯ contained within them all. However, the key of D♯ minor is confirmed by the vocal part (which contains every note of the scale of D♯ harmonic minor and no others) and by alternating tonic and dominant chords in this key (bars 47–50).

Schubert wrenches the music back to B minor by means of another German augmented 6th chord in bar 51. This time it is on the more usual (flattened) sixth degree of the scale (G in the key of B minor, with E♯ forming the interval of an augmented 6th). It resolves to chord Ic of B minor in bars 52–53 and leads to the only definitive perfect cadence in the whole song (V^7–I in bars 55–56).

But Schubert has one last tonal surprise. When the ostinato begins again in bar 56 the bare 5th on C♯ (see bar 4) is replaced by a root-position **Neapolitan chord** (the triad on the flattened supertonic – here, C major) in bar 59. This chromatic stranger then resolves to V^7 of IV, which in turn resolves to IVc (bar 61). Finally, chord IVc is followed by chord I (with a **tierce de Picardie**), thus ending the song with a **plagal cadence**.

Fauré

NAM 39 (page 363) CD3 Track 17
Janet Baker (mezzo-soprano)
Geoffrey Parsons (piano)

Après un rêve is founded on a subtle fusion of modal and tonal melody with subtle chromatic harmony that together obscure the underlying tonal structure of the song.

This can be illustrated in the first nine bars of *NAM 39*. The melody of bars 2–4 outlines the C-minor triad that the piano has already played, but instead of finishing on B♮ (which would suggest an imperfect cadence) the setting of the first line of the poem ends on a modal B♭ in bar 4 that makes no sort of cadence at all.

In bars 5–6 the chromatic D♭s are followed by C–B♮–C, suggesting C minor, but confirmation of this key by the accompaniment has to wait until the V^7–I progression of bars 7–9, by which time the singer has *ascended* through the notes of the *descending* melodic minor scale (bar 7), sounding like the upper segment of the aeolian mode on C. The remaining notes of the mode are heard in bar 9, but these belong to a new phrase that modulates through F minor.

This modal/tonal melody is accompanied by chromatic harmony, (including secondary dominant 9th chords in bars 3–5) before the perfect cadence in bars 7–9. But notice how the dominant 7th in bar 7 clashes with the modal melody and how the cadence in the accompaniment overlaps the vocal cadence (as in Dido's lament).

Despite this wealth of modality and chromaticism, the music is given clear tonal direction by the bass of the first nine bars, which traces a **circle of 5ths** in C minor (C–F– B♭–E♭–A♭–D–G–C). This sort of fusion can be found in many other passages, but now we must look at the tonal structure of the whole song:

	Bar 1	Piano introduction: repeated C minor triads announce the tonic key
A	Bars 2–16	A setting of the first stanza of the poem, consisting of two seven-bar vocal phrases: the first in C minor, the second modulating to the relative major (E♭), followed by a one-bar piano interlude modulating back to C minor for …
A^1	Bars 17–30	A setting of the second stanza of the poem which begins with a repeat of the music of bars 2–11. In bars 26^3–30^2 a sequence based on the triplet figure from bar 7 ends with an imperfect cadence in F minor, which leads straight into …
B	Bars 30^3–38	A setting of the third stanza of the poem. It begins with two four-bar phrases, the first in B♭ minor (containing the climax of the song), the second returning to V of C minor in bar 38. These eight bars are followed by …
B^1	Bars 38^3–47	Two phrases, derived from B (bars 38^3–42^2 and 42^3–47). Despite chromatic harmony, these remain in the tonic key of C minor until the end of the song. The final disappearance of the dream is marked by a long, diatonic perfect cadence (bars 45–48) without any modal or chromatic conflict at all.
	Bar 48	Piano postlude: one tonic chord of C minor.

Like several of the earlier songs we have studied, this one contains a motif common to all three stanzas. It is the winding triplet figure that precedes all four vocal cadences in the first stanza and becomes endemic in the second half of the second stanza and the first half of the third.

Then, like the dream, the triplet figure fades away, with just a last fleeting glimpse of it in bar 45.

Schoenberg

NAM 40 (page 364) CD3 Track 18
Yvonne Minton (reciter)
Michael Debost (flute)
Directed by Pierre Boulez

This expressionist song is entirely **atonal** and without any melodic repetition (other than that in bars 23–24) or motivic manipulation (other than the sequence in bars 22–23). The three stanzas of Giraud's poem are separated by passages for unaccompanied flute but are not, of course, delineated by cadences. The work is **through composed**, with a structure that is dependent on the text. In that respect the nearest parallel is Monteverdi's madrigal – both composers aimed to put the text before the music. But in most respects there is no continuity of structure or tonality between NAM 40 and any other of the secular songs in this Area of Study.

Gershwin

NAM 41 (page 366) CD3 Track 19
Leona Mitchell (soprano)
Cleveland Orchestra and Chorus
Conducted by Lorin Maazel

We have already looked at 'Summertime' in great detail so all we need to do is explore changes and continuities. Like *NAM 37* it is a **strophic** song, though Gershwin, unlike Haydn, changes some of the rhythms to fit the scansion and sense of the second verse. We have noticed, too, that he adds countermelodies and female voices to the second verse and supplies a new ending. Also like the first 16 bars of NAM 37 Gershwin's 16-bar format falls into regular four-bar phrases, though these are not so firmly divided by perfect cadences – hence the greater sense of continuity in *NAM 41*.

Tonally, there are similarities between 'Summertime' and *Après un rêve*. Both are in a minor key and both combine modally-influenced melodies with chromatic harmony. But Fauré's song modulates widely, while Gershwin's is anchored to the key of B minor by the 16-bar blues chord sequence on which both verses are based. Although separated by just 22 years there is, in contrast, a world of difference between the atonal nightmares of Schoenberg's mad clown and Clara's maternal lullaby.

Private study

1. (a) What type of cadence occurs in bars 4^3–5^2 of the recitative in *NAM 36*? (Remember that the second chord is G *major*.)

   (b) Give an example of the same type of cadence from one of the other works in this Area of Study.

2. Explain how the chords in bars 30–39 of *NAM 37* assert the tonality of A major.

3. How does Schubert unify the structure of *NAM 38*?

4. Complete this sentence: The clash between B♭ and B♮ in bar 7 of *NAM 39* is an example of a simultaneous …

Sample questions

In the exam there will be two questions on this topic, from which you must answer **one**.

(a) Compare and contrast the handling of tonality and structure in the songs by Haydn and Fauré.

(b) Contrast the differing approaches to through-composed vocal music seen in the works by Monteverdi and Schoenberg.

(c) Comment on the differing approaches to tonality and structure in Dowland's *Flow my tears* and Purcell's 'When I am laid in earth' (do not include the recitative).

Music for film and television

There are *two* Special Focus works, *NAM 42* and *NAM 45*, both of which must be studied if you are taking the exam in 2008 or 2009.

Special Focus Work 1 for 2008 and 2009

NAM 42 (page 369) CD4 Track 1
Royal Ballet Sinfonia
Conducted by Kenneth Alwyn

Auric, Passport to Pimlico: The Siege of Burgundy

Before starting on this section you should work through (or revise) the information about the context and structure of this music given on pages 108–110 of the AS Guide. Make sure that you understand all of the terminology used on those pages.

Melody and structure

Auric's underscore for this scene depends for its witty effect on the rapid exchange of short motifs, unexpected changes of key and texture, and some glittering orchestration. Although the structure is ultimately determined by the on-screen action that it supports, the music is given an unerring logic by the use of varied repetition, cast in a very classical format of one-, two- and four-bar phrases.

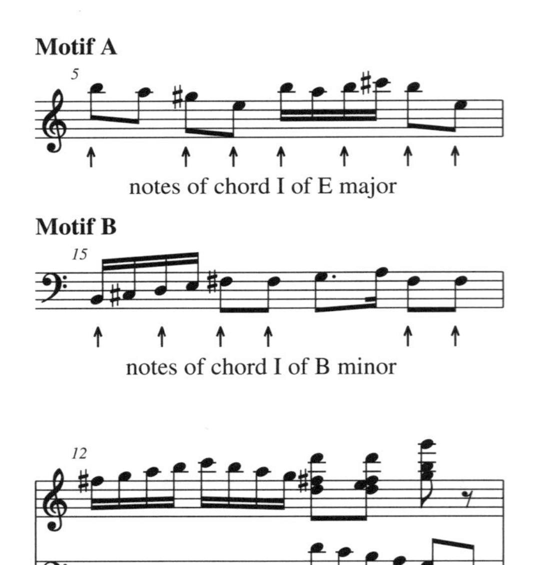

Although keys seem to come and go with extraordinary rapidity, suiting the fast action of the film, they are mostly totally clear due to Auric's preference for:

- Motifs centred on the tonic triad of the current key. Several of these sound like snatches of traditional tunes because, like much folk music, they use a **hexatonic** (six-note) scale.
- Perfect cadences that clearly define the key through the use of a V^7–I progression, despite the frequent use of added notes. Many of these cadences end on the fourth beat in the final bar of a four-bar phrase and are followed by an abrupt transition to a new key.

Both of these points are illustrated *left*. Now we must look in detail at the structure Auric developed from five main motifs.

Bars 1–4, Introduction (E major)

Bar 1. A scalic descent from upper to lower dominant in the horns supports a fall from dominant to tonic on trilling upper instruments and a fanfare-like rhythm on the dominant from trumpets.

Bar 2. A repeat of bar 1 with horns now in parallel 3rds.

Bar 3. To increase a sense of expectation, the music of bar 2 is compressed into half its length (free rhythmic **diminution**) and played twice in this bar.

Bar 4. To add further excitement, the fall from dominant to tonic in the upper parts is reduced to quavers and is heard four times.

Bars 5–8, Motif A (E major)

Remember that if you refer to motifs by letter-names in an exam answer you *must* define which notes the letters refer to – for instance, 'Motif A (the melody first heard in bar 5) …'.

In bar 5 motif **A** (shown *above left*) is stated by flutes and glockenspiel in parallel 5ths and octaves, accompanied by scalic figures in parallel 3rds in the violin parts. This bar is given a varied repeat in bar 6. So far *NAM 42* has been entirely diatonic, but a B♯ in the second violins (4th semiquaver of bar 6) heralds a chromatic idea (lower strings, bar 7) that uses the rhythm, but not the pitches, of motif A. Above this, violins play a sequence of falling 3rds in which

cross-phrasing cuts across the prevailing **quadruple metre** (see *right*). This four-bar unit is then rounded-off with contrary-motion scales and a perfect cadence that ends on the fourth beat of bar 8.

Bars 9–12, Motif A (G major)

These four bars are a varied repeat of bars 5–8, transposed up a 3rd to G major. There is no modulation – Auric just launches straight into the new key on the final quaver of bar 8. There are changes to the melody in bar 10 and to the accompanying parts throughout, with woodwind now providing most of the latter.

Keys which are a 3rd apart, such as E major and G major, have a **tertiary** relationship. Note that the extract starts in E major and ends in C major – another pair of keys that are a 3rd apart.

Bars 13–20, Motif B (B minor / B major)

This section starts with a two-bar link in which brass enter on an F♯ against an **inverted tonic pedal** on G in the upper strings, the dissonance drawing attention to the headline, 'Burgundy Issue Splits Britain'. The key then abruptly shifts to B minor (G major to B minor forming another tertiary relationship) for the introduction of motif B in bar 15. Like motif A it clearly underlines the notes of the tonic triad, but it contrasts by being in the bass and consisting of a rising scalic pattern rather than a falling triadic one.

Bar 15 is answered by a repeated dotted rhythm and chirpy wood-wind decoration in bar 16, and is then restated in the tonic major (B major, bar 17), answered in similar fashion in bar 18.

Brass then start to develop the dotted pattern (bar 19) but the idea is immediately dismissed by the violins' cadential phrase in bar 20, which ends with V^7–I in B major. The chord of B major is the dominant of E major and it prepares the way for a return to the opening key.

Bars 21–26, Motif C (E major)

Motif C is heard in the bass against an **inverted dominant pedal** in the strings. Again this is a motif based on notes of a rising tonic triad, but heavily disguised with chromatic decoration – the chord notes are indicated by arrows in the example *right*. And again Auric spins this one-bar idea into a four-bar phrase by varied repetition. The motif is first repeated in sequence, starting on the last quaver beat of bar 22. Then the ascending chromatic semitone idea from motif C (bracketed) is detached and developed into an answering phrase for piccolo and glockenspiel. This time, though, there is no cadence after four bars. Instead, an ascending chromatic scale in the bass (bar 25) leads to a passage of tonal instability.

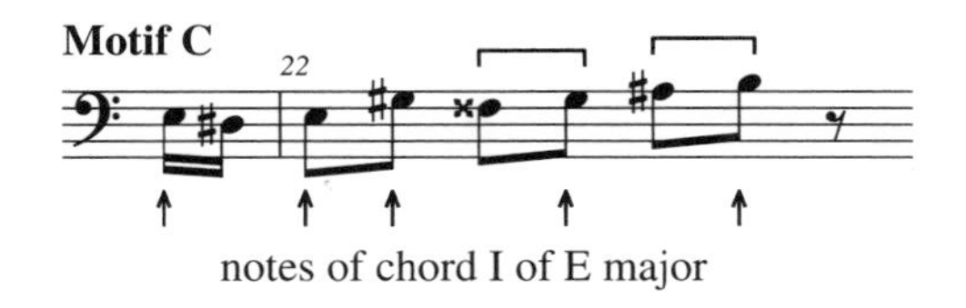

Bars 27–32, Motif D (transition to V of C major)

Motif D (shown *right*) is heard twice in bar 27 and is extended in the next bar. It is heard a compound 5th lower in the bass of bars 29–30, but it gives way to two and a half bars of dominant preparation (bars 30^3–32) for the return of C major in the next section.

Motif D

Bars 33–38, Motifs C and D (C major, ending on V of E♭ major)

Bars 33–34 see a restatement of motif C, shorn of its first three notes, transposed to C major and given a new accompaniment and (in bars 35–36) a new ending to complete a four-bar phrase. Motif D is then heard three times in the bass, starting at the end of bar 36 – but this two-bar link suddenly veers away from C major to finish on the dominant of E♭ major at the end of bar 38.

Bars 39–46, Motif A (E♭ major, then E major)

These two four-bar phrases are a transposed and varied repeat of bars 5–12, but in reverse order. So, bars 39–42 are a transposition to E♭ major of bars 9–12 (with some changes in bar 41). After a perfect cadence in E♭ at the end of bar 42, Auric then leaps straight into E major on the last quaver of the bar for a varied repeat of bars 5–8 in their original key. Notice how the accompaniment at the start of bar 43 is a 3rd lower than in bar 5, in order to emphasise tonic harmony on the first beat of the bar, and how the parallel 3rds are doubled to produce a thicker texture in the first half of this four-bar phrase.

Bars 47–54, Link (E major, then V of C major)

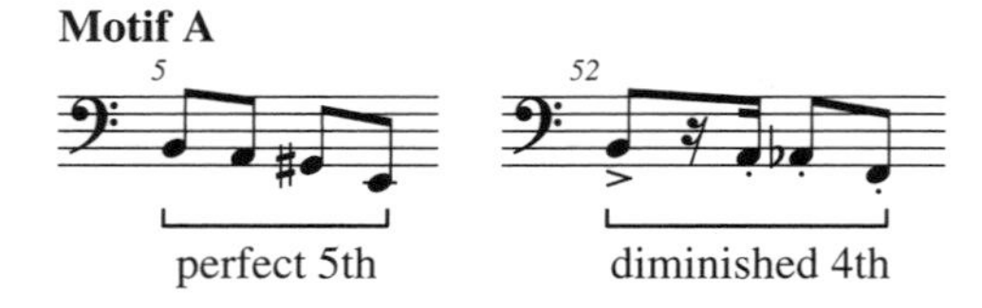

Contrary motion parallel triads in E major in the first two bars of this link hurtle straight into chord V^9 of C major (bars 49–51), the latter decorated with trills between B and C♯ and between D and E (bars 49–50). Auric maintains dominant harmony in the form of chord VII of C major in bars 52–53, again decorated with chromatic trills in the violas. Below this a 'suspense motif' in the bass harks back to the first four pitches of motif A – but they now span a mysterious diminished 4th instead of a perfect 5th because the last of the four has been moved up a semitone (see *left*). In bar 54 a diminished 7th (A♭) is added to chord VII and then the appearance of G (woodwind, then horn) transforms the chord into a dominant minor 9th of C major in preparation for …

Bars 55–65, Motif E (C major)

With considerable tongue in cheek, Auric depicts the arrival of a helicopter with a delicate tune so simple that it could almost be a nursery song. Motif E in bar 55 (shown *left*) is given a varied repeat in bar 56 so that it ends on the dominant. A decorated version of the motif appears in bar 57 and the four-bar phrase is rounded off in bar 58 with a perfect cadence (V9–I) ending, as usual, on the fourth beat of the bar.

A second four-bar phrase begins with another reversal of previously heard material. Bar 59 is a varied repeat of bar 57, and bar 60 is a varied repeat of bar 56 – both are filled-out with extra parts, notably by the oboes in parallel 3rds. Bars 59–60 are then re-orchestrated to form bars 61–62.

A final restatement of motif E (in its bar 57 variant) occurs in the horn part at bar 63, but it is cut short by the trumpet's cadential scale in bar 64 (which is essentially a transposition of bar 8). The final C-major cadence is deliberately weakened by an F♯ from the violas – the only non-diatonic note in the last 11 bars.

Tonality and harmony

Although Auric's preference for **periodic phrasing** (regular phrase lengths terminated by clear cadences) suggests the influence of the classical style, his key scheme does not. The keys of *NAM 42*, outlined above, mostly have a tertiary relationship:

E major – G major – B minor/major – E major –
C major – E♭ major – E major – C major.

This is more a feature of 19th-century music, and the abruptness of most of these key changes is a decidely 20th-century feature – and one that gives this extract much of its sparkling vitality.

Although keys change rapidly and often unexpectedly, each is clearly defined by motifs based on tonic triads and by devices such as pedal points and sections of dominant preparation for a new key – techniques that reflect the classical roots of Auric's style.

But the perfect cadences that reinforce the sense of tonality at phrase ends are not really like those in classical music. Most are extremely rapid, being confined to the last two beats of a 16-beat phrase, and some are coloured by **added notes**. For example, the perfect cadence at the end of bar 12 includes a 9th (E) sandwiched in the middle of its dominant-7th chord and the viola F♯ at the end of bar 64 sounds like a deliberate 'wrong note' to undermine the tonality of the final C-major cadence.

Auric's love of harmonic colour is also seen in his

- Preference for major and minor 7th chords rather than simple triadic harmony – for instance, in bar 64 the first three chords are $I^{maj\,7}$–VII^7–VI^7.
- **Parallel triads**, often in contrary motion, as in bars 47–48.
- Short passages of complex chromatic harmony – for example, the **augmented 6th chord** in the second half of bar 26 resolves irregularly onto B♭^{9} in bar 27, with a dissonant E♮ in an inner part. Similarly, in bars 31–32 the dominant preparation for C major includes the augmented triad of the subdominant (F, A, C♯ at bar 32^{1-2}) over a dominant pedal sandwiched between dominant minor 9ths (bars 31^{3-4} and 32^{3-4}) on either side.

An **augmented 6th chord** is usually built on the flattened 6th degree of the scale (here, C♮) and includes the note an augmented 6th above (A♯). Normally, both chromatic notes would resolve to B as part of chord Ic or V in E major. Auric's resolution to B♭^{9} thus seems delightfully unexpected.

Instrumentation and textures

NAM 42 is presented in **short score**, which doesn't give full details of the orchestration – you may well be able to add more through careful listening. It will be evident, though, that the work is scored for a medium-sized orchestra of woodwind, brass, percussion and strings. Changes in texture and orchestration are as rapid in this work as the contrasts in keys and motifs:

- At the start, **trilling** woodwind and strings, trumpet **fanfares** and cascading horn **scales** (but without any bass instruments) combine to create an exhilarating mood of anticipation.
- The melody in bars 5–6 is orchestrated for flutes and glockenspiel in **parallel 5th and 8ves**. Its busy accompaniment in semiquavers is played by strings in **parallel 3rds**.
- Auric's love of textures involving parallel intervals can also be seen in bar 8, where the contrary-motion scale of E major is harmonised in **parallel 6ths**.
- **Woodwind trills and grace notes** add to the musical activity in order to reflect the lively street scene (bars 9–10).
- A sudden change of texture from **free counterpoint** in bars 5–12 to a single pitch at the start of bar 13 focuses attention on the newspaper headline, and brass enter in stark octaves on a highly dissonant F♯ to punch home its 'shocking' message.

- Low strings and a gurgling bassoon poke fun at the politicians in bar 15 (a **monophonic texture**, despite the octaves). The politicians are answered in the next bar by cheeky comments from different parts of the crowd, illustrated by **antiphonal exchanges** between onbeat strings and offbeat woodwind.
- In bars 21–25 a texture of **melody-dominated homophony** ('tune and accompaniment') features a phrase for bassoon and pizzicato double basses answered four octaves higher by piccolo and glockenspiel. Between the two is sandwiched a rapidly pulsating chordal accompaniment for strings, built around a dominant pedal.
- Tubular bells announce the next headline (bar 31).
- In bars 33–36 a tune in **parallel 3rds and octaves** on woodwind is supported by a chordal accompaniment for strings that clarifies the functional harmony of the passage with clearly separated bass notes.
- The varied repeat of bars 5–6 in bars 43–46 sees a thickening of texture caused by the parallel 3rds being **doubled in octaves**.
- We noticed earlier that parallel triads in contrary motion dominate bars 46–48. The texture between bars 45^4 and 48^2 is not just homophonic, but also **homorhythmic** – in other words, the chords are formed by all parts moving in the same rhythm.
- The off-beat timpani notes in bar 47 are forcefully doubled by bass drum and cymbals (unmarked in *NAM*), and provide one of the few examples of syncopation in the extract.
- The news of a 'deadlock in talks' in the next headline (bar 52) is dramatised by the well-worn combination of trills played by divided violas, and a lugubrious chromatic variant of motif A that descends low in cellos and double basses.

Although many of these devices were the stock-in-trade of film music composers at the time, this doesn't diminish their effectiveness. But Auric's real skill comes in their integration, and in the way he holds our attention through rapid changes in instrumentation and texture (complemented by equally rapid changes of key). For instance, the low-pitched mock-drama of bars 52–53 quickly gives way to the most delicate of orchestral textures in which a piccolo melody is accompanied by pizzicato strings and arpeggiated chords on a **celesta**. This transparent, high-pitched texture provides a vivid contrast with the previous section, as well as ludicrously portraying the 'dainty' arrival of a helicopter!

A **celesta** (printed as 'celeste' in *NAM*) is a keyboard instrument in which the hammers strike metal bars. Compare this doubling of piccolo and celeste with bars 23–25, where the piccolo is doubled by a **glockenspiel** (an instrument with metal bars that are struck directly by the player, using beaters).

As we have seen, Auric makes extensive use of various types of **doubling** in his orchestration. Sometimes melodies are doubled in 3rds or 6ths, but often Auric doubles a part in octaves or even (as in bars 5–6) in 5ths – a technique that can result in distinctive new timbres.

Finally, notice how Auric often lightens orchestral textures by using *pizzicato* strings – some passages are marked in the score, but he also uses pizzicato strings with the opening horn scales and they clarify the bass part throughout much of the extract.

Private study

1. (a) Identify the keys of the following sections in *NAM 42*:
   (i) Bars 1–8 (ii) Bars 9–12 (iii) Bars 19–20.

   (b) What term describes the relationship of these keys?

2. Contrast the textures in bars 19 and 47, describing each with their correct technical term.

3. Identify the chord heard during beats 3 and 4 of bar 54.

4. Bars 55–62 are entirely diatonic. What does diatonic mean?

5. (a) How does a celesta differ from a glockenspiel?

   (b) What precisely is played on the celesta in bars 55–57? (Listen to the recording if you are unsure.)

John Williams, ET (1982): Flying Theme

Special Focus Work 2 for 2008 and 2009

NAM 45 (page 409) CD4 Track 4
City of Prague Philharmonic
Conducted by Paul Bateman

Before starting on this section you should work through (or revise) the information about the context and structure of this music given on pages 114–115 of the AS Guide. Make sure that you understand all of the terminology used on those pages.

Unlike *NAM 42*, which was based on the interplay of short motifs, John Williams' 'Flying Theme' is centred on a single eight-bar melody that is heard five times in the extract, accounting for almost half of its 87 bars. The third of these repetitions is separated from the others by transitional passages on either side. The whole movement starts with an eight-bar introduction and ends with a lengthy coda that makes further references to the main theme (see *right*).

Structure

NAM 45 is not taken directly from the film score of *E.T.* – it comes from a concert suite based on music used in the film.

Bars	*Structure*	
1–8	Introduction	8 bars
9–16	**A** (theme)	8 bars
17–24	**A** (repeated)	8 bars
25–33	**B** (transition)	9 bars
34–41	**A** (in dominant)	8 bars
42–54	**B** (transition)	13 bars
55–62	**A** (in tonic)	8 bars
63–68	**A** (repeated)	6 bars
69–87	Coda	19 bars

The **introduction** consists of a four-note figure for flutes, clarinets and violins, repeated as an **ostinato** over chords $\mathrm{I}^{\text{add 2}}$ (bars 1–2 and 5–6) and $\mathrm{V}^{\text{sus 4}}$ (bars 3–4 and 7–8). Because the notes C, D and G are common to both chords, and the rhythm consists of unvarying quavers, the introduction sounds static, but it obliquely establishes the tonic key of C major. It is also linked to the music that follows by the progression $\mathrm{I}^{\text{add 2}}$–$\mathrm{V}^{\text{sus 4}}$, which anticipates the harmonisation of the first bar of the theme (bar 9).

The **theme** is first heard in bars 9–16 and is repeated, in a more lightly scored version, in bars 17–24. Despite some chromaticism it is essentially in C major.

The **first transition** (bars 25–33) is tonally less stable, but the succession of mainly unrelated triads ends with a diminished 7th chord on the leading note of G major (F♯–A–C–E♭, with E♭ in the bass, in bar 33) that prepares the way for …

The return of the **theme in the dominant key** of G major (bars 34–41). This is the most fully-scored version so far, and includes the three trumpets that were silent in the theme's first appearance.

The **second transition** (bars 42–54) is similar to the first and ends in bars 50–54 with a re-scored repeat of bars 29–33, transposed down a perfect 5th. This means that the diminished 7th in bar 54 is now on the leading note of C major, preparing the way for …

The **fourth statement of the theme** (bars 55–62) now back in the tonic key of C major. This is a repeat of bars 9–16 but with the violins in octaves and some other small changes.

The **fifth statement of the theme** (bars 63–68) is a varied repeat of the second statement, but it is curtailed after six bars in order to make way for …

The **coda** (bar 69 to the end). Initially the tonic key is reinforced by ascending scales of C major and a dominant pedal. But this process is interrupted by the intrusion on the last beat of bar 73 of a very loud E♭ in the bass. This is contradicted at the start of the next bar by an equally loud C-major chord, producing a colossal **simultaneous false relation** between the E♭ in the bass and the E♮ in the tonic chord. Above this discord, the upper woodwind's variants of the opening of the theme features a prominent F♯ that piles on further dissonance.

Williams repeats this passage in bars 76^6–79^5, but then he totally transforms it. The bass admits defeat and sinks to C on the last crotchet of bar 79, leaving pure C-major harmony when the rest of the chord enters in bar 80. And when the variant of the start of the theme appears for a third time in the solo flute and trumpet parts, its previously dissonant F♯ is accommodated within the D^7 chord of bars 82–83. But this chord is purely chromatic – a **tonic pedal** continues from the last beat of bar 79 to the last beat of bar 87, and the movement ends with four bars of serene tonic harmony.

Melody

The periodic phrasing that we saw in much of *NAM 42* is evident again in the structure of John Williams' main theme. It starts with a two-bar idea that outlines the notes of the tonic chord in an elegant arch shape. These two bars are then repeated twice in **free sequence**, followed by a two-bar cadential figure to complete the eight-bar phrase:

When bars 9–10 are freely repeated a tone higher in bars 11–12, the rising 5th of the opening becomes an octave, and the falling 4th at the end of bar 10 is changed to a rising 6th at the end of bar 12. The third statement of the motif is treated even more freely, the E♭ adding a briefly modal tinge. Notice how the succession of top notes (G in bar 9, A in bar 11, B in bar 12 and C in bar 13) climbs inexorably from dominant to tonic of C major, underlining the exhilarating mood of the 'Flying Theme'.

The pattern of varied repetition changes for the last two bars of the theme. Williams shortens the expected semibreve C in bar 14 in order to in order to introduce an anacrusis that propels the phrase to its conclusion. This anacrusis (*y above*) is a rhythmically diminished retrograde (i.e. half note-length and backwards) version of the turn-like figure in bar 9 (*x above*). It leads to a repeat of the falling minor 3rd (E♭–C in bar 15) followed by a cadential figure (*z*) that ends on the leading note.

Although much of *NAM 45* is concerned with varied repetitions of this theme, Williams makes some independant use of the ideas marked *y* and *z*. The first of these reappears in the form of another anacrusis at the end of bar 62, which serves to project the music into the fifth repetition of the theme in the next bar. The distinctive double-dotted rhythm of *z* features prominently in both transitions, at bars 26 (see *below right*), 28, 30, 31, 47, 49, 51 and 52.

The narrow range and mainly stepwise movement of the melody in the two transitions contrasts strongly with the broad sweep and heroic leaps of the main theme. It is based on the two-bar idea first heard in bars 25–26, which is easier to read when re-notated in the key of B major, as shown *right*. This is repeated with fuller scoring in bars 27–28, and then in free sequence an augmented 5th lower in bars 29–30. The second of these bars is repeated in bar 31, after which two bars of quavers provides a link back to the main theme.

The variants of the opening of the main theme used in the coda, starting in bar 75, deserve special mention. The original turn-like figure from bar 9 (*x* in the example *right*) is replaced by six triplet quavers and in both bars includes prominent use of F♯ from the lydian mode on C (C–D–E–F♯–G–A–B–C). In the film score, this variant often accompanies moments of sentiment or sadness. Here it perhaps signals that the magic of the air-borne bicycle ride has come to an end.

Rhythm

The $\frac{2}{2}$ time of the introduction gives way without a change of pulse to $\frac{3}{2}$ time for the main part of the movement. Duple metre returns in the coda, except where references to the opening of the main theme demand the temporary restoration of $\frac{3}{2}$.

Apart from the double-dotted and triplet patterns mentioned earlier, the rhythm is uncomplicated and mostly avoids syncopation. There are continuous quavers throughout almost all of the first 72 bars, the combination of a broad melody and a pulsating accompaniment being one of the fingerprints of Williams' style.

Harmony and tonality

At first glance the overall tonal scheme of starting and ending in the tonic, with a central section in the dominant, seems remarkably conventional. However, Williams tends to use familiar chords in a **non-functional** way – in other words, the harmonies are not there primarily to define keys – and to add dissonant notes to them, so the tonality of the work is not as clear as it at first might seem.

We have already seen that the introduction (and first bar of the theme) are harmonised with the progression I$^{\text{add 2}}$–V$^{\text{sus 4}}$. Because the notes C and G are common to both chords, there is effectively a **double pedal** on tonic and dominant running throughout the introduction and on into the first two bars of the theme, hence the static harmonic mood of this opening.

After another chord of I$^{\text{add 2}}$ in bar 10, Williams keeps the bass on C for one more bar while the harmony above moves to the major version of chord II (D major) – one of his favourite progressions.

This means that the bass note C in bar 11 is the 7th in the chord of D^7, and it resolves by stepping down to B (below a chord of G) in bar 12. However, this is not a modulation – F♯ is cancelled in the very next bar and, in any case, the D^7/C – G/B progression loses clear tonal function through Williams' use of added notes (E in the first chord and F♯ in the second).

But if this is not a modulation, what is the purpose of the chord in bar 11? In terms of C major it is a type of chromatic chord known as a **secondary dominant** – in other words, D^7 is the dominant 7th of the *chord* of G major but not, in this context, of the *key* of G major. We can describe it as 'the dominant of the dominant' or more specifically as V^7d of Vb, with chord Vb itself following in bar 12. Remember that both of these chords contain the added notes mentioned above. However, you can see the underlying harmony of bars 9–16 by reading the trombone, tuba and double bass parts, since all of the added notes are confined to the horns and the right-hand of the piano part.

Williams' preference to anchor the bass part to just three pitches (B, C and D) in bars 9–16, rather than making more use of the roots of different triads to give stronger harmonic direction, is another example of how he uses harmony in a non-functional way.

In bar 13 the C in the bass supports the normal (minor) version of chord II – in other words it is II^7d. Then, to accommodate the E♭ in the melody, another chromatic chord appears in bar 14 – chord ♭VIb (notice that the bass remains stuck on C). Now turn back to the first music example on the previous page, where you will see that this same unusual chord features prominently in the first transition, although there it is in the key of B major. Back in bar 14, notice that Williams doesn't shrink from adding a dissonance to even this chromatic chord – a major 7th (G in the piano and 3rd horn) colours the basic triad of A♭ major.

A whiff of another secondary dominant appears in bar 15 – it is chord $V^{\flat 9}$ of G, but Williams replaces the normal 5th of the chord (A) with A♭ (first horn and piano). And instead of resolving to G in bar 16, the harmony moves straight to the tonic chord of C at the very point where the melody cadences onto the leading note (B), thus concluding the entire eight-bar theme with a very ambiguous cadence that ends on chord $I^{maj\ 7}$.

When you first listened to the theme, did you notice the subtlety of its harmonisation? Probably not, because the listener is swept along by the strength of the heavily-doubled melody, which has harmonic implications far simpler than the complex 20th-century progressions actually used by John Williams.

We cannot analyse the whole of *NAM 45* in this much detail, but there are two other passages to note. In the first transition (bars 25–33) the harmony consists of plain triads without added notes, until the diminished 7th chord in the final bar of the section – although there are, as we saw, chromatic notes in the melody. But tonally this passage is unstable. B major is suggested in the first four bars, but not defined with a cadence, and thereafter the harmony slips through a series of unrelated triads. Finally, in the coda, a **dominant pedal** (bars 69–72, interrupted in bar 71) seems to lead to the tonic key, but its tonal function is frustrated by the bass E♭s and lydian F♯s that ensue. A chord of C major returns at bar 84, over a continuing **tonic pedal**, but there is no cadence to affirm the key, just four bars of sustained tonic harmony.

Texture and instrumentation

John Williams' essentially conservative style is reflected in his use of a traditional symphony orchestra with no unusual or electric instruments and with only very modest use of percussion. Notice, for instance, how the crash cymbal is used to play only two notes in the entire extract – at bar 55, for the most triumphant appearance of the flying theme, and again for its repeat eight bars later.

The textures of *NAM 45* are mainly homophonic – **homorhythmic** in the eight-bar introduction, and **melody-dominated homophony** ('tune and accompaniment') in most of the remainder. In order to give prominence to the main theme on its first appearance it is doubled across three octaves by the woodwind and all of the strings except double basses. The other parts supply a purely supportive chordal accompaniment, articulated in quavers by horns and piano (right hand), but largely sustained in the other parts. Notice that there is nothing particularly idiomatic in the piano part – it is there to fill out the harmony.

E.T. was orchestrated by Herbert W. Spencer, not by the composer (the use of a specialist orchestrator is not unusual in film music). However, John Williams would have been involved in the main decisions about timbres, textures and instrumental effects. For simplicity we have therefore referred only to John Williams in these paragraphs.

When the theme is repeated at bar 17 it is assigned to just unison violins and the texture is lightened with a detached and pizzicato bass line. The violas double the right-hand piano part, playing two semiquavers to each of the piano's quavers, and the clarinets complete the harmonies with a simple quaver pattern. Further variety is provided by a **countermelody** for flutes and bells (heard in alternate bars, starting at bar 18) and a more sustained accompaniment (bassoons and trombones) is added at bar 20.

A further reduction in the density of the texture occurs at the start of the first transition (bar 25). Two flutes play the melody in unison (indicated by 'a 2'), and the chugging quavers are restricted to upper strings and right-hand piano. Gradually the texture fills out again – bassoons and cellos double the flutes at a distance of two octaves below in bars 27–28. The melody then transfers to all four horns and three trumpets in unison, and rolls on timpani and suspended cymbal underpin the crescendo (bars 32–33) that prepares the way for the third appearance of the theme. This is the most fully-scored statement so far, with trumpets (sometimes in unison, sometimes in 3rds) plus bells sharing in the doubling of the melody.

Remember that horns in F sound a perfect 5th lower than written and trumpets in B♭ sound a tone lower. So, while it might not look like it on paper, these parts are in unison in bars 29–33.

The second transition (bars 42–54) is more fully scored than the first. It starts with the melody in octaves on upper strings, supported by most of the rest of the orchestra except upper woodwind, who are held in reserve to take over the melody at bar 46. When they do so, the string parts exploit the contrasts between sustained **tremolo** notes and rising **pizzicato** arpeggios.

The theme is doubled across four octaves when it returns at bar 55, the very high top-violin part being particularly characteristic of the late-romantic style of this type of film scoring.

When the theme is repeated for the last time, Williams adds some brief **imitation** for horns (bar 64).

At the start of the coda **parallel chords** ascend in an imitative texture (bars 69–73) and the lydian version of the 'Flying Theme' is heard twice on upper woodwind against tutti chords, then on solo flute and trumpet in unison. Finally, bells ascend towards distant galaxies on a broken chord of C major.

Private study

1. Complete the blanks in the following account of bars 1–7^3:

   The texture of this section is .... Because there are no chromatic notes the music is entirely .... in the key of C major. The flutes play a four-note .... throughout these bars. It is .... an octave lower by the violins. The clarinets play the same pitches as the .... The sounding pitches of the notes played by horns 1 and 2 in the first bar are .... and .... Dots above and below notes indicate that they should be played .... The cellos play a double .... until the second beat of bar 8. The instruction 'a 2' in the oboe part of this bar indicates that the oboists should ....

2. What helps establish a sense of tonality in bars 1–16 of this work, and what helps to destabilise that sense of tonality? Include the term 'functional harmony' in your answer.

3. What is the main tonal difference between the transitions and the theme?

4. Compare and contrast bars 42–45 at the start of the second transition with bars 25–28 at the start of the first transition.

5. What type of chord is used in bar 54 to introduce another return of the main theme in the next bar?

Sample questions

In the exam there will be three questions on the two special focus works, from which you must answer **two**.

(a) Show how Auric uses repetition in the structure of 'The Siege of Burgundy'.

(b) Discuss John Williams' use of harmony in bars 1–34 of the 'Flying Theme'.

(c) Compare and contrast the variety of musical textures in the two special focus works.

For examination in summer 2008 and 2009

Continuity and change in themes and tonality

You do not need to study this topic unless *Music for film and television* is the Area of Study that you undertook for AS Music and which you are now extending for A2.

Before starting work on this topic you need a thorough understanding of the material on *Music for film and television* in the AS Guide (pages 106–119). Remember that for A2 the topic draws on works from across the **entire** Area of Study, not just those in one of the two lists, A or B.

Remember that tonality refers to the use of (and the relationship between) major and minor keys in music – it has nothing to do with the tone colour of musical sounds. In tonal music, keys are established by cadences, particularly perfect cadence patterns such as V^7–I.

We discussed 'The Siege of Burgundy' in detail on pages 116–120, which you should now revise. In summary, we concluded that:

- Auric captures the lively mood of the film sequence through the use of a number of short, contrasting motifs
- These are often formed from triadic or stepwise patterns based on the first five or six notes of the scale, underlining the strongly tonal style of the music
- Motifs are repeated and manipulated to form phrases that are mainly four bars long
- Some of these melodic phrases are diatonic, others include passing chromaticism, but almost all end with short but clear perfect cadences which confirm the key
- Changes of key are frequent and often seem surprising because they are sudden and unprepared, although this helps reflect the busy action on screen
- Many of the keys have a tertiary relationship, and we noted that the extract begins in E major and ends in C major – a pair of keys that are a 3rd apart.

Auric

NAM 42 (page 369) CD4 Track 1
Royal Ballet Sinfonia
Conducted by Kenneth Alwyn

Bernstein's preference for long melodic lines is in total contrast to Auric's lively treatment of motivic fragments. The opening horn melody begins with a succession of minor 3rds, culminating in a climactic top note in bar 4. Although these are all rising 3rds, this arch-shaped theme has a melancholy quality, largely due to its use of the **blues scale** on F (see *below right* – remember that the horn in F sounds a 5th lower than written).

Bernstein

NAM 43 (page 374) CD4 Track 2
New York Philharmonic
Conducted by Leonard Bernstein

The second part of the melody introduces notes outside this scale (G, A and D sounding pitches in bars 5–6) which hint at a resolution into F major, but the melody is unaccompanied and lacks any sense of definitive cadence (its open-ended quality gives great scope for different treatments later in the suite).

When this theme is heard in two-part canon (bars 7–12), a particularly blues-like clash is heard in bar 11, where the third note of the scale (B♭) in the trombone coincides with the fourth note (B♮, here notated as C♭) in the flutes on the first beat of the bar.

The varied restatement that begins in bar 13 opens with the second half of the theme (bar 13 = bar 4) and ends with a reference to its first half (bar 18 = bar 1). This reversal in the order of previously-heard material is a technique used by Auric (see the note about bars 39–42 of 'The Siege of Burgundy' on page 118), but the effect seems totally different in the context of Bernstein's slow moving theme.

Although the theme in bars 13–19 of *NAM 43* is a 4th higher than the original statement, it is heard over a pedal on F, reinforcing the feeling that that is the tonal centre of the first 19 bars, but there is no cadence in this key – the tonality is deliberately vague.

The Presto Barbaro begins with a riff, which then remains present in one form or another until the coda. The opening interval (G–B♭) reflects the rising minor 3rds heard at the start of the Andante and there is a sense of the tonal centre being G minor because of the

articulated pedal on G in the left-hand piano part. However, there is no cadence in this key and a good deal of dissonance is generated by the constant use of the augmented 4th degree of G minor (C♯) in the second timpani part, and the occasional appearance of the major version of the 3rd degree (B♮) in piano and first timpani.

Remember that the alto saxophone sounds a major 6th lower than written, so the ascending melodic minor scale as notated is G minor: G–A–B♭–C–D–E–F♯–G.

When transposed a major 6th lower, these notes form the ascending melodic scale of B♭ minor: B♭–C–D♭–E♭–F–G–A–B♭.

The alto saxophone solo that starts in bar 42 consists of three four-bar phrases, the first two being similar and the third different. This is a 12-bar blues melodic structure, but there is no sign of a blues chord pattern. The theme is based on the ascending form of the melodic minor scale – a scale widely used by jazz musicians, who often also include a blues-like flattened 5th, as Bernstein does in bars 50 and 51 (D♭, sounding as F♭ in the key of B♭ minor).

Polytonal refers to the simultaneous use of two or more keys.

However, any sense of B♭ minor being the key of this passage is undermined by the impression that the first timpani part revolves around the first and third degrees of G minor, while the second timpani focuses on the first and fourth degrees of C♯ minor. The overall effect is therefore **polytonal** – although note that none of these keys is clearly defined by cadences.

A development of the second and third saxophone phrases starts in bar 54. It is assigned to high wind instruments, transposed up a major 3rd to D minor, but the timpani (now joined by lower strings) remain on their previous pitches, so polytonality continues.

The following bars are concerned largely with the development of short motifs heard earlier. The three-note figure from bar 52 is accompanied by its own inversion in bar 64, and developed over the falling-4th motif (from bar 44) in the bass of bars 66–73. This leads to a central tutti statement of the riff, starting at bar 78, in which the massive superimposed dissonances are **atonal**. A clear sense of tonality is equally evasive in bars 88–105, in which Bernstein develops the falling and rising semitone figures from the saxophone solo (bars 42 and 48).

Finally, the riff ends and the coda (starting in bar 106) opens with a loud and slow restatement of the saxophone motif from bar 52. It is followed by a colossal dissonance that builds upwards from the bass, forming a chord from F, E♭, B, F♯, C and A which is then hammered out in the rhythm of the saxophone motif. When this texture is repeated in the last four bars of the excerpt, the chord is different but the dissonances are as powerful. Because the bass has moved down a semitone between these two discords (from F to E) and the upper part has risen a tone from A to B (forcibly doubled in eight woodwind parts and first trumpet) there is a sense that the music has reached a stopping point. But this is no cadence – the atonality of the final part of *NAM 43* is even more ruthless than the dissonant style of bebop jazz that so influenced Bernstein in the early 1950s.

Goldsmith

NAM 44 (page 388) CD4 Track 3
Conducted by Jerry Goldsmith

The repetition and development of short motifs again forms the main thematic material of *NAM 44*. Particularly notable is the use of the piano figure in bar 4 – it is extended in bars 8–9, it is the basis of the semiquaver riff which starts in bar 11 (and is reused twice later), and it is used to form the ostinato patterns which begin at bar 23.

The other main motivic element is the high sustained violin note that crescendos into an off-beat semitonal dissonance (bars 11–13), a device that is almost the reverse of Bernstein's violin parts on page 384 of the *New Anthology*, except there the dissonances are formed by a tone, not a semitone. This is heard three times at different pitches and is then modified and transferred to trombones from bar 23. In bar 40 the idea is turned on its head – the opening note is reduced to a quaver and the off-beat discord becomes the part of the motif that is sustained, this idea forming the impetus for the repeated semitonal dissonances in the next four bars.

The original form of the motif returns in the horns at bar 45, and forms the foundation for the outburst at bar 52, where the lowest instruments repeatedly rise from E♭ to E♮ against a sustained E♭. Other versions of this motif can be traced throughout the rest of the extract, sometimes much transformed. For instance, in bar 75 the strings open out from a unison G to a minor second on G and A♭, while from bar 84 onwards this idea of an alternating unison and minor 2nd is transformed into a high ostinato pattern of semiquavers in flutes and piccolo.

Goldsmith makes selective use of **serial techniques** in this extract. This is most obvious in the piano part of bars 8–9, where all 12 semitones of the chromatic scale are used in the first 12 notes of these bars. However, Goldsmith had a very ambivalent attitude towards serialism:

For a brief description of **serialism**, see the section headed serial music on page 44 of the AS Guide.

- ✦ He doesn't use this note row systematically throughout the excerpt – it is simply a source for some of the melodic and harmonic ideas employed
- ✦ He doesn't observe the main principle of 12-note music that no one pitch should have pre-eminence over the others.

Before looking at some examples of Goldman's use of the row, you should be aware that in serialism, the notes of a row can appear in any octave. When reading the score, remember that clarinets in B♭ sound a tone lower than written and that the parts for horns and English horns sound a perfect 5th lower than written. Also note that there are *three* English horn parts at the start of the work.

If we examine the use of the note row in the first ten bars of the extract we find that:

- ✦ All 12 notes of the tone row are used to form the three different chords heard in each of bars 1–3 and 5–7 (see *right*). The use of the notes of a tone row to form chords is a serial technique known as **verticalisation**.
- ✦ The piano states the first six pitches of the row in bar 4 and all 12 pitches in bars 8–9.

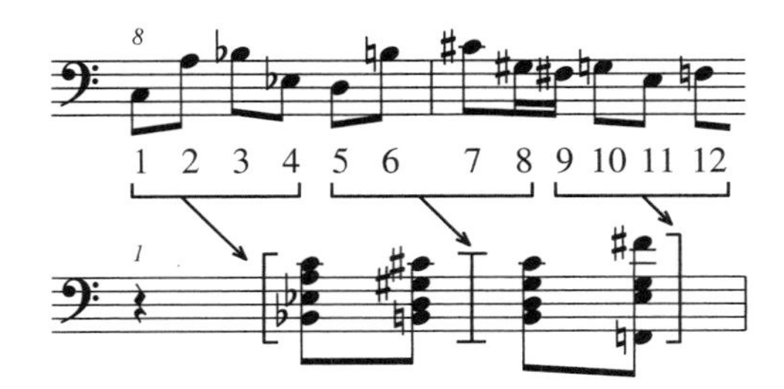

However, the sense of atonality is tempered by an **articulated pedal** on C, played by timpani and piano at the start of every one of the first eight bars. In addition, after stating the 12 chromatic pitches of the row in bars 8–9, Goldsmith adds two more (D♭ and C) which allow the piano solo to return to its starting note (C), and thus reinforcing the impression that C is lurking in the background as the latent tonal centre of the music.

This impression is strengthened still further when a chromatic (but not serial) link in bar 10 takes the music from the tonal centre of C to a new tonal centre on G, starting in bar 11. The first six pitches of the note row are transposed up a perfect 5th to start on G in the left-hand piano part, where they alternate with a minor 3rd on G and E in the right hand to form a one-bar ostinato that is heard throughout bars 11–22.

The idea of moving from an initial tonal centre to the one a perfect 5th higher is one of the planks of tonal music, and is quite unlike traditional serial technique, in which composers consciously try to avoid suggesting such hierarchical relationships.

However, Goldsmith continues to weave serial references into this quasi-tonal fabric. We'll take a look at three short examples taken from the little interjections from piccolo, flutes and xylophone in bars 13–22. It will be much easier to follow the discussion below if you refer to the examples printed *left* as you read it.

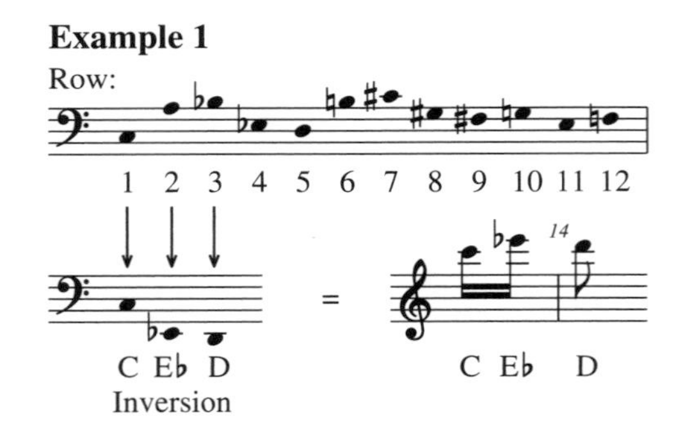

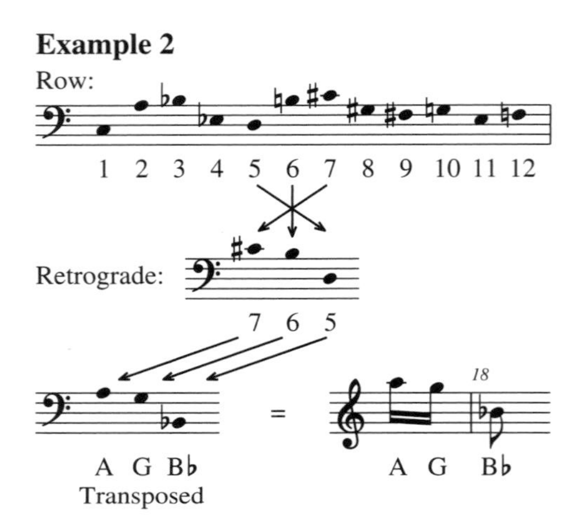

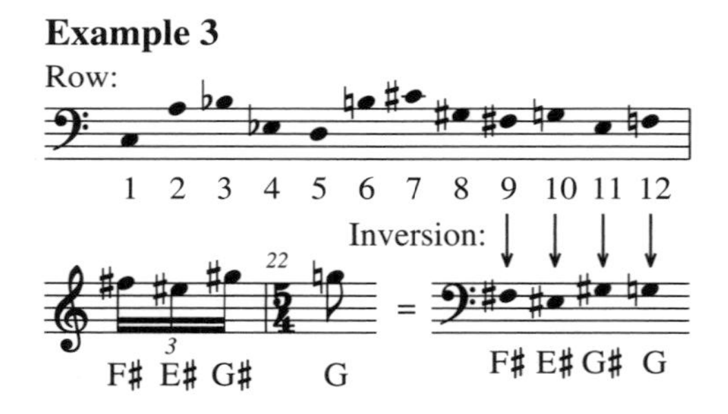

Example 1. The motif in bars 13–14 is formed from the first three notes of the **inversion** of the row. When a row is inverted, rising intervals become falling intervals, and vice versa. So the original row started with a rising major 6th followed by a rising minor 2nd. When inverted, that becomes a falling major 6th followed by a falling minor 2nd.

Example 2. The motif in bars 17–18 is formed from the **retrograde** (i.e. backwards) version of notes 5, 6 and 7 in the row, transposed down by four semitones.

Example 3. The motif in bars 21–22 is an inversion of the last four pitches of the row.

These are all standard procedures in conventional serial music, but what is unusual in *NAM 44* is Goldsmith's application of these manipulations to just a few selected pitches from the row, and his decision to underpin the entire passage by an ostinato figure that incorporates an articulated pedal on G.

In bars 23–38 the first six pitches of the note row are transposed to start on E♭ and form another ostinato, although one that is interrupted for first one bar (bar 26), then two (bars 30–31) and then three (bars 35–37). Sustained E♭s in the trombones give the impression that E♭ has become a new tonal centre, despite the fact that Goldsmith weaves in yet another manipulation of the row.

This is most easily seen in the bassoon part of bars 23–25, which consists of a complete retrograde version of the row, transposed to start on E♭, but mysteriously shorn of its final note (there ought to be a B♭ at the start of bar 26). As if to prove this omission is no accident, Goldsmith then hands the bassoons a complete retrograde inversion of the row (bars 27–29), transposed to start on E♭ (which is enharmonically notated as D♯) and again shorn of its final note (there should be a G♯ in bar 30). Meanwhile, E♭ continues to sound at the start of every bar …

There are many similar examples from later in the excerpt, but by now we have ample evidence of the ways in which a lingering sense of tonality permeates Goldsmith's 'lyrical serialism'.

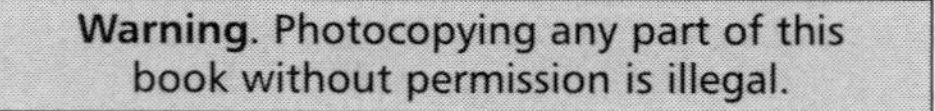

We discussed the 'Flying Theme' in detail on pages 121–125, which you should now revise. In comparison with the short motifs and chromatic intensity of 'The Hunt', John Williams' broad eight-bar theme, presented in the keys of C major and G major seems much more straightforward. However, remember that Williams

- Does not use simple or obvious chord patterns to support his tonal scheme, especially at cadences
- Uses passages of shifting tonality in the transitions, where keys are not clearly defined
- Includes massively dissonant false relations in the coda.

Williams

NAM 45 (page 409) CD4 Track 4
City of Prague Philharmonic
Conducted by Paul Bateman

Pheloung

NAM 46 (page 433) CD4 Track 5
Conducted by Barrington Pheloung

An important feature of the televised *Inspector Morse* series was the use of diegetic music – that is, music which forms part of the action on screen, such as that heard when a character switches on the radio or goes to a concert, rather than background music which is intended purely for the audience and which is not heard by the characters in the drama.

Morse has a particular love of classical music, and so many episodes include substantial excerpts from opera, church or chamber music. Pheloung's choice of an extremely sparse style for the background music helps to avoid any stylistic conflict with the diegetic excerpts from Mozart, Schubert and others with which it shares the sound-track.

NAM 46 is based on the aeolian mode (A–B–C–D–E–F–G) plus two additional pitches (F♯ and A♭) introduced in the second half of the work. In the final bars the music gravitates towards C major, but the tonality remains ambiguous due to a persistent F♯ still sounding in bar 109 and the disappearance of a third from the final chord.

Tonal ambiguity also arises from Pheloung's **non-functional** use of harmony. Chords occur when two or more different notes are heard simultaneously but these arise from the melodic movement of independent parts and do not form harmonic progressions in any conventional sense. There are no cadences (not even modal ones) and chords are often incomplete – for example, the work opens on a bare 4th and ends on an open 5th.

A change of chord is often heralded by one part moving to a dissonance after which the other parts 'catch up' by moving to notes that are concordant with the new pitch. For example, in bar 3 the piano leaps to D, a minor 7th above E in the strings. A beat later, the strings move down to B so that D becomes concordant. The most notable instance of this technique occurs in bar 52, where the piano introduces F♯ against a sustained G in the oboe. After nearly five slow beats, the oboe rises to A, and eventually both parts settle on the notes of a D-major triad until just before the end of bar 64 – but in the absence of any kind of C (sharp or natural) or any sort of cadence, there is no clear sense of modulation.

The music in bars 52–64 shows how Pheloung defines sections by the use of a particular, limited range of pitches. In the first seven bars of the work, the only pitches used were A, B, D and E. In bars 12–31^{2} the only pitches were those from the major pentatonic scale on C (C–D–E–G–A). The strings in these bars are limited to C, D and G, the piano is confined to D, E and A, and the horn spans both groups of notes by using A and G (but no other pitches).

Pheloung's approach to melody is quite unlike that in any of the other works in this Area of Study and stands in striking contrast to the broad sweep of John Williams' 'Flying Theme'. Melodic events in *NAM 46* are often no more than the change from one long note to another against a very static background, rather like the tiny array of rocks on a bed of sand in a Japanese Zen garden.

However, these are not random events. The slow evolution of melodic cells plays an important role in the thematic design of 'Morse on the Case'. For instance, the initial intervals in the piano part (a rising 4th followed by a descending 3rd) are mirrored by an inversion in the strings which is extended into a long sequence of slowly descending 4ths and rising 3rds: E–B–D–A–C–G (the last note in the lower parts only). Meanwhile an extended descending 2nd in the horns (A–G, bars 12–19) is compacted and inverted by the piano and extended to form a three-note figure (D–E–A, bars 17–19) while the first violin answers the horn's falling 2nd with a rising 2nd (C–D, bar 18). The piano then explores the major 2nd played vertically (D and E together, bar 22) which the first violin inverts melodically (D–C, bar 24) at the same time as the second violin returns to the initial rising 4th (G–C).

Bar 26 sees the return of our three-note figure (D–E–A) in the piano, now shrunk to semiquavers, its outer notes also serving as the left-hand accompaniment. Meanwhile the third horn is playing an inversion of this figure (A–G–D) in much longer note values. The close association of tiny intervallic cells like these can be found throughout *NAM 46*, their simplicity often disguised by Barrington Pheloung's use of irregular note-lengths.

Horner

NAM 47 (page 440) CD4 Track 6
City of Prague Philharmonic
Conducted by Nic Raine

Unlike the dissonant, sometimes atonal writing in *NAM 44*, or the modality of *NAM 46*, the music for *Titanic* is unashamedly **tonal**. The first section consists of short passages designed to build-up excitement through the use of techniques such as imitation of rising figures (bars 1–3), repetition of a motif over a rising bass (bars 4–7), ostinato patterns over pedals (bars 8–20) and rising scale figures (starting at bar 21) that culminate in a climax at bar 28.

Equally important in this first section is the use of keys that are a major 3rd apart: E♭ major (bar 1), G major (bar 8) and B major (bar 15). The use of such **tertiary modulations** to produce an exhilarating effect is something of a cliché in film music and one that we met earlier when studying 'The Siege of Burgundy'.

Horner settles on the tonal centre of G major for the first choral section in bars 30–36. This purely diatonic music is underpinned by a **tonic pedal** on G, which briefly gives way for a bass note on the dominant (D) in the second half of bar 33, both features contributing to the strong sense of G-major tonality in this passage.

The music stays in G major for the dance-like refrain beginning at bar 37. It is a theme that appears in different versions at several places in the film. Here the syncopated $\frac{5}{4}$ metre gives it an attractive lilt, but its folk-dance style remains unmistakable. Many of the chords are root-position triads and there is a folk-like reference to the modal flat seventh (a chord of F major) in bars 43–44. The melody is based on the motif heard in bar 37. This is inverted and transposed in bar 38, and restated in varied form a 3rd lower in bar 39. After the imperfect cadence in bar 40, the inverted form of the motif is used to create the sequence in bars 41–43. The third phrase (bars 45–48) sandwiches another version of the inverted motif (bar 46) between two restatements of the original motif.

The choral melody returns (still in G major) at the end of bar 50 but is interrupted in bar 57 by an orchestral variant of the same theme, transposed to the dominant (D major). A quaver figure that tentatively appears in bar 61 gradually takes over, leading to a return of the syncopated folk-dance, now in 6/4 time and in D major. The harmonies are more static here, with a bass on I and V that confirms the new key, although the triad on the flat 7th (C major) is retained to form a modal cadence (♭VII–I) in bars 75–76. After a partial restatement of the folk-dance, Horner slips from D into B major (another tertiary relationship) for the section beginning at bar 86.

This last section is based on another variant of the choral melody. Fragments of it are developed in more varied ways in these final bars – notice the syncopated horn countermelody that briefly emerges in bar 90, the interplay of D♯/ D♮ and the resulting modal-sounding harmonies in bars 93–98, as well as the surprisingly dissonant harmonisation of bars 99–100. Over arpeggiated chords of B major (harps, bars 106–110) and a tonic pedal (strings), a solo horn makes a final reference to the choral melody (now with a chromatic E♯), echoed by flute (doubled by clarinet and glockenspiel). The extract ends on a bare-5th chord (B and F♯).

This version of the choral melody, like the one at bar 51, has the appearance of being augmented, because it is printed with note lengths that are twice the length of those seen in bar 30. However, since the beat is now a minim this is really just a difference in notation.

Private study

1. (i) What makes the opening melody of *NAM 43* sound as though it is based on the blues?

   (ii) This opening melody is treated in canon at bar 7. What precisely is a canon?

2. Every note of the tone row in *NAM 44* is sounded simultanteously on the first beat of bar 42. What term is used to describe notes of a tone row sounded as a chord?

3. Compare the piano part in bars 98–99 of *NAM 46* with that in bars 26–28. How is the piano part of bar 99 varied when it reappears in bar 108?

Sample questions

In the exam there will be two questions on this topic, from which you must answer **one**.

(a) Contrast Williams' use of themes in *NAM 45* with Goldsmith's approach to thematic ideas in *NAM 44*.

(b) To what extent do *NAM 43* and *NAM 46* use tonal techniques?

(c) Compare and contrast the ways in which themes are developed from short motifs in the works by Bernstein and Horner.

Popular music and jazz

There are *three* Special Focus works, *NAM 50*, *NAM 52* and *NAM 57*, all of which must be studied if you are taking the exam in 2008 or 2009.

Most of the music in this area of study was created without the use of detailed notation. The scores in the *New Anthology* are transcriptions, made by notating the music from recordings. It is important to remember that some aspects of live performance, particularly rhythmic placement, are difficult to notate precisely and can often be written in slightly different ways.

Miles Davis, Four

Special Focus Work 1 for 2008 and 2009

NAM 42 (page 468) CD4 Track 9
Miles Davis Quintet

Before starting on this section you should work through (or revise) the information about this extract given on pages 124–125 of the AS Guide. Make sure that you understand all of the terminology used in that section.

Context

Four was originally one of two numbers written by the jazz saxophonist Eddie Vinson for inclusion on Miles Davis' 1954 album *Blue Haze*. It was frequently performed by Davis over the next decade and the extract on CD4 is taken from a live concert at the Lincoln Centre in New York in 1964.

An essential feature of jazz is that every performance is different – often in quite fundamental ways, such as the length of the piece and the ways in which the underlying chord pattern is realised by melodic improvisation. So *NAM 50* doesn't represent a definitive version of *Four* – it is simply the way in which Miles Davis felt moved to interpret the piece on the evening of 12 February 1964.

Four retains some of the hard-edged dissonance of **bebop**, the jazz style pioneered by Charlie Parker in the late 1940s with whom Davis had worked. But it also looks forward to the more intimate style of jazz that became popular in the 1950s. It is essentially an accompanied solo designed to showcase Miles Davis' **virtuoso** skills in improvisation.

Structure

Four is cast in a common type of jazz structure known as a **head arrangement** which is a type of variation form. It begins, often after an introduction (the opening drum solo in *NAM 50*), with a harmonised theme known as the **head**. The sequence of chords that accompanies this theme is called the **changes**. The changes are then repeated a number of times (sometimes with alterations to some of its chords), above which new melodic lines are improvised. Each repeat of the changes is known as a **chorus**.

In *Four* the head consists of 32 bars, divided into four eight-bar phrases in ABAB form:

A (H1) Eight-bar phrase consisting of a four-bar melody that is then repeated in sequence a 5th lower
B (H9) Contrasting four-bar melody which is then repeated
A (H1) Repeat of phrase A
B (H9) Repeat of phrase B but with a new ending.

Each chorus has this same structure, although notice that all 32 bars are written out in full each time, since there are too many alterations in the repeated sections for repeat signs to be used.

Harmony and tonality

Although *NAM 50* is in E♭ major throughout, the harmony appears complex because many chords have added notes and chromatic alterations. However, the underlying chord sequence, which is seen more clearly in the choruses than in the head, is actually fairly simple. In the following table the shaded row shows the basic chord progression with added notes and chromaticisms omitted. The other rows show the actual chords used in the three choruses:

	A								B							
Bar numbers	*1* *17*	*2* *18*	*3* *19*	*4* *20*	*5* *21*	*6* *22*	*7* *23*	*8* *24*	*9* *25*	*10* *26*	*11* *27*	*12* *28*	*13* *29*	*14* *30*	*15* *31*	*16* *32*
E♭ major	I			IV	ii		IV	♭vii	iii		ii	V	iii		ii	V
Chorus 1	E♭ E♭		E♭m^7 E♭m^7	A♭^{7} A♭^{7}	Fm^7 Fm^7		A♭^{7} A♭^{7}	D♭^{7} D♭^{7}	Gm^7 E♭	 C^7	Fm^7 Fm^7	B♭^{7} B♭^{7}	Gm^7 E♭	 B♭^{7}	Fm^7 E♭^{7}	B♭^{7} B♭^{7}
Chorus 2	E♭ E♭		E♭m^7 E♭m^7		Fm^7 Fm^7		A♭^{7} A♭^{7}		Gm^7 E♭	 C^7	Fm^7 Fm^7	B♭^{7} B♭^{7}	Gm^7 E♭	 B♭^{7}	Fm^7 E♭	B♭^{7} B♭^{7}
Chorus 3	E♭ E♭		E♭m^7 E♭m^7	A♭^{7} E♭m^7	Fm^7 Fm^7		 A♭m^7	 D♭^{7}	E♭ E♭		Fm^7 Fm^7	B♭^{7} B♭^{7}	E♭ E♭		Fm^7 Fm^7	B♭^{7} B♭^{7}

We can see from this table that every 16-bar section:

- Begins with two bars of chord I and then moves to the minor form of chord I (with added 7th) in the third bar
- Uses chord ii^7 in bars 5–6 and 21–22
- Contains the progression ii^7–V^7 at the end of its third four-bar phrase (bars 11–12 and 27–28 of each chorus)
- Concludes with either ii^7–V^7 (bars 15–16) or I–V^7 (bars 31–32). This is known in jazz as a **turnaround** – a chord progression, usually ending on chord V^7, which is designed to lead back to the next repeat of the changes.

But as well as similarities there are differences:

- Instead of a change of harmony sometimes the previous chord continues (for example, Chorus 2, bars 4, 8, 20 and 24)
- Sometimes an extra chord is inserted, as in bar 26 of Choruses 1 and 2. This chord (C^7) is known as a **secondary dominant**. It is totally unrelated to the preceding chord of E♭, but it launches a route back to E♭ by means of a partial **circle of 5ths** progression (C^7–Fm^7–B♭^{7}–E♭ in bars 26–29).

A **secondary dominant** is the dominant of the *chord* that follows (here, F minor) rather than being the dominant of a new key.

- Sometimes a chord is changed to one that has a similar tonal function. This is known as a **substitution chord** in jazz. For example, bars 25 and 29 in the first two choruses both contain chord I (E♭) instead of iii^7 (Gm^7). In the third chorus, E♭ has totally replaced Gm^7 at this position in the changes, being used in bars 9 and 13 as well as in bars 25 and 29.

Chords are described as having a similar tonal function if they both come from the same group of chords – either the tonic group (I, iii and vi), or the dominant group (V, vii and V^7) or the subdominant group (IV, ii and ii^7).

Now look at the chord symbols printed above the trumpet stave in the head. They are summarised in the next table:

	A								B							
Bar numbers	*1* *17*	*2* *18*	*3* *19*	*4* *20*	*5* *21*	*6* *22*	*7* *23*	*8* *24*	*9* *25*	*10* *26*	*11* *27*	*12* *28*	*13* *29*	*14* *30*	*15* *31*	*16* *32*
E♭ major	**I**			**IV**	**ii**		**IV**	**♭vii**	**iii**		**ii**	**V**	**iii**		**ii**	**V**
Head	E♭ E♭		E♭m^7 E♭m^7	A♭^{7} A♭^{7}	Fm^7 Fm^7		A♭m^7 A♭m^7	D♭^{7} D♭^{7}	Gm^7 Gm^7	F♯m^7 B^7 F♯m^7 B^7	Fm^7 Fm^7	B♭^{7} B♭^{7}	Gm^7 Gm^7 F♯m^7 B^7	F♯m^7 B^7 Fm^7 B♭^{7}	Fm^7 E♭	B♭^{7} E♭

We can see that the head is based on the same chord sequence as the choruses, but there are two important differences:

- ✦ Bars 10, 14 and 26 each contain two different chords (thus quickening the harmonic pace) which form the progression F♯m^7–B^7. Although totally unexpected in this key, at such a fast pace this has the effect of only momentarily defocusing a sense of tonality.
- ✦ The entire chord progression in bars 13–16 (the 'first time' bars) is condensed into just two bars, over a chromatically descending bass, on the repeat (bars 29–30). This allows tonic harmony (E♭) to replace the turnaround for the short solo break in bars 31–32.

Much of the dissonance typical of bebop arises from the technique of **playing away from the chord**. There are a number of examples throughout *Four*, including:

- ✦ Bar 1.4, where the chord is A♭^{7}. The bass plays notes either side of the root – G, B♭ and B♭♭ (=A♮) – but entirely avoids A♭ itself.
- ✦ Bars 3.9–3.10, where the chord is E♭ but Miles Davis begins in A major, even touching on a highly dissonant E♮ in bar 3.10, and then includes both G and A♮ above the Fm^7 chord in the next bar.

The first eight bars of the head reveal how the basic harmonies of *Four* are elaborately varied from the outset. The chord pattern of the first four bars is | E♭ | E♭ | E♭m^7| A♭^{7} |. The pianist begins by adding a major 7th and a major 9th to the tonic chord (E♭$^{\Delta 9}$) and then piano and bass rise through the chromatic progression Fm^7–F♯$^{dim\,7}$ to a first inversion of E♭$^{\Delta 9}$ (G in the bass) in bar H.2. All four chords are very short and are **pushed** (that is, played just before the beat). The combination of all these factors results in the E♭ tonality of the music emerging only gradually, rather than being stated obviously from the outset.

When the opening four bars are repeated sequentially in bars H.4–H.8, the melodic sequence in the solo part is a perfect 5th lower. However, the free harmonic sequence in the accompaniment begins a major 2nd higher, (chords based on F, G, A♭ and F, rather than on E♭, F, F♯ and E♭) thus adding to the harmonic complexity. The solo melody in bars H.5–H.6 outlines the notes of an E♭-major triad, so at first sight it seems to bear little relation to the underlying F-minor harmony. However, it actually centres on notes that are a 7th, 9th and 11th above the root (see *left*), thus maintaining a relationship, albeit a dissonant one, with the underlying harmony.

Such melodic focus on the upper extensions of chords (particularly the 7th, 9th, 11th and 13th), rather than on the notes of the basic triad, is one of the main characteristics of bebop, pioneered by Charlie Parker with whom Miles Davis worked in the 1940s.

Melody and rhythm

The theme is based on the three-note scale figure heard at the start of the head, and has a modest compass of a 10th, in the middle range of the trumpet. The fragmentary, scalic nature of this material is the trigger for an exploration of scalic figures over a much greater melodic range in the first two and a half choruses. Many of these involve chromatic patterns, although Davis has a particular preference for a gapped chromatic descent that avoids the flattened 7th (D♭), as in bars 1.1, 1.14, 1.29, 2.2–2.3 and 2.22.

The predominantly quaver-based scalic style of improvisation gives way to longer note values where Davis needs space to demonstrate other aspects of his trumpet technique (see Instrumentation *below*). Towards the end of *NAM 50* longer note lengths are used for the first significant exploration of wide leaps in bars 3.19–3.24. As the extract fades out, quavers return, but in a new pattern of repeated notes on single pitches.

Although the **C** time signature suggests $\frac{4}{4}$, the tempo is so fast that *Four* is felt as being **duple metre** (two minim beats per bar). The rhythm is highly **syncopated**, particularly in the head where many of the chords are **pushed** (that is, sounded just before a downbeat). This, together with melodic phrases that neither start nor end on the first beat of a bar, makes it difficult to sense the pulse in the first half of the head. A clearer sense of the beat arrives with the tentative introduction of a **walking bass** in the second half of the head, and thereafter the regular crotchets of this walking bass combine with the drum part to provide a firm rhythmic backing against which Miles Davis can develop his own syncopations.

Instrumentation and texture

Of the five instruments in this excerpt, the tenor saxophone is heard only in the head. There it **doubles** the trumpet an octave lower, indicating that the head is a pre-composition, even though the choruses are improvised.

The type of piano playing in the extract is known as **comping** – a jazz term derived from 'accompanying' and indicating a chordal, non-melodic style of accompaniment. The part is rhythmically varied – often syncopated and staccato – but it doesn't have a soloistic role in this excerpt from the complete piece.

The bass part is played **pizzicato** on a double bass. After the composed head it maintains a walking bass pattern that elaborates the harmonies of the changes. Occasionally the bassist explicitly outlines the harmony with a simple broken-chord pattern, such as the G-minor triad in bars 1.9–1.10^{2}, but more commonly harmony notes are filled-in with passing notes and other forms of melodic decoration to produce a more conjunct line. Like Miles Davis, bassist Ron Carter focuses on higher chord extensions rather than the chord itself, as in bar 1.8, where E♭ is the 9th, and B♭ the minor 13th, of D♭7. Carter entirely avoids the root and 3rd of the chord in this bar. As mentioned earlier, he also occasionally plays away from the chord entirely, as in bar 1.4 where the bass notes are a semitone below, and a tone and semitone above, the root of the chord.

The drummer sets the tempo in his introductory solo, after which he plays a supportive role, maintaining a steady beat played with sticks on a ride cymbal, and punctuating melodic phrases with short fills and rim shots on the snare drum.

Miles Davis uses a range of extended instrumental techniques in his playing, including

- A deliberately **split note** (bar H.31)
- A short downward slide called a **fall-off** (bar 1.15)
- **Pitch bend** (bars 1.19–1.20)
- A **ghost note** (the bracketed note in bar 2.1)
- A **quarter tone** (indicated by an arrow on the ♮ in bar 2.31)
- **Half-valving** (partially opening a valve to produce a note of thin tone and uncertain pitch, indicated by diamond-headed notes in bar 3.32).

The texture of the head and choruses can be described as **melody-dominated homophony**, with a tune in the trumpet part and an accompaniment provided by a walking bass part and comped piano chords. Variety is provided by the doubling of the melody at the lower octave by tenor saxophone during the head, and by occasional changes in the tessitura of the parts, such as the high bass part (indicated by an ottava sign) starting in bar 1.21 and the very high trumpet part at the start of the third chorus.

? Private study

1. What is meant by the following expressions used in jazz?
   (i) the changes (ii) playing away from the chord
2. What type of chord is played by the pianist on the last quaver of bar H.1?
3. Explain each of the following terms: (i) secondary dominant (ii) substitution chord (iii) head arrangement (iv) comping
4. What do you understand is meant by the word 'virtuosity'?
5. When bars H.1–H.4 are repeated in sequence to form bars H.5–H.8, what is the main difference between the melodic sequence in the trumpet part and the free harmonic sequence in the accompaniment?
6. Comment on the differences between the four 'first time' bars at the end of the head, and the four bars that replace them when the head is repeated.

Special Focus Work 2 for 2008 and 2009

NAM 52 (page 477) CD4 Track 11
Carl Perkins (vocal, guitar)
James 'Buck' Perkins (rhythm guitar)
Lloyd 'Clayton' Perkins (upright bass)
W. S. Holland (drums)

Carl Perkins, Honey Don't

Before starting on this section you should work through (or revise) the information about this song given on pages 126–127 of the AS Guide. Make sure that you understand all of the terminology used in that section.

Context

Honey Don't was one of four songs recorded by the Perkins Brothers in late 1955 at Sun Studios in Memphis, Tennessee, where Elvis Presley had recorded his earliest songs. The original recording was in mono (not stereo) and involved making several complete takes of the entire song on a single track, since the studio did not have one of the new multi-track tape recorders that were just starting to appear around this time.

The best of the takes was selected for release in January 1956 as the B side to Carl Perkins' *Blue Suede Shoes*. It was issued in the still relatively new format of a seven-inch vinyl single (playing at 45 rpm) and in the much older, and fast disappearing, format of a ten-inch shellac record (playing at 78 rpm).

Due to the success of *Blue Suede Shoes*, which became a number one hit, the record had sold more than a million copies by May 1956. But by then a serious car accident had brought a premature end to the performing career of the group. Although Carl survived, he was to see his most famous song, *Blue Suede Shoes*, covered by Elvis Presley. *Honey Don't* was also later to be covered by others, including the Beatles in 1964.

Instrumentation and texture

Carl Perkins sang the vocal and also played the lead guitar part on an electric guitar, using a plectrum (also known as a guitar pick). The distinctive echo on the guitar part was produced by feeding the signal through a device equipped with a loop of tape on which the sound was recorded and immediately replayed via a series of closely-spaced playback heads, producing repeated tiny delays of the original signal.

The lead guitar has a short solo at the start and two solo **breaks** (starting in bars 30 and 74). Both of these feature patterns in **parallel 4ths**, played on the two top strings of the guitar (which are tuned a 4th apart). During the verses the lead guitar punctuates phrases, as in bars 7–13. Elsewhere it doubles (and occasionally elaborates) the bass part, as in bars 14–29.

Jay Perkins plays the entirely chordal rhythm guitar part on an acoustic guitar. During the verses it punctuates phrases in parallel with the lead guitar. Elsewhere it fills out the backing with four strums per bar of the current chord.

The bass part is played pizzicato by Clayton Perkins on an **upright bass** (that is, a double bass) – the electric bass guitar was not widely used before the 1960s. During the verses the bassist plays the root notes of the chords in the same punctuating rhythm as the two guitars. Elsewhere, he plays a **walking bass** in crotchets. Unlike the walking bass in *Four*, this consistently and clearly outlines the harmony by arpeggiating notes of the current chord.

The x-headed notes in the bass part (for example, in bars 32–36) indicate places where the string has been plucked so hard on the previous note that it snaps back to produce a percussive hit on the fingerboard. This technique, known as **slapping**, is one of the characteristic sounds of rockabilly bass playing.

Sometimes the bass part is entirely triadic, as in bars 38–45. When decoration is introduced, it is simple and leaves the functionality of the harmony totally clear. For instance, in bars 37–38 the progression from dominant (B) to tonic (E) is filled-in with descending passing notes. The main form of decoration, though, can be seen in bars 16–17, where the bassist adds a minor 7th (D♮) to the chord of E major, approaching and quitting it by means of passing notes on C♯. The resulting arch-shaped walking bass pattern, which is a cliché of much popular music of the 1950s, is heard three times and is then applied to the chord of A major in bars 22–23.

The Perkins brothers were used to performing country music in the traditional manner without a drummer. Shortly before their second recording session they realised that their new rockabilly style would benefit from the sort of drum backing commonly used in rhythm and blues, and so they drafted in W. S. Holland, a friend of Clayton Perkins. Astonishingly, Holland had never touched a drum kit until the week before the recording.

Despite Holland's inexperience, he went on to become one of the most influential drummers in early rock, earning the nickname 'Fluke' as a result of this meteoric rise to fame. He was still recording in 2006.

The drum part is in the style of rhythm and blues, and is based on the pattern first heard in bars 4–5:

- Bass drum on beats 1 and 3
- A strong **backbeat** on beats 2 and 4, played on the snare drum
- A cymbal pattern with **swung quavers** on beats 2 and 4.

In the verses variety is produced by reserving the bass drum for the first beat of alternate bars and for reinforcing the punctuating rhythm that occurs between phrases (as in bars 7, 9, 11 and 13).

As explained on page 127 of the AS Guide, the passages in which the lead guitar plays a decorated version of the bass part create a **heterophonic texture** between these two specific parts.

The texture of the song (excluding the short introduction) can be described as **melody-dominated homophony**, in which variety is achieved by replacing the voice with the lead guitar in the instrumental breaks and by placing much of verse 3 (bars 49^4–57^3) in a higher vocal register than the first two verses. Otherwise, there is little variety in the texture, with each of the accompanying instruments maintaining basically similar patterns throughout.

Tonality, harmony and structure

Although composed only a year after the original version of *Four*, the harmony of this rockabilly song is much more straightforward than the complex modern jazz style of *NAM 50*. Like *Four*, it is in the same key throughout but its use of simple **functional harmony** (mainly chords I, IV and V^7 in root position) makes the home key of E major crystal clear. And although *Honey Don't* includes some chromatic inflexions, these are far simpler than those in *Four*.

The final chord is coloured by an added 6th (E^6), but this simple embellishment makes no impact on the clear chord progressions of the rest of the song.

At the heart of these differences is the fact that *Honey Don't* is a popular song of its day, aimed at a wide market, while *Four* is a sophisticated piece of modern jazz aimed at a specialist audience of keen fans.

But *Honey Don't* has a sophistication of its own. It has a **verse-and-chorus** structure, in which an eight-bar verse and a 16-bar chorus together form a 24-bar unit that ingeniously spans two 12-bar blues chord progressions:

	Verse								Chorus			
Bars 6–17:	E	E	C	C	E	E	C	C	B^7	B^7	E	E
Bars 18–29:	E	E	E	E	A	A	E	E	B^7	B^7	E	E
	Chorus (continued)											

The second of these progressions (bars 18–29), is a fairly standard 12-bar blues pattern in E major, although the influence of western harmony is felt in the strongly functional harmony of the last four bars, where B^7–B^7–E–E is preferred to the V–IV–I–I (B–A–E–E) pattern that would be more typical of a traditional blues.

The first of the 12-bar blues progressions *above* is more unusual because a chord of C major replaces the key chord in bars 3–4 and 7–8 of the pattern, between which the harmony returns to E major.

We encountered substitution chords in *Four*. Here, the appearance of chord ♭VI (C) reflects the influence of American country music, the style from which (with rhythm and blues) rockabilly evolved, although this chord also conveniently supports the conventional blue third (G♮) of the melody in these bars.

The use of eight- and 16-bar sections is an inheritance from older styles of western popular music. In contrast, the 12-bar blues was a structure associated with black music. By creating a fusion of the two, Perkins was able to broaden the appeal of his rockabilly style.

Introduction (bars 1–5)
The lead-guitar solo announces the dominant (B) and tonic (E) in a pattern of 4ths above a descending chromatic bass (B–A♯–A♮). This prepares for the entry of the rest of the band in bar 4, who immediately confirm the tonic chord of E major and outline two bars of the bass and drum pattern that will dominate the rest of the song. The clear tonal direction of this opening is nothing like the elusive sense of tonality created by the complex harmony at the start of the head in *Four*.

Verse 1 (bars 6–13) and chorus (bars 14–29)
The first appearance of the main 24-bar pattern described *above*.

Verse 2 and chorus (bars 6–29 repeated)
A repeat of the first verse, with some changes to the vocal melody, mainly to incorporate the different scansion of the new lyrics. Both text and music are repeated in the chorus, which has a slightly modified ending indicated by the 'second bars' sign.

Instrumental 1 (bars 30–49)
The guitar solo starting in bar 30 uses a clever contraction of the 24-bar chord scheme, cutting the first blues pattern down to eight bars and substituting B^7 for C in the eighth bar (bar 37) in order to move straight into the second pattern:

Bars 30–37:	E	E	C	C	E	E	C	B^7				
Bars 38–49:	E	E	E	E	A	A	E	E	B^7	B^7	E	E

Verse 3 (bars 49^4–57^3) and chorus (bars 57^4–73)
The melodic outline of this verse differs from the first two because Perkins creates a climactic effect by centering it around E an octave higher than previously. It is not a simple transposition, though. For example, when the chord changes to C major in bars 52–53 and 56–57, the vocal part rises a major from C♮ to E, losing the characteristic blues effect of the falling minor 3rd from G♮ to E in the first two verses. Verse 3 also differs from verse 2 (although not verse 1) by starting with an anacrusis (or 'pick-up') at the end of bar 49 – a feature that Perkins also reflects at the start of the chorus.

However, despite these differences, the chords are the same as the earlier verses, and the rhythms are similar, so this section still sounds like a modified verse rather than new material.

Instrumental 2 (bars 74–83) and coda (bars 83–96)
These two final sections together span another modified repeat of the complete 24-bar chord pattern. The instrumental, which reuses the parallel 4ths idea of the first break, sees the first blues pattern reduced to ten bars by omitting the eighth and tenth bars of the

chord sequence. The coda uses the second blues pattern, extending it to 13 bars by prolonging the final chord. The end of the song is signalled by a brief chromatic descent (B–B♭–A–G♯) in bars 94–95 of the lead guitar part.

The end of the instrumental overlaps with the start of the coda in bar 83. This bar is extended to six crotchets beats in $\frac{3}{2}$ time in order to incorporate a longer anacrusis ('Well, little honey') at the start of the vocal.

Melody

The vocal melody is firmly centred on E (the tonic) and is mostly **disjunct** with leaps to and from other chord notes. Much of the melody uses just four pitches (E, G♮, B and D♮) from the blues scale on E with its distinctive **blue notes**, G♮ (the minor 3rd) and D♮ (the minor 7th). Perkins occasionally uses the raised form of these two pitches (G♯ in bars 39–40 and a possibly unintentional D♯ in bar 58). Both C♮ and C♯ also appear, but the second and fourth degrees of E major (F♯ and A) are entirely avoided in the vocal part.

The vocal melody in the verses consists of four two-bar phrases, and the marked differences between these in the three verses suggests that much of the vocal part might have been **improvised**.

Notice that Carl Perkins starts the first and second choruses on E, despite the underlying chord of B^7 (bar 14), but in the third chorus the same harmony pulls him down to D♯ (bar 58).

The melody in the choruses is fragmentary (mostly one-bar patterns separated by rests) and is even more tightly glued to the tonic. In the first two choruses, two-thirds of the pitches are E and in the third chorus decoration is removed to produce a **monotone** (a repeated single pitch) on E from bar 60 to the first beat of bar 65.

The word-setting throughout the song is **syllabic** (one note per syllable) and the inclusion of nonsense syllables, such as 'ba ba ba' in the third chorus, reinforces the feeling that Perkins improvised some of the vocal part, adapting melodic formulae from the blues to fit the pre-set chord pattern.

Rhythm

Honey Don't has a clear quadruple-metre pulse (except for the single bar of $\frac{3}{2}$ time mentioned above) that is reinforced by the simple drum patterns and the steady crotchets of the rhythm guitar and walking bass. The punctuating rhythm between phrases in the verses provides variety and withing each crotchet beat, shorter rhythms are **swung**, as had been the practice in most popular music for many years.

The main feature of the swung rhythm is the pattern  which is notated as ♪. ♬ in the score.

Against this firm backing Perkins makes much use of **syncopation** in the vocal part (for example, bars 15, 17, 21 and 23), becoming increasingly adventurous in the final chorus – compare bars 61–64 with bars 17–20, noticing how he fills beats that were previously silent. Similarly, Perkins makes much use of syncopation in the patterns of parallel 4ths for lead guitar in the instrumental breaks.

?

Private study

1. How many *different* chords are used in *Honey Don't*?
2. Compare the use of a walking bass in *NAM 50* and *NAM 52*.
3. What influences of the blues can you find in *NAM 52*?
4. What term describes the type of word setting in *Honey Don't*?

Oasis, Don't Look Back in Anger

Special Focus Work 3 for 2008 and 2009

NAM 57 (page 509) CD4 Track 15
Oasis

Before starting on this section you should work through (or revise) the information about this extract given on pages 131–132 of the AS Guide. Make sure that you understand all of the terminology used in that section.

Context

Oasis is a rock group formed in Manchester in 1991 by Noel Gallagher (lead guitarist) and his younger brother Liam (vocalist). The band also includes rhythm guitar, bass guitar and drums, the players of which have changed over the years. Oasis rose to fame in 1994 with the release of their first album, *Definitely Maybe*, and quickly became known as one of the leading bands in the Britpop movement of the mid-1990s. Britpop was a reaction against the electronic dance music and American grunge bands that were then in vogue, and found its inspiration in the music of guitar-based British pop groups of the 1960s, such as the Beatles and the Kinks.

Don't Look Back in Anger comes from Oasis' second album, *What's the Story (Morning Glory)?*. Released in October 1995. it went straight to number one in the UK album charts, and four of its tracks became hit singles, including *NAM 57*, which was released as a single in February 1996. *Don't Look Back in Anger* has become a much-loved number at Oasis' live concerts, at which the audience is often encouraged to join in singing the chorus. It reflects several important musical features of the Britpop style:

- A lyrical vocal melody
- Regular four-bar phrasing
- Simple root-position chords
- A verse-and-chorus structure
- An instrumentation based around guitars and drum kit.

The lyrics, too, are characteristic of Britpop, with their nostalgic tale of a relationship that has faded away.

Noel Gallagher's song-writing was influenced in particular by the Beatles, and this song includes two acknowledgements of the debt:

- The alternation of broken chords of C major and F major for piano in the introduction, along with the little semiquaver figures at the end of the second and fourth bars, recalls the introduction to John Lennon's song *Imagine* (although there are several differences in detail).
- The lyric in bars 13–16 is said by Noel Gallagher to be a quotation of John Lennon's own words, taken from his privately tape-recorded memoirs.

Texture and instrumentation

The texture of the song is **melody-dominated homophony**, in which the voice is supported by a chordal accompaniment on piano, guitars and organ. A dense **wall of sound** is created through the use of a busy and low bass part (as in bars 13–24), repeatedly strummed guitar chords (the quaver and semiquaver rhythms shown in bar 5 form a template for much of the rest of the song), the use of a low register for the piano (both staves are in the bass clef) and a recording that is bass-heavy and uses a good deal of reverberation.

The scoring is reduced from bar 59 onwards, and the heavy bass fades away, resulting in a much more transparent texture for the ending, although all instruments return for the quiet final chord.

From bar 13, the texture is thickened by strings in octaves, and later in four-part chords, again in a low range. These appear to be sampled sounds, played on a **mellotron**, an instrument that uses a keyboard to trigger the playback of sounds recorded on loops of tape. The mellotron was used by a number of British pop groups in the 1960s and its presence here is another indication of Oasis' respect for the music of that era.

Variety is provided by the instrumental section in bars 33–34, in which the singer makes way for a lead-guitar solo improvising on the chords of the first half of the chorus. The lead guitar also provides a link (bars 33–35) before the second verse, and often plays short **licks** between vocal phrases, as in bars 14, 16, 18 and 24. The mild distortion on this part is another technique that is more redolent of the 1960s than of the heavily-distorted guitar parts common in the 1970s and 80s.

The bass-guitar part is entirely functional, being mainly confined to the root of the current chord, with only minimal decoration.

The drums enter in the middle of bar 4 with a **pick-up** (anacrusis) to introduce the vocal. They maintain a steady beat throughout most of the song, with bass drum on beats 1 and 3 and snare drum emphasing the **backbeats** (beats 2 and 4). However, the part is a good deal more complex than the drum part in NAM 52, and both bass and snare drum have additional notes in each bar. Short **fills** on the tom-toms project the music forward at the end of sections (as in bars 12 and 24), and there is a one-bar solo drum break in bar 44. Continous semiquavers on tambourine are added to the basic drum-kit part in several sections.

Tonality and harmony

The song is in C major throughout, with a clear sense of tonality resulting from the use of repeated progressions of **root-position chords**. Each is four bars long, and together they form the building blocks of the entire song:

Pattern A	C G	Am E	F G	C Am G
Pattern B	F Fm^7	C	F Fm^7	C
Pattern B^1	F Fm^7	C	G	G♯dim
Pattern C	Am G	F	G	G

If pattern A sounds familiar, it is because it is a variant of the chord progression heard 28 times in succession in Pachelbel's famous Canon in D which, in the key of C major, is:

| C G Am Em | F C F G |

Pachelbel's harmonies have, in fact, become a standard chord progression used in many pop songs, most notably in The Farm's 1991 hit, *All Together Now*, revived as England's anthem for the Euro 2004 football cup. Noel Gallagher's version differs from Pachelbel's towards the end and also in his choice of the major version of chord III (E major instead of E minor) as the fourth chord.

There are only two other chromatic chords in the entire song:

- Fm⁷ in pattern B is a substitution chord for F major
- G♯ dim at the end of pattern B¹ acts like a secondary dominant to lead into the chord of A minor at the start of pattern C – G♯ dim is chord vii in the key of A minor, but there is no modulation to this key because G♮ returns almost immediately.

All of the other chords are diatonic. In marked contrast to *NAM 50*, few chords have 7ths or any other sort of added note, but the vocal melody adds frequent passing dissonances.

Structure

The chord patterns discussed *above* are arranged as follows to create a **modified verse-and-chorus form** for the entire song:

		Bar numbers	*Chord pattern*
Introduction	4 bars	1–4	B (but with chords of F instead of Fm⁷)
Verse 1	8 bars	5–8	A
		9–12	A
Pre-chorus	12 bars	13–16	B
		17–20	B¹
		21–24	C
Chorus	8 bars	25–28	A (with new melody)
		29–32	A (omitting 4th bar)
Link	4 bars	32–35	A (last bar of chorus overlaps with start of link)
Verse 2	8 bars	Repeat of bars 5–12 with new words	
Pre-chorus	12 bars	Repeat of bars 13–24	
Chorus	8 bars	Repeat of bars 25–28 followed by	
		29–32	A (now completed in the 2nd-time bar)
Pre-chorus (instrumental)	12 bars	33–36	B
		37–40	B¹
		41–44	C
Chorus	8 bars	45–48	A
		49–52	A
Chorus	9 bars	53–56	A
		57–61	A¹ (C G | Am | F | Fm⁷ | Fm⁷)
Coda	4 bars	62–65	A² (C G⁷ | Am E | F G♯dim (G⁷ᵇ⁹) | C)

Because of the way the final chorus merges into the coda, it could equally well be argued that the latter starts with the change to a slower tempo in bar 58.

In the previous choruses the **title hook** (that is, the phrase sung to 'Don't look back in anger') ended over a chord of F major. In bar 60 a modification of pattern A leaves the voice suspended over a chord of Fm⁷, the chromatic chord that earlier coloured pattern B. As in bars 13, 15 and 17, it resolves to the tonic chord, but here we can savour its evocative effect more thoroughly, since it is sustained for two full bars at a slow tempo.

The final appearance of pattern A in bars 62–65 is also modified. In the second half of bar 64 the expected chord of G is replaced by G♯ dim – the chromatic chord from the end of pattern B¹. But here it is heard simultaneously with a chord of G^7 in the lead guitar, and when the bass enters on a G♮ at the end of the bar, it becomes clear that the two chords together form a dominant minor 9th ($G^{7\flat 9}$) in which the minor 9th (A♭) is enharmonically spelled as G♯ (see *left*). This dominant dissonance gives a poignant twist to the final vocal motif '... least not today' before resolving to the tonic and thus allowing the song to come to rest on a quiet chord of C major.

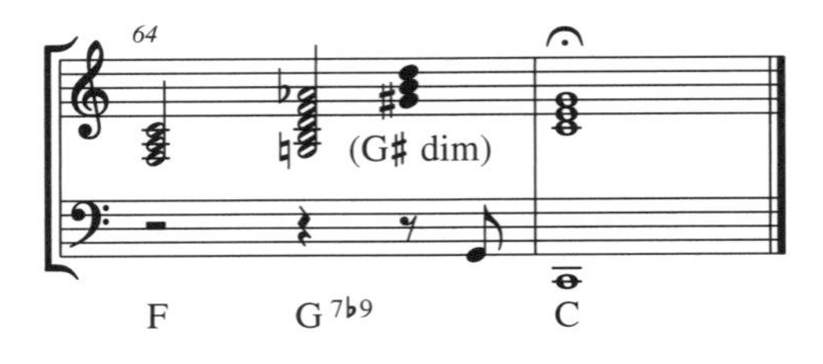

Melody

The melody is sung by Noel Gallagher (not Liam, who is usually the lead vocalist of Oasis) and the recording of the vocal part is double-tracked to thicken the sound (which is why it occasionally seems as if more than one person is singing).

Another feature unique to verse 2 is the pair of short guitar interjections printed on the string stave in bars 10–11. They illustrate the reference to a 'rock and roll band' in the lyrics of the second verse.

The vocal melody in the verses uses the **major pentatonic** scale on C (C–D–E–G–A). This scale also forms the basis of the melody in the pre-chorus, although Gallagher includes a blues-like E♭ in bars 17 and 20. Notice that in the second verse, the E♭ in bar 20 is replaced by a G♯ which resolves to a climactic top A in bar 21.

The note F is added to the basic set of five pitches in the melody of the chorus, the result being a **hexatonic**, or six-note scale. However, although the leading-note (B) is avoided throughout the vocal solo, it is firmly embedded in the dominant chords that form the first half of the perfect cadences in the accompaniment (V–I in bars 28^4–29^1 and 31^3–32^1), thus making the tonality crystal clear.

The word-setting is mainly **syllabic** with short falling **melismas** at the ends of many phrases in the verses (on 'mind', 'find', 'play', 'been' and 'seen' in verse 1). Most phrases combine stepwise movement with small leaps and most have a **falling contour** – a feature that contributes to the melancholic, nostalgic character of the song.

The verses have a narrow vocal range of a 6th, as does the pre-chorus (except for the extension to a top G♯ and A, mentioned earlier, when the latter is repeated).

Tessitura refers to the part of the overall range in which the melody mainly lies.

The chorus is distinguished by the use of a higher **tessitura** and it starts with an aspirational upward leap of an octave (bars 24–25) but after that, even this lyrical melody descends (to the lower dominant, G in bar 28). When the first four bars of the chorus are repeated, the ending is changed to reach higher, to a top A in bar 30, for the **title hook**, 'don't look back in anger' – but again the melody falls back down the scale, this time to the tonic (C).

The lead-guitar melody in the instrumental break (bars 33–44) features semiquaver movement and crushed notes (𝅘𝅥𝅮). Given the moderate tempo it tends to sound melodic rather than virtuosic, but it covers a range of almost three octaves, moving into the high register in the second half. Like the vocal version of the pre-chorus it is based on the major pentatonic scale of C, with occasional use of the 'blue third' on E♭.

Private study

1. Listen to the recording of *NAM 57* and then decide whether the quavers are swung or played straight (i.e. as written).
2. The bass guitarist mainly plays just the root of the current chord, but there are a few places where the root is decorated with other notes. In bars 17–28, give the number of a bar where the root is decorated with:

   (i) lower auxiliary notes *and* a chromatic passing note

   (ii) added 6ths *and* a harmony note that is *not* the root

   (iii) just an additional harmony note.
3. How do the following sections relate to the rest of the song?

   (i) the introduction (bars 1–4)

   (ii) the instrumental in bars 33–44.
4. What is meant by the 'title hook'?
5. Which percussion instrument, not normally part of a drum kit, features in this song?

Sample questions

In the exam there will be three questions on the three works you have studied, from which you must answer **two**.

(a) Compare the style and structure of the solo vocal melodies in *NAM 52* and *NAM 57*.

(b) Discuss the role of the bass in all three special focus works.

(c) Describe the structure of *Don't Look Back in Anger*.

Continuity and change in structure, tonality and texture

For examination in summer 2008 and 2009

You do not need to study this topic unless *Popular music and jazz* is the Area of Study that you undertook for AS Music and which you are now extending for A2.

Before starting work on this topic you need a thorough understanding of the material on *Popular music and jazz* in the AS Guide (pages 120–132). Remember that for A2 the topic draws on works from across the **entire** Area of Study, not just those in one of the two lists, A or B.

Tonality refers to the use of (and the relationship between) major and minor keys in music – it is nothing to do with the tone colour of musical sounds. In tonal music, keys are established by cadences, particularly perfect cadence patterns such as V^7–I.

West End Blues

NAM 48 (page 461) CD4 Track 7
Louis Armstrong (trumpet and voice) with clarinet, trombone, piano, banjo and drums.

Louis Armstrong begins with a spectacular solo that deliberately delays offering a clear definition of the key. His improvisation first suggests C minor, then E♭ minor and B♭ minor, before the band enters on an augmented triad on the dominant (B♭–D–F♯) in bar 6. It is not until bar 7, when this chord resolves on to tonic harmony, that it becomes clear we are to hear a blues in E♭ major.

West End Blues is an early example of a **head arrangement** – a structure we encountered earlier in Miles Davis' *Four*. The changes are formed by the 12-bar blues progression heard in bars 7–18 which, being based on the three primary triads of E♭ major, firmly establishes the tonality after the ambiguous introduction:

bars	*7*	*8*	*9*	*10*	*11*	*12*	*13*	*14*	*15*	*16*	*17*	*18*
chord	E♭ I	E♭ I	E♭ I	E♭^{7} I^7	A♭ IV	A♭ IV	E♭ I	E♭ I	B♭^{7} V^7	B♭^{7} V^7	E♭ I	E♭ I

Bars		
1–6	Solo trumpet	Introduction
7–18	*Tutti*	Five choruses
19–30	Trombone	of a 12-bar blues
31–42	Clarinet/voice	in E♭ major, the
43–54	Piano	last extended to
55–68	*Tutti*	form a short coda

There are then four more choruses of the **blues changes**, often with chord substitutions (especially by the solo pianist in bars 43–54). The last chorus has an extended final phrase (bars 63–68) which acts as a short coda. The complete structure is summarised *left*.

The music remains in E♭ major throughout but the improvising musicians add a rich vocabulary of **chromaticism**. Some of this results from the use of **blue notes** – the flattened 3rd of E♭ major (G♭, sometimes notated as F♯) and the flattened 7th (D♭). However, some chromatic notes occur in **chord substitutions** that actually serve to strengthen E♭ as the tonal centre of the music. For example, instead of repeating the chord of E♭ in bar 20, the pianist plays a **falling 5ths progression** designed to emphasise the importance of E♭ in the next bar (F^7 B♭^{7} | E♭). A similar progression occurs in bars 51–53, where the chord of F (bars 51–52^2) is a secondary dominant that resolves to B♭^{7} (bar 52^3) and then to E♭ (bar 53).

The chord of F^7 here is another example of a **secondary dominant** – see page 135.

In other cases, chord substitutions in *West End Blues* colour the harmony but without obscuring a clear sense that E♭ is the tonic, such as the use of the minor version of chord IV (A♭m) in bars 24 and 36. This is far removed from the complex chord substitutions in the much later *Four*, where successive unresolved dissonances sometimes result in the tonal centre being only a distant memory.

Even at the very end of *NAM 48*, where accidentals proliferate, it is not hard to hear that the work ends with a decorated **plagal cadence**, basically IV–I (or A♭–E♭) – and it is possible to see it, too, if you read the B♮ as C♭ because the last three chords can then be recognised as the progression A♭^{7}/C – A♭m^7/C♭ – E♭^{6}.

The structure of *West End Blues* is defined by contrasts in texture:

- The unaccompanied trumpet melody in the introduction opens the work with a **monophonic** texture
- The texture formed by the three frontline players in the head (bars 7–18) is traditionally known as **New Orleans counterpoint** although in this piece the clarinet and trombone are really just accompanying Armstrong's trumpet melody
- **Melody-dominated homophony** occurs in bars 19–30 (notice that the pianist is **comping** – see page 137)
- The accompanied duet in bars 30^4–42 features **dialogue** in **call-and-response** style between clarinet and voice
- The melody-dominated homophony of the piano solo in bars 43–54 features the charcateristic wide leaps of a stride-bass part in the left hand.

Ellington's *Black and Tan Fantasy* is another **head arrangement** based on the 12-bar blues. The structure, shown *below right*, is similar to *West End Blues* in that the head is played *tutti* (by all), and is followed by choruses that each feature a different soloist, ending with another *tutti*. However, it differs from Armstrong's work in having no introduction, by including a 16-bar section that is *not* based on the 12-bar blues, and by having a coda that interrupts the final chorus (with a quotation from Chopin's funeral match), rather than extending it.

There is also a significant difference in tonality: *West End Blues* remains in E♭ major throughout while the *Black and Tan Fantasy* begins in B♭ minor, shifts to the **parallel tonic major key** (B♭ major) at bar 13, and then returns to B♭ minor for the four-bar coda.

The 12-bar blues progression in the head (bars 1–12) establishes the key of B♭ minor with chords I, IV and V^7 in root position. The modulation to B♭ major is triggered when the chord of $G\flat^7$ in bars 13–14 is treated as an augmented 6th chord (see *right*) that resolves to B♭ major in bar 15. The harmony then becomes increasingly chromatic, with a **circle of 5ths** in bars 19^2–21^1 that ingeniously ends back on $G\flat^7$ in bars 21–22.

When the blues progression returns it is initially diatonic, despite occasional blue notes in the melody (bars 29–52). However, the piano solo provides the opportunity to explore chromatic **chord substitutions**. Ellington includes diminished 7ths (bars 58 and 63^3) and a **circle of 5ths** (bar 59^3–64) in his improvisation on the blues changes, although these all lead back towards B♭ as the tonal centre, confirmed by the perfect cadence (V^{79}–I) in bars 64^4–65.

The texture of the *Black and Tan Fantasy* is essentially one of **melody-dominated homophony**. In the first 12 bars the melody is harmonised mainly in **parallel 6ths** and is heard over a bass **riff** that changes pitch to match the chord changes. The backing to the saxophone solo alternates between sustained harmonies and chords in shorter note lengths. The accompaniment remains purely supportive, even in the piano solo, where Ellington uses a **stride bass** not unlike that of the piano solo in *West End Blues*.

Black and Tan Fantasy

NAM 49 (page 465) CD4 Track 8
Duke Ellington and his orchestra

Bars		
1–12	*Tutti*	12-bar blues (B♭ minor)
13–28	Sax	16 bars (B♭ major)
29–52	Trumpet	12-bar blues (B♭ major)
		12-bar blues (B♭ major)
53–64	Piano	12-bar blues (B♭ major)
65–75	Trombone	12-bar blues (B♭ major)
76–86	Trumpet	Start of a 12-bar blues (B♭ major), interrupted after seven bars by a modulation to …
87–90	*Tutti*	Coda (B♭ minor)

It is no coincidence that in both *NAM 48* and *NAM 49* the more complex chromatic harmony occurs during a piano solo. This is because an unaccompanied pianist can introduce complicated chord substitutions without the danger that they might create unintended dissonances with other parts.

The type of sustained accompaniment seen in bars 13–17 and 21–23 is sometimes described as a **pad** in pop and jazz.

Four

NAM 50 (page 468) CD4 Track 9
Miles Davis Quintet

We discussed this work in detail at the start of this chapter (which you should now revise) so we just need to compare *Four* with the other two jazz works we have studied:

- It is another head arrangement but with choruses based on a 32-bar chord pattern in ABAB form rather than on a 12-bar blues
- Like *West End Blues*, it is in E♭ major throughout, but complex chords and chromaticism make the tonality far less obvious
- The bass part resembles the crotchet-based rhythms used in *NAM 48* and some sections *NAM 49*, but it has the melodic countours of a walking bass rather than consisting of mainly repeated roots (Armstrong) or roots and 5ths (Ellington)
- Like *NAM 49*, the texture is melody-dominated homophony, but the limited forces used in *Four* offer less opportunity for variety, except by changes in tessitura and by octave doubling between trumpet and saxophone in the first chorus.

I'm Leaving You

NAM 51 (page 471) CD4 Track 10
Howlin' Wolf (vocal, harmonica)
Hosea Lee Kennard (piano)
L. D. McGhee (guitar)
Hubert Sumlin (guitar)
S. P. Leary (drums)

Bars		
1–2	Introduction	
3–14	Verse 1	Six choruses of a 12-bar blues in G major
15–26	Verse 2	
27–38	Verse 3	
39–50	Instrumental	
15–26	Repeat of verse 2	
27–36	Repeat of verse 3	
51–52	new ending for verse 3	
53–58	Outro (fade-out)	

This rhythm and blues song is in **strophic form** – in other words, each verse is sung to basically the same tune. It uses six choruses of a 12-bar blues in G major, prefaced by a short introduction and rounded-off by a coda that fades out (see *below left*). The replacement of the singer by an instrumental solo in one of the verses is typical of many rhythm and blues songs, and is a feature that was also adopted in early rock 'n' roll. We saw the same idea used in *Don't Look Back in Anger*, where one of the pre-chorus sections was treated as an instrumental. Here, though, Howlin' Wolf joins the lead guitarist with vocalisations to 'Whoo' (you could describe this as a type of scat – a term used in jazz to mean singing to nonsense words) and with interjections on the harmonica.

The label **stop chorus** at the start of verses 2 and 3 in the score refers to the fact that the accompaniment stops (that is, it includes rests) in order to focus attention on the singer. Note that the term 'chorus' is used here in the same sense that it is used in jazz, meaning the changes (here, the 12-bar blues chord sequence). Be careful not to confuse this use of the word with the type of chorus that follows the verses in verse-and-chorus form.

In early blues-based music, melodies tend to emphasise the 12-bar structure of the chord pattern by falling into three clear four-bar phrases – something that was evident throughout most of *NAM 48*, although less marked in *NAM 49*. Here, Chester Burnett's vocal line often transcends the four-bar units of blues harmony – the first phrase is five bars long, and is followed by three two-bar phrases, plus a rest to complete the 12-bar period. The numerous small differences in the melody of each verse are a clear indication that it is essentially improvised around a basic composed structure.

Although the chord sequence in *I'm Leaving You* is very similar to the 12-bar blues patterns of *West End Blues* and *Black and Tan Fantasy*, it makes much freer use of 7ths and 9ths in the backing. In the two earlier works, such dissonances tend to arise through clashes between the solo melodies and the harmony, rather than appearing in the accompaniment itself.

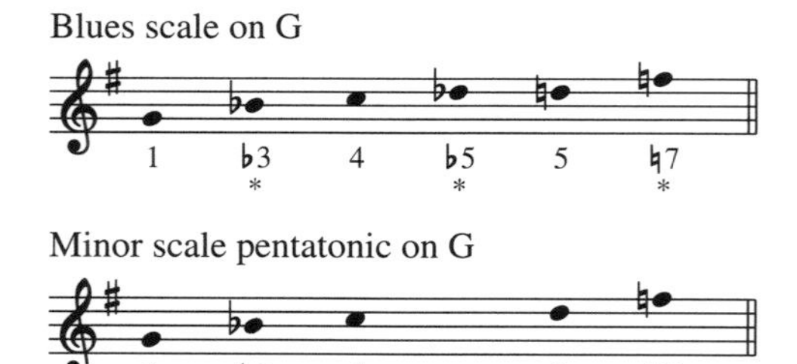

Further dissonance arises from the use of the blues scale, which contains all three **blue notes** of the key (indicated by asterisks in the example *left*) and the **minor pentatonic scale**, which is the same as the blues scale except that it has no flat 5th. Both Howlin' Wolf and the lead guitarist draw on pitches from these scales and also freely mix major 3rds with their blue-note equivalents, for example, B♭ and B♮ in bar 6. However, most of the vocal melody is based on the figure heard in bar 3 – essentially a falling triad of G minor (D–B♭–G). This, together with the frequent use of chords G^7 (which includes F♮) and C^9 (which includes B♭), gives a strong tinge of **blues modality** to the song. This is reinforced by a lack of clear perfect cadences that would define the tonality as G major. When the dominant 7th (D^7) is used, it is most commonly followed by C^9 (bar 12) or G^7 (bar 51) rather than by a simple tonic triad.

The texture of this song is, like many of the works in this area of study, largely **melody-dominated homophony**. However, there is also frequent **dialogue** between voice and guitar, particularly well illustrated by their repeated overlapping phrases in the fade out.

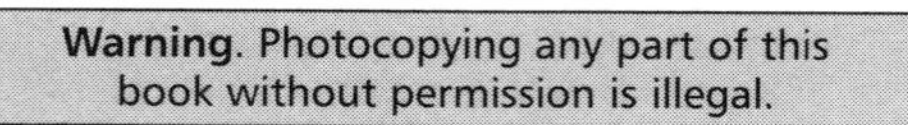

We discussed *Honey Don't* in detail on pages 138–142 (which you should now revise) so we will just summarise a few of the most important points here:

Honey Don't

NAM 52 (page 477) CD4 Track 11
Carl Perkins (vocal, guitar)
James 'Buck' Perkins (rhythm guitar)
Lloyd 'Clayton' Perkins (upright bass)
W. S. Holland (drums)

- The song has a **verse-and-chorus** structure in which the 24 bars formed by an eight-bar verse and 16-bar chorus span two 12-bar blues progressions. Like a number of works we have studied, it begins with a short introduction and ends with a short coda.
- Like *I'm Leaving You*, variety is provided by an instrumental based on the same harmonies, although here there are two such sections, and both involve some modification of the original chord pattern.
- The song is in E major throughout with mainly functional harmony (chords I, IV and V^7 in root position). Neither the one simple substitution chord (C major) nor the occasional use of blue notes obscures the strongly tonal feel of the song.
- This tonality is reinforced by a walking bass which outlines the current chord with only minimal decoration, unlike the walking bass in *Four*, which often avoids obvious chord notes.
- Like many of the works in this area of study, the texture consists of melody-dominated homophony, to which is added a touch of heterophony in the relationship between lead guitar and bass.

Waterloo Sunset

NAM 53 (page 483) CD4 Track 12
The Kinks

Waterloo Sunset is a strongly tonal song with no blue notes or suggestions of modality. It begins with an eight-bar introduction in which the key of E major is defined through four bars of **dominant preparation** (B^7) below which the bass descends stepwise in repeated quavers from upper dominant to lower dominant. As this opening resolves to the tonic in bar 5, the lead guitar plays a four-bar phrase that will be repeated by the lead vocalist to form the first phrase of the verse.

Each of the verses consists of four four-bar phrases, in the pattern AABA. This is known as **popular song form**, a structure that rose to prominence decades earlier in the music of Gershwin, Porter, Berlin and other song-writers of the 1920s and 1930s. Each of the three verses uses the same music, with only minor differences in the backing, so we can say that the overall form of the song is **strophic** (see *right*).

Bars		
1–8	Intro	8 bars
9–24	Verse 1 (AABA)	16 bars
25–32	Middle eight …	8 bars
33–34	and turnaround	2 bars
	Verse 2, middle eight and turnaround (formed by a repeat of bars 9–34)	
35–50	Verse 3 (AABA)	16 bars
51–60	Coda	10 bars

The A phrase starts with a five-note **hook** (a memorable motif) set in verse 1 to the words 'Dirty old river'. This is repeated in descending sequence for 'must you keep rolling' and again, slightly varied and extended, for 'flowing into the night'. This four-bar phrase is then repeated with new lyrics to form the second A phrase.

Traditionally, the third phrase (B) contrasts with the A phrase in melody, harmony and lyrics. We can see this in bars 16–19 of *Waterloo Sunset* – the hook line is dropped, the lyrics suddenly become defiantly positive ('But I don't need no friends'), the melodic line heads for an aspirational top G# on 'need' and the first use of chromatic harmony appears in bar 18.

Finally, the verse ends with a return to phrase A, modified at the end, starting in bar 20.

The melody of phrase A uses the **major pentatonic scale** on E (E–F♯–G♯–B–C♯) and its harmonisation with chords I, V^7 and IV makes the E-major tonality totally clear. In contrast, the B phrase (known as the **bridge**) uses chord ii (F♯m) and its secondary dominant, chord V of ii (C♯ major). However, it ends on a dominant 7th (B^7) which leads back to the tonic at the start of the final A phrase (V^7–I in bars 20–21), again reinforcing the tonality of the song.

This 16-bar verse is followed by two more structural features found in much older popular song. The first is a **middle eight** (bars 25–32). This again asserts the tonic by means of a falling 5ths progression in its first four bars (F♯–F♯–B–E). When this passage is repeated in bars 29–32 the last two chords are replaced by two bars of B^7 and the harmony then remains on this dominant 7th in bars 33–34, forming the second traditional structural feature – a short section known as a **turnaround** because it prepares (by means of V^7) for the tonic key to come back round at the start of the next verse.

The backing in bars 31–34 is the same passage of dominant preparation that formed the introduction. Ray Davies ingeniously links this to the first part of the middle eight by extending the descending scale in the bass of bars 29–30 into a complete scalic descent of one and a half octaves, ending on the dominant in bar 34^3.

It remains only to look at the coda (bars 51–60) in which the events of the introduction are reversed. Here the instrumental version of phrase A comes first, accompanied by a more sustained descending bass pattern. This is then followed by repeated dominant 7ths which match those of the opening, although now the bass remains on the dominant throughout. Paradoxically, though, a fade-out ensures that we never get to hear a final tonic chord, despite the obviously tonal nature of the entire song.

With the exception of the two-bar turnaround, all the phrases are four-bars in length. Such regular periodic phrasing can make a song sound predictably sectional, but this is disguised by the long pick-up (or anacrusis) of four quavers used in the hook, which crosses the gap between sections, and by guitar licks which fill silences in the melody at the ends of phrases, such as in bars 11, 15 and 23.

The texture of this song is again **melody-dominated homophony**, with backing vocals and guitar licks providing additional interest. Rather like the relationship between the bass guitar and lead guitar parts in much of *Honey Don't*, there is a **heterophonic** relationship in the middle eight of this song in the way that the bass shadows the lead vocal by playing the same descending scales but in a different rhythm.

A Day in the Life

NAM 54 (page 487)
This song is not included on the CDs that accompany the New Anthology.

This track differs in many ways from all of the other works in this area of study, not least because it was designed as the finale of a long concept album rather than as a stand-alone song that could be performed live or issued as a single. It also differs in its unusual genesis and structure, in which a G-major song in **modified strophic** form by John Lennon is interrupted by a contrasting (although related) verse in E major by Paul McCartney, creating an overall **ternary form** and introducing a duality of key that is not entirely obliterated by the **atonality** of much of the coda.

The structure of *A Day in the Life* is summarised *right*. It begins with an introduction in which an acoustic guitar outlines the chord pattern (G–Bm–Em–Em^7–C) that will be used at the start of each of the following verses.

Bars		
1–4	Intro	4 bars
5–14	Verse 1	10 bars
15–23	Verse 2	9 bars
24–34	Verse 3	11 bars
35–46	Transition	12 bars
47–57	Bridge	11 bars
58–67	Transition	10 bars
68–78	Verse 4	11 bars
79–89	Coda	11 bars

When the voice enters this chord pattern is underpinned by a decorated descending scale of G major in the bass but, despite this, the tonality is often ambiguous. The dominant chord of D major is totally avoided in the verses, and the harmonic progressions often sound modal, especially with the inclusion of a **modal**-sounding F major, the chord on the flattened leading-note.

The vocal line is slightly different in each verse, reflecting the essentially improvisatory nature of the singing. In verse 2 the previously ten-bar length of the verse is foreshortened to nine bars (neither verse being anywhere near as symmetric as the four-bar phrase lengths we saw in *Waterloo Sunset*). At the end of the second verse the note B is decorated with a semitonal figure in semiquavers (bar 22). This is inverted and greatly extended at the end of verse 3 although it still hovers around B, like so many of the melodic motifs in the song. This trilling figure is extended by the orchestra into an almost pitchless spiral of sound for the transition in bars 35–46, after which it becomes clear that B was being set-up as the dominant for the bridge in E major (bars 47–57).

McCartney's bridge focuses on the tonal area of E major although, as in Lennon's verses, there is a strong modal element, with prominent use of D♮, the characteristic flat 7th degree of the **mixolydian mode** on E (see *right*). The two sections are also complementary in other respects. Like Lennon, McCartney uses repetitive intervals (mainly 3rds) rather than stepwise melody, and assymetric structures made up of 2½-bar phrase lengths. And while Lennon's motifs mainly centre on the 4th between B and upper E, McCartney's focus on the 5th between B and lower E (thus reversing the normal role of the two singers, in which McCartney usually took the high notes).

Mixolydian mode on E:
E–F♯–G♯–A–B–C♯–D–E.

The second transition (bars 58–67) is underpinned by massive root-position harmonies that turn on its head the conventional **circle of 5ths** patterns, for here the 5ths rise instead of fall, twice outlining the pattern C–G–D–A–E.

The final verse is musically similar to verse 3 and the reappearance of the orchestral spiral in bar 78 links the coda to the first transition, but this time it leads to a dramatic silence followed by the brilliant light of E major, reverberating for 42 seconds.

The texture is mainly **homophonic**, with variety being provided by the contrasting style of the two singers, and by the inclusion of the sometimes atonal orchestral effects.

You Can Get it if You Really Want

NAM 55 (page 496) CD4 Track 13
Desmond Dekker and the Aces

The D♭-major tonality of *You Can Get it if You Really Want* is made obvious by the repeated use of

- A rise from leading note to tonic in the introduction
- A stepwise descent to the tonic (F–E♭–D♭) in its melodic motifs
- Harmonic progressions built mainly on chords IV, I and V$^{(7)}$ in root position.

The lead vocal keeps largely to notes of the **major pentatonic scale** on D♭ (D♭–E♭–F–A♭–B♭) but the V^7–I progressions in bars 13–14, 25–26, 35–36 and 53–54 firmly assert the tonality of the music. There are no blue notes, and the only chromaticism occurs in the instrumental, where the surprise appearance of the **unrelated chord** of E major in bars 37, which is followed by a descent down part of a **whole-tone scale** in bar 39: A♭–G♭(=F♯)–E♮–D♮. When the effect is repeated four bars later, the wind section harmonises this descent with parallel root-position chords.

Bars		
1–3	Intro	3 bars
4–13	Refrain	10 bars
14–25	Verse 1	12 bars
26–13	Refrain (repeat)	10 bars
14–25	Verse 2 (repeat)	12 bars
26–35	Refrain	10 bars
36–43	Instrumental	8 bars
44–53	Refrain	10 bars
54–57	Outro (repeat to fade)	

The song has a **verse-and-chorus** structure (shown *left*), prefaced by an intro and concluded with an outro (a coda that fades). An instrumental is used instead of a third verse, but it doesn't use the same chord pattern as the verses, like the instrumental sections in earlier songs we have studied. The texture is **homophonic** with **close-harmony backing vocals** to supporting the lead vocal. There is **dialogue** between voice and trumpets in the verses and between lead vocal and backing singers in the outro.

Tupelo Honey

NAM 56 (page 501) CD4 Track 14
Van Morrison

Bars		
1–4	4 bars	Introduction
5–12	8 bars	Verse 1
13–20	8 bars	Chorus
5–12	8 bars	Verse 2
13–20	8 bars	Chorus
21–36	16 bars	Instrumental
5–12	8 bars	Verse 3 (= verse 2)
13–20	8 bars	Chorus
37–44	8 bars	Middle 8, played as ‖:37–40:‖:41–44:‖:37–40:‖
5–12	8 bars	Verse 4 (= verse 1)
13–20	8 bars	Chorus
45–52	8 bars	Chorus (varied repeat)
53–56	4 bars	Coda (repeat to fade)

This song is in **verse-and-chorus form** (with an introduction, an instrumental, a middle eight and a coda). It looks complicated because there are many repeats in the score and because neither of the two sections marked 'Coda' is actually a structural coda. Also, it is difficult to follow aurally because there is little melodic or harmonic differentiation between sections. The diagram *left* unpacks the repeats and shows the structure, but you will need to get used to following the score in the *New Anthology* while listening to the recording.

The lead vocal uses the **major pentatonic scale** on B♭ (B♭–C–D–F–G) but the other parts use all of the notes of a B♭-major scale. The harmonies are based on a repeating chord pattern that is only a little more complex than those in *NAM 55*: I–iii–IV–I–(V). This gives the song an hypnotic quality and anchors it to the key of B♭ major throughout – *Tupelo Honey* is **entirely diatonic**, with no blue notes, chromatic notes or modulation to other keys.

The inclusion of a short flute solo at the beginning is unusual in a pop song, although the flute appears in a number of Van Morrison's songs and reflects the composer's roots in Irish folk music. Here it is used to introduce a two-bar **hook**, played twice, variations of which permeate the song – compare it with the second-verse vocal in bars 7–8, for instance, or compare its second, third and fourth notes with the first three notes of the chorus.

In much of the song the lead guitar is used as a melody instrument, largely in the upper part of its range. Initially it is in **dialogue** with the flute or voice, but from bar 21 it takes part in a complex web of **counterpoint** with high acoustic guitar, saxophone and bass.

There is a gradual increase in the density of the music through the song, and the decoration of its one basic pattern becomes increasingly impassioned – especially in the instrumental, but also in Van Morrison's increasingly elaborate vocal decoration (culminating in top B♭s at the start of both the middle eight and the coda). The high tessitura of the vocal and guitar parts, set against a low bass and with piano in the middle, gives the song its warm, rich texture.

Don't Look Back In Anger

NAM 57 (page 509) CD4 Track 15
Oasis

We discussed *Don't Look Back in Anger* in detail on pages 143–146 (which you should now revise) so we will just summarise a few of the most important points here:

- The song is in modified verse-and-chorus form, in which the verse and chorus share the same chord progression but are separated by a pre-chorus based on a different progression. It consists mainly of four-bar phrases.
- It starts with an introduction, ends with a coda and includes an instrumental version of the final pre-chorus. All of these sections are based on the chord patterns of the main part of the song.
- The song is in C major throughout with root-position chords and very limited used of chromatic harmony, resulting in a strongly tonal feel.
- The lead vocal is based on a major pentatonic scale (hexatonic in the chorus) with very occasional blue notes.
- The texture consists of melody-dominated homophony with a chordal accompaniment, to which lead-guitar licks provide additional melodic interest.

Private study

1. Explain the difference between diatonic and chromatic.
2. Write out examples of (i) a major pentatonic scale starting on C and (ii) a minor pentatonic scale starting on A.
3. On what type of chord does the band enter in *NAM 48*?
4. Compare the use of guitars in *NAM 55* with the way they are used in *NAM 56*.
5. Explain the meaning of the terms 'atonality' and 'dialogue', giving an example of each from the works in this area of study.
6. In popular song form, explain the purpose of (i) the bridge and (ii) the turnaround.

Sample questions

In the exam there will be two questions on this topic, from which you must answer **one**.

(a) Compare and contrast structures based on the 12-bar blues in *West End Blues* and *I'm Leaving You*.

(b) Discuss the approaches to texture and tonality in Ellington's *Black and Tan Fantasy* and Van Morrison's *Tupelo Honey*.

(c) Comment on the different approaches to verse-and-chorus form seen in *Waterloo Sunset* and *You Can Get it if You Really Want*.

World music

There are *three* Special Focus works, *NAM 58*, *60* and *62*, all of which must be studied if you are taking the exam in 2008 or 2009.

Special Focus Work 1 for 2008 and 2009

NAM 58 (page 519) CD4 Track 16
Ram Narayan (sarangi)
Charanjit Lal Biyavat (tabla)

Rag Bhairav

Before starting on this section you should work through (or revise) the information about the context and structure of this music given on pages 140–141 of the AS Guide. Make sure that you understand all of the terminology used in that section.

All Indian words are transliterations and you may find alternative spellings and some vowels marked with diacriticals (signs such as the accents in French) in different books.

The classical music of northern India was originally perceived as an art form for the educated. Traditional performances were, and still are, similar to those of western chamber music, involving a small and knowledgeable audience in close proximity to the performers. In Indian music both audience and performers sit on the floor; most listeners understand the parameters set by the *rag* and the *tal*, and place great store in the way these are used in the improvisation. Each *rag* is intended to express a particular mood and many are associated with set times of the day or seasons – *Rag Bhairav* is intended for performance at dawn. These days, though, you could well hear *Rag Bhairav* being sung or played in a film or being used as the basis for a popular Indian song.

The three main elements of *NAM 58*, explained in the AS Guide, are the *rag*, the *tal* and the drone (played by the *tampura*). The pitches used in the improvisation are known as the **that** – a term broadly equivalent to a scale or mode in western music. They are given at the head of the music, on the stave which shows the tuning of the sympathetic strings of the *sarangi*. Some *rags* use only a selection of pitches from the *that*, but *bhairav* uses **sapurna jati** (all seven pitches), both in ascending and descending passages.

The improvised melody is built around **pakad** – groups of notes that characterise the *rag* and which the musician constantly develops and embellishes with microtonal inflections, vibrato and slides. For example, a phrase beginning with the pitches shown *left* first appears at 3^3 and then returns, in different rhythmic guises at 6^9, 7^1, 17^{32}, 22^{15}, 28^{34} and starting on the last two notes of stave 34. See if you can spot how the melodic figure at the start of stave 19 is used (some clear examples are at the starts of staves 21, 23, 29, 31 and 33, but there are many more).

In this section, locations such as 3^3 mean stave 3, note 3.

When following the score, remember that the flats at the start of each stave (A♭ and D♭) are not a key signature in the western sense but they are there to remind you that these two pitches are flattened in this particular *that*.

Rag Bhairav starts with a slow, improvised section known as the **alap**, to set the mood. After this there is a gradual build-up of intensity through the rest of the work. The music starts to develop a sense of pulse and becomes melodically denser in the central section (the **jhor**) but there is no regular metre until the start of stave 19 where the *tabla* enter with the 16-beat cycle of **tintal**, divided into four **vibhag** of four beats each.

This marks the start of the concluding section (the **jhala**) and is the point at which the music focuses on a memorised composition (known as the **gat**) rather than entirely free improvisation. Notice how the *sarangi* and the *tabla* come together on the first beat of the *tal*, and how the pace builds up not only through an accelerating pulse but also through the use of shorter note-lengths and a wide range of pitches in this final section. *NAM 58* is a complete piece, but very much a miniature one. In live performance all three sections would normally be considerably longer.

Each of the three instruments in *NAM 58* have specific roles:

- The bowed sounds of the *sarangi*, enhanced by the resonance of its sympathetic strings, improvises on the *rag*
- The plucked strings of the *tampura* provide drones
- The *tabla* player adds rhythmic improvisation, synchronising with the other musicians on the first beat (**sam**) of each *tal*.

The wide pitch-range (three octaves) and resulting variety of timbre of the *sarangi* is a striking feature of the music, but also notice how the two small drums of the tabla vary in timbre, according to the finger and hand strokes of the **bols**, and the different pressures exerted on the drum heads to vary the tone.

The texture is **monophonic** (a single melody), despite the drone – the entry of the *tabla* for the *jhala* adds variety to this texture, but doesn't change its basic monophonic nature.

Yellow Bird

Special Focus Work 2 for 2008 and 2009

NAM 60 (page 528) CD4 Track 18
Red Stripe Ebony Steelband

Before starting on this section you should work through (or revise) the information about the context and structure of this music given on pages 134–135 of the AS Guide. Make sure that you understand all of the terminology used in that section.

Yellow Bird was originally a calypso, a type of song from Trinidad that was used as a way to spread anything from news and political comment to salacious gossip by supplying new and topical words to simple, traditional tunes. Calypsos can be slow and in a minor key, but the best-known types are in a major key, with triadic melodies that can be harmonised with the common chords I, IV and V. They are usually in **duple metre** (*Yellow Bird* is effectively in $\frac{2}{2}$ despite its $\frac{4}{4}$ time signature) and the rhythm is frequently syncopated, a particular feature being the use of the pattern ♪♩ ♪, which is a characteristic of the Afro-Brazilian dance, the samba. All of these features can be seen in *NAM 60*.

The steel pans used in the *New Anthology* arrangement are a more recent Trinidadian tradition, although their origin can be traced back to the tamboo-bamboo bands of the late 19th century. Modern steel bands tend to play a wide repertoire of music, of which calypso is only a small, but important part.

The song and its arrangement are very straightforward, the piece making its impact with a tuneful and **mainly diatonic melody** (C♯ is the only chromatic note) that is in just the right range to be sung or hummed, and the engaging **tremolo** effect of long notes being rolled on the pans. The piece is harmonised almost entirely with the **primary triads** of G major (I, IV and V) decorated by occasional 7ths and chromatic notes. There is no modulation but the secondary dominant (G^7) in bars 8, 12, 33 and 37 adds a touch of chromaticism to the otherwise diatonic harmony.

The opening section (A) consists of four **four-bar phrases** and uses both **melodic sequence** (bars 9–10) and **varied repetition** (compare bars 10 and 11). The B section in bars 17–25 has an extra bar of V^7 harmony (in bar 24) to break-up the periodic phrasing. Overall the form is AABAAB – notice the tiny **countermelody** that rises above the tune in bars 28–29 and 32–33, giving this repeat some variety.

Each part has its own clearly-defined function, which is maintained throughout the arrangement. The basses play chordal notes in a tango rhythm which never varies. The four-pan cello is a simple harmony part that moves in semibreves and minims. The double tenor plays a **counter-rhythm** in the first seven bars of the A sections adding 6ths to the tonic chords and 7ths to the dominant chords, but it is confined to semibreves elsewhere. The melody is assigned to the upper instruments throughout, sometimes in 3rds. A part for kit drums (not printed in *NAM 60*) underpins the **homophonic texture** of the entire piece.

Special Focus Work 3 for 2008 and 2009

NAM 62 (page 532) CD4 Track 20
Mustapha Tettey Addy

Agbekor Dance

Before starting on this section you should work through (or revise) the information about the context and structure of this music given on pages 138–139 of the AS Guide. Make sure that you understand all of the terminology used in that section.

Although totally different in character to *Yellow Bird*, this ritual war dance is, like *NAM 60*, scored for a group of mainly similar instruments. Those used here (described in detail in the AS Guide) all have a percussive timbre: the *atsimevu* (or master drum), the *sogo* (a smaller drum) and the *gangkogui* (a double bell that can produce two distinct pitches). Also like *NAM 60*, each part has a fixed and unchanging role to play within the instrumentation.

The *gangkogui* plays a repeating pattern called a **time line** – an ostinato that acts as a reference point for the other parts. Although the time signature reflects the fact that the very fast pulse falls into 12-beat units, they are not articulated as four groups of three, as they would be in the normally 'divisive' rhythm of $\frac{12}{8}$ time. Instead, they are articulated as an **additative rhythm** in a pattern of notes that are 2+3+2+2+3 quavers in length (see *left*) – one of the most common rhythms in African drumming.

The *sogo* plays its own rhythm against the time line – the basic pattern heard at the start attracts two variants (bars 12^2–13^1 and 26^2–27^1) both of which alternate with the original version in the second half of the piece. The master drummer, as befits his status, has a much wider variety of patterns than the other two players and also directs the performance. The complexity of the resulting **polyrhythmic texture**, with its frequent **cross-rhythms**, makes a stark contrast with the metrical pulse, simple rhythms and clear homophony of *Yellow Bird*.

Private study

1. (i) What is a *tampura*?

   (ii) What is the role of the *tampura* in *NAM 58*?

2. (i) What is an *atsimevu*?

   (ii) What is the role of the *atsimevu* in *NAM 62*?

3. Which elements in *Yellow Bird* do you consider to have been influenced by western music?

4. What are the musical characteristics of each of the three main sections of a rag?

Sample questions

In the exam there will be a total of three questions on the three works you have studied, from which you must answer **two**.

(a) Write an account of the structure of *Rag Bhairav*.

(b) Discuss the instrumentation of *NAM 62*, giving details of both the instruments themselves and the way they are used in the *Agbekor Dance*.

(c) Contrast *NAM 58* and *NAM 60*, showing how each work is representative of its local musical culture.

Similarities and differences in the handling of melody, rhythm and metre

For examination in summer 2008 and 2009

You do not need to study this topic unless *World music* is the Area of Study that you undertook for AS Music and which you are now extending for A2.

We have already discussed the handling of these elements in the three special focus works (*Agbekor Dance*, of course, is essentially rhythmic and includes very limited pitched material). So here we will confine ourselves to brief notes on the other three works. Make sure you have a thorough understanding of the material on *World music* in the AS Guide (pages 133–143). Remember that for A2 the topic draws on works from across the **entire** Area of Study, not just those in one of the two lists, A or B.

Baris Melampahan

NAM 59 (page 522) CD4 Track 17
Gong Kebyar de Sebatu

The melodic material is based on pitches 1, 2, 3, 5 and 6 of the seven-note *pelog* scale. This subset is called the *pelog selisir*, and is subtly different from the more familiar five-note gamelan tuning called *slendro*. A tradition in *Gong Kebyar* is to tune each pair of metallophones slightly differently, causing a beating effect called *ombak* when they play the same note. *Ombak* can clearly be heard in *NAM 59*, and helps give the music its shimmering quality.

Balungan instruments play the main theme (the 'nuclear melody'), the *Panususan* instruments simultaneously decorate it, creating a heterophonic texture, gongs divide the sections, and drums and cymbals add contrast. The rhythmic cycle of the *gongan* is clear in this piece, since the four-beat groups in the *ketag* tend to dominate the texture and give a firm sense of pulse to this dance music.

Tom McElvogue's (jig) and New Irish Barndance (reel)

NAM 61 (page 530) CD4 Track 19
Niall Keegan (Irish flute)

The melody of the jig consists of eight-bar phrases in the pattern AABBBAABB. The repetitions are invariably decorated in different ways, and the constant variation of ideas results in similar figures permeating both sections. However, you should be able to spot that the A sections start with an upward leap of a 5th from G to D (bars 1, 9, 33 and 41) and end with a V–I cadence in G major, while the B sections start on a high G (bars 17, 25, 49 and 57) and ends with a vii–I cadence in G. Between the cadences the leading note (F♯) is often altered to F♮ just before the cadential progression itself, a modal inflection common in Irish music. The compound duple metre features occasional dotted rhythms and ornamentation.

The A♭ in bar 57 is a chromatic passing note and is neither modal nor a feature of traditional Irish music.

The last note of the jig overlaps the first note of the reel, which has a melody of four-bar phrases that form, in bars 65–96, the pattern AABBAABB. After bar 96, as the speed increases and the elaboration and recycling of similar ideas becomes more intense, the dance structure is overtaken by a whirl of virtuoso ornamentation. There are occasional chromatic notes, but the music is tied to G major by the use of the pitch G at the start of at least every other bar. The jig is in simple quadruple time, with persistent use of dotted rhythms, occasional triplets and a long *accelerando* to add to the excitement.

Se quema la chumbambá

NAM 63 (page 534) CD4 Track 21
Familia Valera Miranda

The vocal melody consists of four-bar phrases based on repetitions of the chord pattern I–V^7–V^7–I in G minor. It is cast in a call-and-response format in which the *pregón* improvises on the melody from the second verse onwards. The triadic cuatro melody that accompanies the voices adds a minor 9th (E♭) to the D^7 chords. Bars 1 and 3 of both melodies are characterised by a silence on the first beat followed by a syncopated rhythm.

Although the simple duple metre is clearly outlined by the on-beat rhythms of the maracas and bongos, all of the other parts include syncopation, particularly in the the clave's pervasive rhythmic ostinato (♩. ♩. ♩ | 𝄽 ♩ ♩ 𝄽). This is one of the most charateristic rhythms in Latin-American music and is known as '3:2 son clave' because there are three notes in the first bar and two in the second. Syncopation, including cross-rhythms caused by crotchet triplets, also plays an important role in the cuatro solo (page 536 of *NAM*).

Private study

Write a short account to compare the role of the clave part in *Se quema la chumbambá* with the role of the *gangkogui* part in *Agbekor Dance* and the role of the gong players in *Baris Melampahan*.

Sample questions

In the exam there will be two questions on this topic, from which you must answer **one**.

(a) Contrast the melodic structures in *NAM 63* with the jig (only) in *NAM 61*.

(b) Comment on the different approaches to rhythm and metre in *Baris Melampahan* and the reel (only) in *NAM 61*.

(c) Compare the approaches to both melody and rhythm in *Yellow Bird* and *Se quema la chumbambá*.